Crossover Cinema

Cinematic products in the twenty-first century increasingly emerge from, engage with, and are consumed in cross-cultural settings. While there have been a number of terms used to describe cinematic forms that do not bear allegiance to a single nation in terms of conceptualization, content, finance, and/or viewership, this volume contends that *crossover cinema* is the most apt contemporary description for those aspects of contemporary cinema on which it focuses. This contention is provoked by an appreciation of the cross-cultural reality of our postglobalization twenty-first-century world.

This volume both outlines the history of usage of the term and grounds it theoretically in ways that emphasize the personal/poetic in addition to the political. Each of the three sections of the volume then considers crossover film from one of three perspectives: production, the texts themselves, and distribution and consumption.

Sukhmani Khorana lectures in media and communication in the Faculty of Law, Humanities and the Arts, University of Wollongong, Australia.

Routledge Advances in Film Studies

1. **Nation and Identity in the New German Cinema**
   Homeless at Home
   Inga Scharf

2. **Lesbianism, Cinema, Space**
   The Sexual Life of Apartments
   Lee Wallace

3. **Post-War Italian Cinema**
   American Intervention, Vatican Interests
   Daniela Treveri Gennari

4. **Latsploitation, Exploitation Cinemas, and Latin America**
   Edited by Victoria Ruétalo and Dolores Tierney

5. **Cinematic Emotion in Horror Films and Thrillers**
   The Aesthetic Paradox of Pleasurable Fear
   Julian Hanich

6. **Cinema, Memory, Modernity**
   The Representation of Memory from the Art Film to Transnational Cinema
   Russell J. A. Kilbourn

7. **Distributing Silent Film Serials**
   Local Practices, Changing Forms, Cultural Transformation
   Rudmer Canjels

8. **The Politics of Loss and Trauma in Contemporary Israeli Cinema**
   Raz Yosef

9. **Neoliberalism and Global Cinema**
   Capital, Culture, and Marxist Critique
   Edited by Jyotsna Kapur and Keith B. Wagner

10. **Korea's Occupied Cinemas, 1893–1948**
    The Untold History of the Film Industry
    Brian Yecies with Ae-Gyung Shim

11. **Transnational Asian Identities in Pan-Pacific Cinemas**
    The Reel Asian Exchange
    Edited by Philippa Gates and Lisa Funnell

12. **Narratives of Gendered Dissent in South Asian Cinemas**
    Alka Kurian

13. **Hollywood Melodrama and the New Deal**
    Public Daydreams
    Anna Siomopoulos

14. **Theorizing Film Acting**
    Edited by Aaron Taylor

15. **Stardom and the Aesthetics of Neorealism**
    Ingrid Bergman in Rossellini's Italy
    Ora Gelley

16. **Postwar Renoir**
    Film and the Memory of Violence
    Colin Davis

17 **Cinema and Inter-American Relations**
Tracking Transnational Affect
Adrián Pérez Melgosa

18 **European Civil War Films**
Memory, Conflict, and Nostalgia
Eleftheria Rania Kosmidou

19 **The Aesthetics of Antifascism**
Radical Projection
Jennifer Lynde Barker

20 **The Politics of Age and Disability in Contemporary Spanish Film**
Plus Ultra Pluralism
Matthew J. Marr

21 **Cinema and Language Loss**
Displacement, Visuality and the Filmic Image
Tijana Mamula

22 **Cinema as Weather**
Stylistic Screens and Atmospheric Change
Kristi McKim

23 **Landscape and Memory in Post-Fascist Italian Film**
Cinema Year Zero
Giuliana Minghelli

24 **Masculinity in the Contemporary Romantic Comedy**
Gender as Genre
John Alberti

25 **Crossover Cinema**
Cross-Cultural Film from Production to Reception
Edited by Sukhmani Khorana

Crossover Cinema
Cross-Cultural Film from Production to Reception

Edited by Sukhmani Khorana

NEW YORK AND LONDON

First published 2013
by Routledge
711 Third Avenue, New York, NY 10017

Simultaneously published in the UK
by Routledge
2 Park Square, Milton Park, Abingdon, Oxfordshire OX14 4RN

First issued in paperback 2016

Routledge is an imprint of the Taylor and Francis Group, an informa business

© 2013 Taylor & Francis

The right of the editor to be identified as the author of the editorial material, and of the authors for their individual chapters, has been asserted in accordance with sections 77 and 78 of the Copyright, Designs and Patents Act 1988.

All rights reserved. No part of this book may be reprinted or reproduced or utilized in any form or by any electronic, mechanical, or other means, now known or hereafter invented, including photocopying and recording, or in any information storage or retrieval system, without permission in writing from the publishers.

Trademark Notice: Product or corporate names may be trademarks or registered trademarks, and are used only for identification and explanation without intent to infringe.

Library of Congress Cataloging-in-Publication Data

Crossover cinema : cross-cultural film from production to reception /
   edited by Sukhmani Khorana.
      pages cm — (Routledge advances in film studies; 25)
   Includes bibliographical references and index.
 1. Motion picture industry—Economic aspects—Foreign countries.
I. Khorana, Sukhmani, 1984– editor of compilation.
   PN1993.5.A1C795 2013
   384'.83–dc23
   2012051235

ISBN 13: 978-1-138-24325-5 (pbk)
ISBN 13: 978-0-415-63092-4 (hbk)

Typeset in Sabon
By Apex CoVantage, LLC

This book is dedicated to all the passionate filmmakers trying, against the odds, to make border-crossing cinema.

Contents

Acknowledgments   xi

PART I
Producing a Hybrid Grammar

1. Crossover Cinema: A Genealogical and Conceptual Overview   3
   SUKHMANI KHORANA

2. *My Tehran for Sale*: A Coproduction with Poetry at Stake   14
   GRANAZ MOUSSAVI

3. Maps and Movies: Talking with Deepa Mehta   27
   SUKHMANI KHORANA

4. *Los Libertadores* as Crossover Cinema   36
   NOAH ZWEIG

PART II
Reading outside the Canon

5. Hong Kong Film as Crossover Cinema: Maintaining the HK Aesthetic   51
   PETER C. PUGSLEY

6. On No Longer Speaking Chinese: Crossover Stardom and the Performance of Accented English   66
   OLIVIA KHOO

7. Bridging Pop Culture and Identity Politics: Fatih Akin's Road Movie *In July*   83
   AISHA JAMAL

8 Film Policy and the Emergence of the Cross-Cultural:
    Exploring Crossover Cinema in Flanders (Belgium)   94
    GERTJAN WILLEMS AND KEVIN SMETS

PART III
Watching Other Worlds

 9 Leaping the Demographic Barrier: Theoretical Challenges for
    the Crossover Audience   107
    ADRIAN M. ATHIQUE

10 Seduced "Outsiders" versus Skeptical "Insiders"?
    Slumdog Millionaire through Its Re/Viewers   123
    SHAKUNTALA BANAJI

11 *Control Room*: Film and Websites   140
    EMANUELLE WESSELS

12 *Desi* Turns Malay: Indian Cinema Redefined as Crossover in
    the Malaysian Market   153
    SONY JALARAJAN RAJ AND ROHINI SREEKUMAR

    Contributors   167
    Index   171

Acknowledgments

This book would not have been possible without the constant encouragement and mentorship I received from Professor Graeme Turner during my time as a postdoctoral research fellow at the Centre for Critical and Cultural Studies, University of Queensland. The Centre has been a dream workspace, and all my colleagues were of immense help, especially on days when chapters arrived in disarray or reference checking took its toll. I also wish to thank all the contributors to this collection not only for taking the time to write and revise their chapters, but also for their solidarity and enthusiasm in bringing discussions of crossover cinema to life. Finally, I am extremely grateful to Kirsty Leishman for being a model research assistant, to my doctoral supervisors for supporting me in my early work on diasporic film studies and practice, to audiences at the 2011 Screen Conference and the 2012 Crossroads in Cultural Studies Conference where I presented versions of this concept, and to the Routledge team for their faith in this project.

Part I
Producing a Hybrid Grammar

1 Crossover Cinema
A Genealogical and Conceptual Overview
Sukhmani Khorana

In this collection, the term *crossover cinema* is used to encapsulate an emerging form of cinema that crosses cultural borders at the stage of conceptualization and production and hence manifests a hybrid cinematic grammar at the textual level, as well as crossing over in terms of its distribution and reception. It argues for the importance of distinguishing between crossover cinema and transnational cinema. While the latter label has been important in enabling the recognition and consideration of the impact of post–World War II migration and globalization on film practice and scholarship, and while it constituted a significant advance on the term with which is so often conflated, *world cinema*, this chapter argues for a repositioning of the former term as more definitive of the contemporary cultural epoch. The extension of scope in this manner more accurately reflects the highly contingent ways in which global flows in both production and consumption have shaped cinema—not only in the locations of so-called Third Cinema but also in the West. Such a repositioning enables us to think of cross-culturally conceptualized cinema as lying beyond the exclusive art house category that often restricts (a) its reading by film scholars and critics; (b) its publicity discourses and availability in mainstream cinemas; and (c) its reception by various audience communities. There is also an appropriate political objective in the adoption of the term *crossover* to describe cross-culturally conceptualized cinema. This is because with an extended scope, it joins forces with the broader project of internationalizing cultural studies, that is, to keep the competing forces of cultural indigenization and capitalist internationalization from becoming synonymous with globalization (see Abbas and Erni 2005).

In reviewing and reconceptualizing crossover cinema, this chapter attempts to locate it so that on the one hand, it is appropriately specific, while on the other hand emphasizing that it is both situated and global by virtue of its ability to transgress genre, audience, and cultural borders. Such an approach foregrounds the production contexts within which crossover cinema is generated and also argues that the notion of "crossing over" best describes the personal/poetic and political border crossings being constantly undertaken and negotiated by filmmakers with cross-cultural affiliations and influences, and thereby manifested in the hybrid content and form, as well as the distribution and reception, of the films themselves.

I will demonstrate that since the nature of global flows, and ways of defining and associating with home and host cultures, has been transformed in the wake of globalization, it has become imperative to examine the new breed of transnational creative practitioners and their cinematic practices as crossover rather than as simply understood through their national/ethnic origins or identities. Importantly, the potential of such cinema to cross over implies not simply another passing cinematic fad, but a major structural shift in global media industries on one level, while at another level it acknowledges new kinds of creative collaborations that are holistic and replete with the promise of awakening us to the essentialism that persists in certain cultural processes and products.

CROSSOVER CINEMA: FROM JARGON TO *JAGARAN* (HINDI FOR "AWAKENING")

The aim of this anthology is not so much to be geographically representative, but to provide a glimpse of the kind of cinema (and ways of making meaning from its textual and extratextual elements) that is cross-culturally conceived, yet not relegated to the margins of mainstream public culture by virtue of its ability to cross over. Unlike "world cinema" or "transnational cinema," for instance, there is no argument to be made about the inclusion of crossover cinema in mainstream cinema culture. In reconceptualizing crossover cinema, I am appropriating a term that has so far had a very particular location, but also simultaneously a very unattached resonance. As a moniker hitherto applied to films associated with or emerging from the Indian subcontinent that are able to appeal to Western audiences, crossover cinema has a rather rooted history, albeit with little explication of its content or the setting out of its practice-based parameters. Similarly, Ranjit Keval Kumar's (2011) PhD thesis on crossover and makeover trends in new Indian cinema also acknowledges the muddling of the terms *Bollywood*, *Indian*, and *crossover* film and argues that crossover is an emerging genre in its own right. In a similar vein, American distributor Miramax attempted a model crossover hit in the 1990s by reediting Hong Kong films to create a balance between distinctiveness and accessibility (Dombrowski 2008). This shows a similar rooted yet outward tendency, drawing on the South Asian usage of the term, but again it remains ambiguously defined and poorly executed.

I argue that despite the above limitations, *crossover cinema* as a conceptual term and as an indicator of an emerging form is ripe for usage in the contemporary cinematic context. However, it must be emphasized that unlike the South Asian or Hong Kong use of the term, *crossover cinema* in this collection of chapters does not derive its primary point of difference from other kinds of cinemas through its crossover in audience terms alone.

Instead, it is the site of cross-cultural conceptualization and production that is taken as the principal foundation and that then leads to textual hybridity and wide-ranging audience appeal. This is not done to privilege an auteurist account of such cinema, but rather to highlight the process of creating a film that is not conventionally grounded in a single national/cultural/generic source.

The first usage of the term in South Asia can be traced back to the early years of the twenty-first century with the border-crossing popularity of films made by Indian diasporic directors (such as Gurinder Chadha's [2002] *Bend It Like Beckham* and Mira Nair's [2001] *Monsoon Wedding*) and English-language films by India-based filmmakers (like Nagesh Kukunoor's [2003] *Bollywood Calling* and Rahul Bose's [2001] *Everybody Says I'm Fine*). At the same time, the nation's most prolific commercial film industry, Mumbai-based Bollywood, borrowed the term soon after and began using it to describe its own global, neoliberal outreach. Not surprisingly, this led to widespread confusion and an opinion piece in the *Times of India* dubbed the trend "Crossover Cinema" (Nair 2003). However, ambivalence toward the term continues into the present within Indian film and media circles; Bollywood superstar Shahrukh Khan recently declared, "It disturbs me that all Indian filmmakers are chasing an elusive dream of crossover cinema" (cited in *Mid-Day* 2011).

The previous comment implies not that Indian filmmakers are chasing a supposed genre called crossover cinema, but rather that, according to Khan, their search for a Western audience may not come to fruition. In other words, there is a conflation of the term with a particular segment of the global audience, and a particular marketing strategy, and this has gone relatively unquestioned in film scholarship. For instance, when discussing the globalization of Bollywood, renowned film scholar Daya Kishan Thussu (2008, 106–7) distinguishes between diasporic and Indian films but still defines crossover primarily as Bollywood's attempted foray into traditional Hollywood territory. Such usage needs to be qualified. Bollywood has a long history of transnational appeal in nations as diverse as Malaysia and the former Soviet Union (see Iordanova 2006), and the crossover cinema is by no means defined by its attempt to make it into Hollywood. Further, it is worth noting that such formulations implicitly defer to Hollywood as a media center; the global reach of Hollywood is hardly ever described as a crossover. What I am suggesting here is that being cross-cultural in terms of the text, the intertext and the extratext is intrinsic to a crossover film. Such a film does not assume a Western audience at the outset but rather is forged from multiple cultural affiliations and eventually appeals to a range of viewing communities among whom the Western audience is only one possibility.

What, then, exemplifies a crossover film? And, is it opening up cinematic and discursive spaces that are based on a cross-cultural, cross-platform paradigm? I would like to begin your journey through the anthology with the previous questions, while also offering the suggestion that Danny Boyle's

(2008) *Slumdog Millionaire* is a possible, if arguably contested, template. Although *Crouching Tiger, Hidden Dragon* (Lee 2000) was widely lauded as a crossover phenomenon after Miramax's initial unsuccessful attempts to generate a Hong Kong–based worldwide hit, it still only made it to the Best Foreign Film category of the Academy Awards. *Slumdog Millionaire*, on the other hand, literally crossed over to the main (nonforeign) group. This is not to suggest that the Academy Awards is an objective barometer of crossover success, or that it is transparently representative of the best of global cinema. However, it is crucial that the latter film's cross-cultural affiliations no longer rendered it foreign, and this is an important indicator of its crossover production, content, and appeal.

In her review of *Slumdog Millionaire*, which locates it in the viewership context of post–financial crisis America, Kavoori (2009) refers to the film as "a classic crossover text," adding that it uses "the specifics of Indian locale to speak to wider (global) concerns of personal responsibility in a heartless world; the need for agency in an alienated society and perhaps most critically, the renewal of 'love' as a category for understanding the self" (260). Not only is this reading demonstrative of the situated knowledge theorized as being critical to a holistic consideration of crossover cinema, but it also shows that transnational appeal needs to be both globally and locally dispersed rather than invested in an elite Western milieu. This collection is merely the beginning of an endeavor to free up the term so that it can have multiple cinematic roots and routes. The word *crossover* refers to more than an arbitrary attempt to join discrete entities; in this context, the term indicates cross-cultural affinities that both travel and stay.

PERSONAL/POETIC AND POLITICAL: THEORIZING CROSSOVER CINEMATIC PRACTICE

In order to free up the term *crossover*, it is crucial that its usage in film theory and practice is understood as a manifestation of cross-cultural affinities that are not merely political but also personal/poetic. The aim of this and the following section, then, is to first articulate such a theoretical framework and, subsequently, enact all the dimensions of a conversation about crossover cinema that itself crosses over disciplinary and methodological boundaries.

In an essay titled "Ethnicity in an Age of Diaspora," diasporic Indian scholar R. Radhakrishnan (2003, 119) begins with a personal scenario in which his eleven-year-old son asks him whether he is Indian or American. Terming the scenario "both filial and pedagogic," Radhakrishnan tells his son that he is both (122) and embarks on a polemical journey about identity and the shifting contours of its relationship with ethnicity and location. Such an autobiographical, yet contextually relevant, beginning is an apt metaphor for this chapter due to both its personal particularity and its wider political implications. It also leads us to question the use of the personal/poetic anecdote as a springboard for reflections on the cross-cultural condition that otherwise adhere to conventional academic discourse.

The answer to the previous question lies in the nature of contemporary transnational formations, which, like Radhakrishnan's filial-pedagogic scenario, are both experiential and theoretical. For this reason, Sunil Bhatia and Anjali Ram (2001) recommend a process-oriented approach to acculturation research "where the focus is on understanding how immigrants living in hybrid cultures and diasporic locations are constantly negotiating their multiple, and often conflicting histories and subject positions" (3). Similarly, in the introduction to an edited volume titled *Theorizing Diaspora*, Jana Evans Braziel and Anita Mannur (2003) call for a need to move beyond the construction and consolidation of cross-cultural identities to ask how these identities are "practised, lived, and experienced" (9). Therefore, as Radhakrishnan's story illustrates, I contend that for a well-rounded understanding of crossover cinematic practice, it is crucial to examine the ongoing performativity of the creative self.

In addition to considering the personal through its performativity, it is important to remember that the transnational selves that are performed display affiliations to two or more cultures or nations. The politics of these belongings are deeply intertwined with the performativity of the personal. Gina Wisker (2007) notes this entanglement of the personal and the political in her commentary on the identities of diasporic writers: "As they dialogue with the adoptive homeland, they change themselves, the new homeland, and their versions and memories of the other homelands, and as they dialogue with the other homelands they renegotiate meaning in their minds and actions" (29).

Migrant scholar Ien Ang (2001) theorizes her own identity through a similar consideration of performativity and context when she notes, "If I am inescapably Chinese by descent, I am only sometimes Chinese by consent. When and how is a matter of politics" (51). While the postcolonial notion of "negotiated belonging" and the postmodern conceptualization of "performativity" help to adequately theorize the political and personal elements of crossover cinematic practice, respectively, they do not aid in moving beyond the two entities represented by the nation of origin and the adoptive homeland. The idea of "hybridity" theorized by Homi Bhabha (2004) as the "Third Space of enunciation" is useful in amalgamating the two entities, but it does not necessarily entail the formation of an identity and accompanying practice that transcends the sum of its parts. This idea is reinforced by Werbner (1997) who, in her introduction to a collection of essays on cultural hybridity, proposes "critical self-distancing from their own cultural discourses" as an alternative to Bhabha's "interruptive hybridity from the margins" (14). In other words, it is crucial, especially in light of a society that is not just postcolonial and marginal, but increasingly global and local, to employ a theory of resistance that both examines the discourses of constitutive cultures and is able to transcend these through distanciation or the creation of a mode of its own.

8 Sukhmani Khorana

To articulate this mode, the remaining chapters of the first part of this collection (on conceptualization and production) include a reflective chapter on the poetic and political negotiations around making an Iranian-Australian coproduction by Granaz Moussavi, a film site interview on the advantages and disadvantages of occupying the diasporic space with Academy Award–nominated director Deepa Mehta, and an account by Noah Zweig of how the "pink tide" in Latin America could be linked to the emergence of particular kinds of crossover films. These chapters, although varied in form and voice, also perform an enactment of the personal/poetic and political aspects of crossover cinematic practice, or a "both and" approach. By *poetics*, I mean not just the aesthetics of this kind of cinema, but the larger inventiveness of which the aesthetics forms a part. This is similar to David Bordwell's (2007) use of the term *poetics* when studying both film as art and the very evolution of such theorizing. While Moussavi, Mehta, and Zweig are primarily concerned with the creative process and the conditions of production, they also briefly reflect on the composition of the screen texts and the audiences for the films under consideration. These aspects of crossover cinema, however, are more fully explored in the two subsequent parts of the collection. What the above reflections demonstrate is merely the primal significance and flow-on effects of the conceptualization and production stage in the life cycle of the crossover film.

The previously mentioned "both and" approach is not new in the field of transnational and migration studies. It has been adopted by scholars such as Ann-Marie Fortier (1999, 42) who, in her study of the Italian émigré culture in Britain, concludes that cultural identity in migration is both deterritorialized and reterritorialized. In a similar vein, Wisker (2007) cites the example of British-Indian screenwriter and comic Meera Syal whose "satiric and comic voice steers a course between gentle mockery and farce, undercutting the Othering and ignorance which stereotyping feeds by dramatizing examples of Asian culture" (98–99). What I propose in this chapter, therefore, is also that textual readings of the hybridity of crossover film texts must pay close attention to the multiple cinematic affiliations of the filmmaker(s). The second part of this collection attempts such close textual/intertextual analysis through Peter Pugsley's account of contemporary Hong Kong cinema's adoption of a transnational aesthetic and narrative palette, Olivia Khoo's examination of the recent phenomenon of using Chinese actresses to perform an "accented English," Gertjan Willems and Kevin Smets's consideration of the emergence of diasporic and intercultural strands within Flemish cinema, and Aisha Jamal's reading of a European crossover road movie made by migrant German filmmaker Fatih Akin. The politics of language, location, travel, and narrative style is therefore implicated in the analysis of crossover films in this section.

A holistic approach to studying crossover cinema also necessitates a reading of extratextual elements, such as the crossovers performed in relation to discourses of cross-cultural audience reception, digital distribution platforms, and global marketing strategies. This is of consequence not merely in terms of preexisting audience communities based on national, ethnic, class, or gender categories, but also with regard to the fragmentation and new viewership patterns brought about by postbroadcast television and the Internet. Therefore, in the final part of the collection, Adrian Mabbott Athique's contribution postulates the theoretical challenges of conceptualizing the crossover audience, Shakuntala Banaji's chapter shows what such a group may look like through qualitative interviews with international viewers of *Slumdog Millionaire*, Emanuelle Wessels examines the website of the crossover film *Control Room* as a medium for ongoing ethical viewer participation, and Sony Jalarajan Raj and Rohini Sreekumar read the historical and contemporary reception of Indian cinema in the Malaysian market as the enactment of a crossover. Again, the emphasis in this section is not on speculating on the kind of cross-cultural film that is likely to be a box-office and/or online success. Rather, the objective here is to begin to understand what interests spatially and temporally dispersed audiences in certain crossover texts, whether such discourses can be framed within an ethics and/or politics of viewership, and if the organizational and people-to-people networks underpinning cross-cultural reception need further attention.

The simultaneous yet contextual consideration of the personal/poetic and the political in each section of the collection aids in the generation of situated readings and practice. In their edited volume of essays by scholars with cross-cultural affiliations, Evans Braziel and Mannur (2003) perform the crucial task of emphasizing the historical and cultural specificity of any new becomings:

> Diasporic traversals question the rigidities of identity itself—religious, ethnic, gendered, national; yet this diasporic movement marks not a postmodern turn from history, but a nomadic turn in which the very parameters of specific historical moments are embodied and—as diaspora itself suggests—are scattered and regrouped into new points of becoming. (3)

Commenting on the representation of the black postcolonial subject in the "Third Cinemas" of the Caribbean, Stuart Hall performs a similar theorization of diasporic identity and representation in his specific Jamaican-British context. He suggests, "Perhaps instead of thinking about identity as an already accomplished fact, which the new cultural practices then represent, we should think, instead, of identity as a 'production', which is never complete, always in process, and always constituted within, not outside representation" (Hall 1996, 110). While Hall refers to identity itself as a production, this volume takes the specific becomings embodied in crossover cinematic practice, distribution, and reception as its focus. This is not done to emphasize cinematic practice over identity formation but is a pragmatic choice as visual practice is a rendering of the processes of performing, negotiating, and inventing cross-cultural identities that makes it possible to study and theorize about the previously mentioned processes (and not just the products).

An example of a situated performing, negotiating, and inventing is evident in *Shooting Water*, a memoir written by Indian-Canadian filmmaker Deepa Mehta's daughter Devyani Saltzman (2006). It combines the writer's own tales of self-discovery during the filming of *Water* (Mehta 2005) with observations on the wider sociopolitical situation in South Asia. Mehta's films are similarly considered in my interview with her (in the first part of this volume) as embodying the personal/poetic journey of the filmmaker and manifesting the turbulent politics prevalent at the time of their inception. Such an entangling of the personal/poetic and the political is discursively performed in the following section in that it produces cultural understandings that are situated (hence partial), yet with the depth and potential to cross over.

FIRANGS AND SLUMDOGS: TOWARD CROSSOVER CONVERSATIONS

In 2008, on reaching the midpoint of my PhD candidacy (on diasporic cinema and creative praxis) at the University of Adelaide, and after spending more than five years pursuing tertiary studies and media-related work in Australia, I decided to visit India during the nonholiday season—that is, the Indian monsoon and the Australian winter. What led to the specific time and nature of this journey? It came about for a combination of reasons—not teaching during the semester in question; feeling overwhelmed by the multiple theoretical underpinnings of my doctoral project; seeking visual inspiration for the documentary I was about to begin shooting; and most importantly, making sure that I was not growing apart from my family, my home, and my childhood version of India.

The last reason reminded me of Sri Lankan–Canadian writer Michael Ondaatje's (1984) temporary return journey to his homeland to come to grips with his family and nation, poetically documented in his memoir *Running in the Family*. Given the context of my reasons, I was slightly taken aback when my mother, habitually quick to comment on any changes in physical appearance, pointed out that I appeared *firang* (Hindi for "foreign"). She explained that it was obviously not my skin color or clothes and jewelry, but something in my accent and general demeanor that was not quite her lived understanding of being "Indian."

A visit to my youngest sister's boarding school (also my alma mater) and a brief conversation with her sixteen-year-old friends led them to conclude that I looked like an Australian tourist. Again, I was surprised because I made it a point to wear chic Indian fusion garb while in India—three-quarter black pants with a sleeveless ethnic tunic, silver necklace and earrings, and kohl-lined eyes. Perhaps it was the digital video camera always slung across my right shoulder, giving the impression I was constantly documenting moments and sights that were ordinary to all those around me. Both the observations of my mother and my sister's friends made me wonder if my "Indianness" had already been hyphenated, if not usurped by the act of living, studying, and working in Australia. I, like nearly twenty million people of Indian origin living in the diaspora, had not necessarily grown apart from India but acquired an additional layer of cultural identity and hence become cross-cultural in my personal/poetic and political affiliations. This newly acquired layer led me to foreground my old (yet not fixed) layer in some scenarios and relegate it to the background in others. I am, therefore, becoming different from my India-based family and friends even as I share my ancestral history and ongoing yet varying interest in Indian cultural and political events with them. Herein I see a cross-cultural identity at play: performing, negotiating, and inventing.

On my return to the Australian summer two months later, I interviewed members of the Indian diaspora in Adelaide for the documentary component of my doctorate, wrote the bulk of my thesis, and continued to work my way through familial and social becomings. It is perhaps no coincidence that my personal-political negotiations and poetic recreations, although ongoing, peaked at the same time as the release of the film *Slumdog Millionaire*, which, as explained earlier in this chapter, traverses national and cinematic boundaries. The release and success of the film renewed my confidence in the disciplinary, cultural, and creative significance of the project at hand; in addition, it inspired me to consider a wider scholarly consideration of crossover cinema beyond the South Asian diaspora. Although Boyle's film does not strictly fit the definition of diasporic cinema, it provides a significant model of cross-cultural cinematic content and talent that has also successfully crossed over into the realm of the mainstream audience.

Perhaps the notion of a cinematic practice that crosses over in terms of culture, genre, and reception platforms need no longer be a novelty or an anomaly. It may be a phenomenon that is gaining wider acceptance in mainstream film culture, as well as film and cultural studies scholarship. It may also be an indication for film practitioners coveting transnational and mass audiences that there are means to achieve the same. With this crossover potential in mind, I continue to find myself talking about *Slumdog Millionaire* (and subsequent films of the kind, such as Argentinean filmmaker Gustavo Taretto's [2011] *Medianeras*, British director Michael Winterbottom's [2011] *Trishna*, and Swedish/British documentary *Searching for Sugar Man* directed by Mark Bendjelloul [2012]) with family and friends in Australia, in India, and in other parts of the world. While my reading of crossover cinematic practice is situated in specific Indian, Australian, and academic discourses, it somehow also transcends these locations so that our mutual film discourse becomes a crossover conversation itself, something to be celebrated (albeit critically).

REFERENCES

Abbas, Ackbar, and Erni, John Nguyet. 2005. *Internationalizing Cultural Studies: An Anthology*. Malden: Blackwell Publishing.
Ang, Ien. 2001. *On Not Speaking Chinese: Living between Asian and the West*. London: Routledge.
Bendjelloul, Mark, dir. 2012. *Searching for Sugar Man*. New York: Sony Pictures Classics.
Bhabha, Homi. 1994. *The Location of Culture*. London: Routledge.
Bhatia, Sunil, and Ram, Anjali. 2001. "Rethinking Acculturation in Relation to Diasporic Cultures and Postcolonial Identities." *Human Development* 44(1): 1–18.
Bordwell, David. 2007. *Poetics of Cinema*. London: Routledge.
Bose, Rahul, dir. 2001. *Everybody Says I'm Fine*. India: Pinnacle Entertainment.
Boyle, Danny, dir. 2008. *Slumdog Millionaire*. Los Angeles: Fox Searchlight.
Chadha, Gurinder, dir. 2002. *Bend it Like Beckham*. United Kingdom: Redbus Film Distribution.
Dombrowski, Lisa. 2008. "Miramax's Asian Experiment: Creating a Model for Crossover Hits." *Scope: An Online Journal of Film and TV Studies* 10. http://www.scope.nottingham.ac.uk/article.php?issue = 10&id = 988. Accessed April 10, 2011.
Evans Braziel, Jana, and Mannur, Anita. 2003. "Nation, Migration, Globalization: Points of Contention in Diaspora Studies." In *Theorizing Diaspora*, edited by Jana Evans Braziel and Anita Mannur, 1–22. Oxford: Blackwell Publishing.
Fortier, Ann-Marie. 1999. "Re-membering Places and the Performance of Belonging(s)." *Theory, Culture & Society* 16(2): 41–64.
Hall, Stuart. 1996. "Cultural Identity and Diaspora." In *Contemporary Postcolonial Theory: A Reader*, edited by Padmini Mongia, 110–21. London: Arnold.
Iordanova, Dina (with contributions from Juan Goytisolo, Ambassador K Gajendra Singh, Rada Sesic, Asuman Suner, Viola Shafik, and P. A. Skantze). 2006. "Indian Cinema's Global Reach: Historiography through Testimonies." *South Asian Popular Culture* 4(2): 113–40.
Kavoori, Anadam. 2009. "Film Review: Why the Sun Shines on Slum Dog." *Global Media and Communication* 5: 259–62.
Kukunoor, Nagesh, dir. 2003. *Bollywood Calling*. Mumbai: Eros International.
Kumar, Ranjit Keval. 2011. *Crossovers and Makeovers: Contested Authenticity in New Indian Cinema*. PhD thesis, University of Wollongong. http://ro.uow.edu.au/theses/3417. Accessed October 22, 2012.
Lee, Ang, dir. 2000. *Crouching Tiger, Hidden Dragon*. Hong Kong: EDKO Film.
Mehta, Deepa, dir. 2005. *Water*. Toronto: Mongrel Media.
Mid-Day. 2011. "It Disturbs Me to See Filmmakers Chasing Crossover Cinema." http://www.mid-day.com/entertainment/2011/mar/180311-Bollywood-Shah-Rukh-Khan-crossover-cinema.htm. Accessed April 5, 2011.
Nair, Mira, dir. 2001. *Monsoon Wedding*. Universal City, CA: USA Films.
Nair, Suresh. 2003. "Crassover Cinema." *The Times of India*. http://timesofindia.indiatimes.com/india/Crassover-cinema/articleshow/287078.cms. Accessed April 5, 2011.
Ondaatje, Michael. 1984. *Running in the Family*. London: Picador.
Radhakrishnan, R. 2003. "Ethnicity in an Age of Diaspora." In *Theorizing Diaspora*, edited by Jana Evans Braziel and Anita Mannur, 119–31. Oxford: Blackwell.
Saltzman, Devyani. 2006. *Shooting Water: A Mother-Daughter Journey and the Making of a Film*. New Delhi: Penguin Books.
Taretto, Gustavo, dir. 2011. *Medianeras*. Buenos Aires: Aura Films.

Thussu, Daya Kishan. 2008. "The Globalisation of 'Bollywood'—The Hype and Hope." In *Global Bollywood*, edited by Anandam Kavoori and Aswin Punathambekar, 97–113. New York: New York University Press.
Werbner, Pnina. 1997. "Introduction: The Dialectics of Cultural Hybridity." In *Debating Cultural Hybridity*, edited by Pnina Werbner and Tariq Modood, 1–26. London: ZED Books.
Winterbottom, Michael, dir. 2011. *Trishna*. New York: IFC Films.
Wisker, Gina. 2007. *Key Concepts in Postcolonial Literature*. Hampshire: Palgrave Macmillan.

2 *My Tehran for Sale*
A Coproduction with Poetry at Stake

Granaz Moussavi

The aesthetics, form, and content of Persian poetry have evolved through a long history of cultural development, invention in language, and creative innovation, shaped in response to local, regional, and global shifts in power. Within Iranian society, poetic games play an integral role in how certain communities—religious, political, and artistic—imagine and enact their shared histories and world perspectives.

My Tehran for Sale is a feature film conceived and developed on the basis of my research into poetic cinema. As a practice-led research project, I was from the outset concerned to demonstrate my understanding of poetic aesthetics and how they may be recuperated through film. However, I have seen my role as being more than a poet and emerging filmmaker traversing disciplinary bounds. How I saw my research interests and the ideas that I tried to manifest visually was to reflect on my position as a practitioner who has lived and worked across cultural contexts, negotiating the conditions for innovation in dissimilar social realities and creative conditions. Therefore, "the private/personal is political" is part and parcel of *My Tehran for Sale*.

First and foremost, my personal life and artistic output has been significantly shaped by the turbulent experiences of revolution, war, and immigration. I have found poetry to be a necessary survival mechanism—it has provided me with the means to forge and express a contemporary Iranian identity that stands against the concrete definitions circulating both within and outside of a highly regulated and politicized society. Prior to making the film, I invested two years into researching Persian poetics and how it has evolved through a tradition of constant innovation in response to shifting social and political pressures, sustaining the Persian (Iranian) imaginary even through the trauma of invasion, a colonialism that was never fully realized, and an imported modernity.

Though Persian poetry has been elevated to a position of critical influence and acclaim within global creative discourse, it remains largely unknown to international audiences. The barriers of language are compounded by the complexities of expression and intertextuality advanced through Persian poetic discourse. Even within Iran, many cultural nuances and manners of

Figure 2.1 Granaz Moussavi on the set of *My Tehran for Sale*.
Source: Author's own.

storytelling become difficult to relay through ordinary modes of expression—this is true even in relation to the modernized forms of poetry developed by *Nimaic* poets and their successors.

Cinema holds unique potential for local communities to build an alternate realm of communication within the global sphere. By inventively playing with the conventions associated with dominant modes of storytelling in cinema, artists may succeed in preserving residues of traditional cultures, including ethnic poetic traditions, innovating new cinematic languages that are open to be read and interpreted by diverse audiences.

Partly, I was curious about the possibilities of combining the film and exegesis and placing in dialogue distinct traditions of poetic cinema defined at various scales of affiliation. As much as I was inspired by the films of Sohrab Shahid-Sales, Forough Farrokhzad, Abbas Kiarostami, and others, I was interested in importing the conscious poetic approaches of Pier Paolo Pasolini (1988) and Maya Deren (1970)—among other Western and international poetic filmmakers—as a means to translate the local poetry invested in Iranian art-house cinema into a form surpassing language and cultural barriers accessible to Iranian and international audiences.

In my view, the substantial gap in the literature on Iranian poetic cinema and the potential for proper investigation of the subject is hampered by tendencies to see Iranian culture and its cinematic expression as representing an "exotic Other," or as a nativist response to creative innovation originating within modern Western or European experiences.

The experience of producing a poetic film across cultural borders, under the terms of "coproduction," illustrates the central theoretical framework that I propose: that is, distinct bodies of poetic cinema are the outcomes of an innovation process staged at once at a local and cross-cultural scale. And that the process of poetic innovation is improvised by the creative involved as a response to the immediate challenges and expectations arising from within the social reality with which they are affiliated. Poetic innovation through cinema is *reiterative*: the creative figure may draw on poetic traditions that are embedded in the history and culture of that society, just as they may draw on an array of cinematic techniques and cultural materials.

Also, I discuss in connection with the development of *My Tehran for Sale* that poetic ideas, aesthetics, and techniques offer an armory of tools that are useful for testing the limits of expression and experimentation within specific social and professional contexts.

CROSS-CULTURAL AFFILIATIONS AND THE TERMS OF "COPRODUCTION"

The production of *My Tehran for Sale*, as an unusual coproduction located within the Australian film industry, could not have been possible without ongoing and crucial support from the Adelaide Film Festival (AFF). Acquiring additional support from the South Australian Film Corporation (SAFC) followed the initial financial investment of the AFF in the idea. The creative strategies behind the film's development were broadened so the film would meet criteria as a "coproduction" between Australia and Iran. However, the film was always technically referred to as a "collaboration" considering the sensitivities associated with the term *coproduction* given that Iran was under sanction. In fact, *My Tehran for Sale* would be the first noted Iranian-Australian feature film coproduction (collaboration) in history.

The early emphasis on this project as a coproduction had a range of outcomes in terms of shaping the creative and professional strategies invested in the work. One of these outcomes was a strengthening of my artistic and professional affiliations within Iran's alternative film industry. In order to secure the Australian funding, at least a third of all money invested in the project had to be provided by an Iranian party, and as I was a first-time feature filmmaker with no directorial credits to my name, I was advised to acquire the backing of a well-known Iranian producer. I engaged Bahman Ghobadi—an award-winning Iranian film and documentary maker of Kurdish descent who had established Mij Film, a film production company, in 2000.

This decision, however, compromised the uniqueness of *My Teheran for Sale* as a small production made by a no-name director (myself) in its approach to narrative, use of location, and even some costume design, since Ghobadi also produced his *No One Knows about Persian Cats* a few months after our production.

The engagement of Ghobadi in this project was built on a personal experience of collaborating with him on a series of projects that have extended across Australian and Iranian borders. I worked as an assistant and onset digital editor during the production of his third feature film, *Turtles Can Fly*; I cowrote with him and Sepideh Shamlou a yet-to-be-made film with a working title of *Love without L.O.V. . . .*; and I acted as his minder and interpreter during his visit to the AFF in 2006, during which we established with my local producers his involvement in *My Tehran for Sale*.

My hope for this mode of production was to open a dialogue to cut across the internally regulated cultural and political borders of Iran and also challenge knowledge and stereotypes of Iranian people and culture operating across public stages within the international sphere.

The central criteria set out by the SAFC script assessors and advisors was modification of the script; they argued that it would need to be developed in certain ways that made the ethnic poetic approach and Iranian content more meaningful for mass audiences (and Australian audiences specifically). This meant, first, making the film more explanatory and insightful about the details of restricted life in Iran today, and second, relating the film's themes and content to Australian experiences and concerns.

To give just one example of how this shaped my creative strategies, through the script-editing process I decided to highlight in the film narrative a conflict that remains central to Australia's cultural and political conflict and contested national identity—the issue of asylum seekers, their treatment in detention centers and the psychological pressures, impacts, and responses these conditions elicit. I was especially interested to explore the imperative on illegal arrivals to formulate personal biographies, narratives that often oscillate between truth and untruth, just as poetic films may highlight the false economy of truth and fiction circulating within the cinematic space.

THE PROCESS OF SCRIPT WRITING

The poetic foundations of *My Tehran for Sale* are found in a poem that I wrote on my lived experience of exile, titled "Sale" (Moussavi 2000, 8–10). The script-writing process was a combination of my work as a poet and almost a decade of conversations with Marzieh Vafamehr and other friends in Iran, as well as a number of Iranian people in exile, through which I have shaped true-to-life stories about people I have encountered across the borders.

After my synopsis won the national pitching competition supported by Australian law firm Holding Redlich, the project attracted Cyan Films (also facilitated and encouraged by the AFF) as potential producers, and the script-writing process gained its initial momentum. In March 2007, I completed the first draft—a forty-nine-page script composed of a nonlinear narrative and a weave of side stories featuring minor characters. This version was designed with a film-within-a-film style, with Marzieh role-playing a prostitute pimped by Saman for the sake of a "film" being made by an Australian crew. Marzieh's gaze direct to camera and dialogue heard offscreen when the camera was supposedly switched off would hint at Marzieh's real-life persona as a participant in the film crew even as the lines between these embedded realities would be brought into question.

The revelation that Marzieh has been infected with HIV would act as a catalyst for destabilizing the perceived separation between fiction and reality, opening space for further poetic readings of the film. The final scene of the script was a crane shot of Marzieh stuck in heavy traffic on a Tehran street.

THE AUSTRALIAN CONTEXT

In their critiques of the film through its various stages of production, the major Australian investors supporting *My Tehran for Sale* urged for stronger and more conventional and expository approaches to narrative development. My biggest challenge through the process of script editing was to write the drafts in a way that satisfied the investors while advancing the poetic qualities of the film.

This was a greater struggle when it came to conforming with the "central conflict theory," that is, the central conflict as the driver of narrative progress and audience engagement. Raul Ruiz critiques this theory as originating out of U.S. culture and indicating cinema's role in the cultural politics of globalization. The modification of the script required more involving drama that would address Marzieh's motivations and actions in resolving key problems with which she is confronted through the course of the narrative. The emphasis on clarity of events, "expositions," and more linear storytelling was clearly in opposition to my initial radical and more experimental view on poetic qualities.

My Tehran for Sale, in its final form, reflects my attempt to resolve investors' demands for narrative resonance and strength with specific elements and devices that create a poetic quality and subvert conventional narrative forms. The film employs a nonlinear story line, with events interrupted and expanded over the course of the film, leading to an open ending. Around the central story line—Marzieh's relationship with Saman and her journey for personal and cultural freedom by leaving Iran for Australia—the narrative thread develops through a collage of minor events. These side stories—peripheral events brought into cinematic focus—provide documentary-style glimpses of the underground lifestyle and social pressures experienced by youths and artists in Tehran.

The film opens by crosscutting between a rave in Tehran, raided by police, and a scene of Marzieh in an Australian detention center. Under questioning, Marzieh constructs her story, conveying how she survived the raid and punishment by lashing that followed. Then the film title is introduced, superimposed over an extreme long shot of Tehran in the early morning, with city noises and a vague sound of "call out to pray" spiritual verses (sound of *Azan* from mosques) echoing out, punctuating the stillness of dawn.

The incorporation of the detention center scene helped me to build narrative strength but also strengthened the framework for poetic innovation: I broke down the scene and distributed it throughout the script, creating a time shift that would engage the imagination of the audience, which would receive information gradually and be required to put the pieces together. The narrative development also set the ground for me to introduce oneiric and ambiguous qualities, as I became interested in exploring the imperative on illegal arrivals to formulate personal biographies—narratives that oscillate between truth and fiction just as poetic films may highlight the false economy of truth and fiction circulating within the cinematic space.

The film continues as a documentation of lifestyles set across various internal and external locations in Tehran—in front of the Australian embassy, street life and traffic, the house next door to Marzieh where she babysits the young girl Niloufar, a medical clinic in Tehran that Marzieh attends for health checks to meet visa requirements. In all these scenes, Marzieh is present amongst others, but there is no specific focus on her story. As minor or peripheral characters present themselves and their stories, Marzieh's character is built up slowly.

For the first seventy-five minutes of the film, there is no central conflict driving a three-act structure. Instead, in the second section, a sudden climax arrives with a letter delivered to the couple's door informing them that Marzieh's medical tests returned an HIV-positive result. The final section of the film contains scattered scenes of Marzieh saying good-bye to the city and the underground life that she both loves and hates, putting her belongings on sale and raging at the Australian detention officers for their unjust treatment of her case while she considers voluntarily going back to the place from which she has risked her life to escape.

In their feedback, readers for the funding bodies specifically targeted the use of multiple points of view and peripheral stories observed and acted out by supporting characters. I insisted on keeping this specific device, not simply because it subverts the principles of linear, character-based narrative, but because it helps build the dichotomy of the film as both fiction and documentary, thus creating potential for a heightened interactive experience. The poetic collage structure raises awareness of the ways we are accustomed to seeing life represented through films and other media, and it illuminates the potential for other, more radical forms of seeing. As Rumi (2003) says, the work of poetry is "[an] ear that interprets mystery, a vein of silver in the ground, and another sky!" (64).

For the same reason, I purposefully left the ending open, a possibility again emerging out of the strengthening of narrative for Australian audiences. In the final scene, Marzieh wanders through Tehran streets to the music and lyrics of

Mohsen Namjou, an artist popular in the Iranian underground. The position of this scene in the narrative thread is left undetermined, and the film thus remains unresolved, or "unfinished" in the terms of Kiarostami. The scene may be interpreted as taking place in the past, before Marzieh left the country, or in the present, indicating that Marzieh has been deported back to Iran.

POETIC CINEMA AS CREATIVE PROCESS

Poetic cinema refers not to a specific genre or unified movement, but rather to varied traditions of innovation enacted at different scales of affiliation. In contrast to other film movements, which are often advanced through the reproduction and evolution of genres and styles, poetic cinema is the outcome of an iterative process of creative innovation, which advances residues of traditional culture through new assemblages that resonate with indeterminate meanings.

In an artistic sense, the challenge for poetic filmmakers is thus to experiment within parameters set according to their network of professional affiliations and intended audiences, with the aim to advance a process of poetic innovation. As a first-time filmmaker who is also interested in film scholarship, I was aware that the established ideas and techniques for recuperating poetic aesthetics into film constitute tools for improvisation and poetic assemblage in response to the social realities and creative conditions in which the filmmaker operates.

NEGOTIATING TABOOS: THE IRANIAN CONTEXT

In contemporary Iran, one of the aspects of the innovation of poetics through cinema continues in response to censorship driven by political authorities and cultural taboos generated at a more social, even grassroots level. The incorporation into cinema of poetic language, aesthetics, and techniques comes forth in tackling the obstacles of censorship because they open up the film structure and narrative to multiple interpretations, thus enabling creative practitioners to highlight the social margins and voices otherwise considered taboo.

When the social and political implications of a narrative are materialized in the final form of a film, it becomes more difficult to ascertain whether it is "crossing the red lines"—a phrase employed within the Iranian department responsible for censorship. As Hamid Dabashi (2001) states in his study *Close-Up: Iranian Cinema Past, Present, and Future* with regard to Kiarostami's elliptical style:

> To put art, the visual and performing arts in particular, consciously at the service of social and political causes ultimately and paradoxically

ossifies and thus intensifies precisely those forces that have conditioned those causes. A far more radical and effective negation of those forces is to abandon the site of their authority. (280)

Kiarostami's "unfinished" style is constructed through the use of dark screen, offscreen space, and unresolved endings, with these techniques designed to increase the level of interactivity and open up the overall structure of the filmic text so viewers will read between the lines. In Iranian poetic cinema more generally, filmmakers push the limits of public discourse by creating alternate modes of expression offering multiple layers of interpretation governed by complex rules.

The experimentation in forms and modes of communication, language games, and innovative ways of expression find their origins in Persian poetic traditions, and more specifically in the modern innovations of the *Nimaic* poets. Their poetic forms departed from the rigidities of classical aesthetics, advancing cultural residues while offering new kinds of voices for expressing radical contemporary ideas and affiliations. Nima's poetry especially manifested a new sense of subjectivity in which modernity and cultural identity could be reimagined.

Is it possible to map a theoretical framework that sees poetic films as affiliated to distinct bodies, their creative and professional relations emerging from the unique social realities in which they are produced? My own experience illustrates that the element of process is integral to this linkage.

In order to realize this coproduction in the Iranian context, the team needed to improvise around the severe control that is exerted over all aspects of filmmaking, from script writing to the shoot. This influence may even be cast over the reception of a film, as festival attendees may measure the film's credibility against the moral systems and ideologies advanced by the clerical rules of the country.

Upon beginning production in Iran, the social restrictions were immediately apparent on a practical level. An offer to use an apartment in Ekbatan as the setting for Marzieh's apartment seemed perfect. In the 1970s, the Ekbatan urban village was built by a vast team of architects and engineers—many Western educated or professionals lured from overseas. The development was funded by the shah to express the modernization and economic prosperity under his government. The location overlooked Tehran's Mehrabad airport, as well as the Azadi tower (a monumental signature of Tehran)—it would have conveyed well the sense of a Tehranian girl leading a modern life behind tall walls and closed doors, yearning to fly out of the country. But I was informed that filming in Ekbatan was not easily allowed, meaning I would have to shoot on a tight schedule.

Another issue concerned cultural conventions about female modesty, in particular the coverage of hair. I designed all the female characters' costumes to show minimal skin. In the rave scene and in the gathering party scene, I used fake hair wigs for the girls and bandanas and headbands instead of a conventional *hijab*, or head veil (which is routinely used in mainstream Iranian films). In the case of Marzieh, I decided to shave her hair to bypass issues around hair coverage because it was not always appropriate to portray her wearing a fashionable hair covering—for instance, in bed early in the morning.

As anticipated, these kinds of practical and social considerations lead the film toward alternate modes of expression—the very poetic, irregular, nonlinear, subjective, chaotic, and oneiric qualities that Pasolini observes are essential to the aesthetics of poetic cinema. Thematically, *My Tehran for Sale* captures the realities of urban living for young people in Iran. To do so, it relies on ambiguities that subvert the narrative representation of that reality, positing the film as a text to be actively read and interpreted like a poetic text.

Perhaps the strongest example of how these practical improvisations resulted in the innovation of a poetic cinema style concerns the film's representations of relationship intimacy. Showing a couple in bed or a male and a female sharing physical intimacy is an absolute taboo and forbidden in Iran. Any direct indication of physical intimacy would endanger the safety of the actors and the rest of the crew, including myself. Consequently, I struggled with finding ways to represent the development of Marzieh's relationship with Saman.

Addressing the morality and censorship codes that impacted on classical Hollywood, Susan Hayward notes that the enforcement of such codes led to the development of a unique cinematic style. She clarifies that "in order to convey what cannot be said, primarily on the level of sexual and repressed desire, décor and mise-en-scène had to stand in for meaning" (Hayward 2000, 107). My solution was to utilize visual metaphors, distorted shot compositions, low-key lighting, and cinematographic methods that would limit the relay of information while hinting at further interaction between characters.

In the opening sequence of the film, set outside the rave, Marzieh and Saman are positioned in the background of a long shot. They are seen to be sharing a cigarette, while in the foreground horses move in the quiet of the night. Saman drags Marzieh by her sleeve to the closest stable and closes the door, but the camera doesn't move. It captures the horses' movements under moonlight, dust flying in the air, while Marzieh and Saman's intimate moments are inside the stable, behind its closed door, offscreen and unseen. The film cuts away to the rave scene.

When the audience finally glimpses within the stables, the representation of intimacy is at once magnified through body language and sparse sound design, and distorted through the use of low-key lighting. The audience never sees physical touch or actual intimacy—this information is left offscreen, implied in part through creation of a cinematic "void."

The use of metaphor in dialogue contributes to building a more open mode of expression. Marzieh and Saman speak of flying together, suggesting togetherness (intimacy), freedom (sexual liberation), and climax. The use of poetic language prepares the viewer for a more poetic communication through film, encouraging them to fill in the blanks by reading between the lines, engaging beyond the logic of conventional narrative.

ASSEMBLAGE AND CULTURAL INTERFACE

As stated, my aim for *My Tehran for Sale* was to improvise a new cinematic language that abridges cultural perspectives and influences, and thus to assemble a "border-crosser" audience held together by a cross-cultural poetic cinema. The theoretical grounding for this challenge was drawn from the cultural theory of Deleuze and Guattari, and in particular their concept of "assemblage."

In their use of the term, Deleuze and Guattari draw attention to the dynamics of collective and individual meaning making. Assemblage is a process involving the interweaving of concepts and categories, the mixing and combining of genres and the interconnection of forms. Through this process, individuals and collectives effectively blur the lines of culturally concrete definitions. Assemblage dismantles binary categories such as "us" and "others," "real" and "representation," "fact" and "fiction."

In Deleuze and Guattari's (2004) theory, as set out in their book *A Thousand Plateaus*, the language system to which all speakers of a language belong, or the "collective agencement of enunciation," precedes the process of assemblage. The individual subject is oriented in relation to objects through a "social agencement of desire"; they intermingle these orientations in further actions of enunciation, this constituting an assemblage (Deleuze and Guattari 2004, 98).

In the development of *My Tehran for Sale*, the concept of assemblage provided the theoretical basis for a cinematic strategy to examine life across cultural borders, elevate awareness of the technologies of representation used, and at the same time encourage audiences to engage beyond binaries such as "us" and "others," "real" and "representation."

In developing a poetic cinematic text, assemblage came to mean interweaving unrelated poetic devices and expressions into a new body of meaning; and beyond simply enunciating existing language systems developed through singular poetic cinema traditions, it meant improvising new syncretic systems of meaning achieved through a collage of established forms and ideas.

Challenged from the outset to improvise poetic outcomes using conventional cinematic forms, I was empowered by the theory of assemblage to reimagine *My Tehran for Sale* as a dynamic patchwork of technical elements and cultural materials drawn from Iranian and Western traditions. These language objects would be enacted (or enunciated) together as a form of poetic cinema through a dynamic process of meaning making. This process would extend from the film's production to its reception. As Deleuze and

Guattari (2004) note, "A technical element remains abstract, entirely undetermined, as long as one does not relate it to an assemblage it presupposes" (397–98).

Throughout the script-editing process, I reevaluated the stylistic aspects that I valued highly and the methods that I could use in order to relate Marzieh's journey. I thought that the use of abstract images and time shift in the representation of film events, adding to a gradual revelation of the story through various side stories (thus avoiding a three-act structure), would add poetic values to the film and playfully subvert the conventions of cinema expected by the mainstream film industry and audiences in Australia. Henri Bergson (1911), in his article "The Cinematographical Mechanism of Thought and the Mechanistic Illusion," suggests that the structures of intellect and perception in Western cultures are attuned not to process but to "the logic of solids," with this mode of perception operating, in his view, as a kind of "cinematographical apparatus" (306).

While indulging in creative improvisation of filmic elements through production, it was not my intention to entirely omit this logic of solids, which finds expression in the linearity of conventional narrative genres and styles. Rather, I hoped to draw this logic into a collage with poetic aesthetics, thus advancing and intermingling residues from varied cultural traditions. The effect would be not to negate the strength and resonance of the narrative but to raise awareness of its functioning, just as poetry broadly may be said to examine the essence of logic, reality, and time. As Odilon Redon once wrote, poetry is bound to put "the logic of the visible at the service of the invisible" (quoted in Hauptman 2005, 59).

To this end, I sought throughout the film development process to preserve a raw style, utilizing digital "home video" technology, wobbly handheld images, unpolished diegetic sound design, long takes, and multiple points of view—effectively placing the film between documentary and fiction without the need for an explicit film-within-a-film structure. Even as I sought to strengthen the narrative, I avoided stepping into a purely formalist approach to narrative organization. The illusion of events randomly occurring and being captured by my camera, interwoven through a range of technical elements, would in its own right create a more flexible cinematic language, open interpretability of the narrative, and elevate awareness of the fictive frame.

POETIC ASSEMBLAGE AND CULTURAL INTERFACE

Roland Caputo (2003) observes that Kiarostami developed a distinctive cinematic style through the interweaving of technical elements that relate to the different social uses of film and video technology. In doing so, Kiarostami acts as a dialectician between two metaphors—cinema as "window" and cinema as "frame" onto reality. In the production of *My Tehran for Sale*, I have sought to render these same dynamics and tensions as the means to create an interface between distinctive social realities, reflecting the terms and aims of this project as a coproduction.

During the script-editing process, I became increasingly interested in how the assemblage of poetic aesthetics and conventional narrative structures could be used to portray details about underground life in Tehran. Much of this assemblage was finalized in the editing process. I sought to portray public life in Iran's urban center through a slow rhythm without sudden cuts, as if the characters were stuck in constant traffic. This was juxtaposed with the chaotic fast rhythm of scenes representing the youthful abandon of Tehran's underground culture, featuring quick jump cuts between images. This juxtaposition was designed to map the underground life as a world within a world, a double life framed by frustrations at the excessive measures of control exerted within the society and the inventive search by youth for new cultural freedoms and modes of expression. The result of the struggle, however, is a phase of social decadence.

In the opium scene, I paid specific attention to the visual rhythm connecting abstract images of objects and expressions. In this scene, I freed the narrative from any direct communication through dialogue, avoiding any compulsion to be expository in the relay of "important" narrative information, focusing instead on correlating images and sounds so as to build a poetic conveyance. To affect a surrealistic and hallucinatory style, I adjusted the camera to a fast-motion mode when capturing the scene and slowed the footage down in editing. The series of slow-motion images were compiled and edited in a random fashion, with extreme jump cuts between close-ups of Marzieh, images of paraphernalia used for smoking opium, and floating, handheld close-ups of other people present in the scene. I complemented this irrational, chaotic, and surrealistic style by reversing background dialogue in the sound-editing stage. The actors' incomprehensible, out-of-sync speech patterns compromise realism while empowering artifice.

The overall effect was to express Marzieh's shifting subjective and formal relations to the embedded world of which she was a part—that is, her frustration, pain, and disconnection from what is rapidly revealed as a dysfunctional environment plagued by contradictions and double standards. The point of the scene in narrative terms was advanced through a largely improvised assemblage of poetic techniques and aesthetics, which introduced oneiric and ambiguous qualities into the formal fictive frame. Finally, the scene was overlaid with a melancholic song by Namjou as a mood-making device toward creating a heartfelt, deeply subjective and yet formalized poetic scene.

By incorporating surrealistic and oneiric signs and techniques, I managed to destabilize the status of reality perception and invoke the audience's active participation in the process of meaning making. For instance, in Marzieh's flashback, a traveling shot shows Sadaf, Marzieh, and Saman sitting next to one another amongst other rave attendees waiting in turn to be lashed. However, when the shot returns along the same track, they have been replaced with strangers. In actuality, it is forbidden for men and women to be seated next to one another in a punishment hall or lashed in a mixed-gender group.

Thus, it is left to the audience to determine the status of the flashback—as a representation of the "real," of memory, or of imagination. On the one hand, such interpretation impacts on the overall meaning derived by the audience (the problems confronted by Marzieh in Tehran, and the likelihood she will be deported). On the other hand, the viewers' interpretation of the poetic frame is colored by their interpretation of the narrative, which brings into relief their own cultural and political positioning. The viewer must decide if the flashback is an impaired version of reality due to Marzieh's memory loss in detention, or the possibility of her distortion of events to seek refuge in a country with complex cultural politics surrounding issues of migration and asylum seekers.

Essentially, at the heart of this enterprise, assembling filmic techniques, including narrative structures and poetic devices, is the potential to heighten interactivity within the cinematic space, as the assemblage process works to transform cultural texts and imaginings and open them to original readings and enunciations.

REFERENCES

Bergson, Henri. 1911. "The Cinematographical Mechanism of Thought and the Mechanistic Illusion—A Glance at the History of Systems—Real Becoming and False Evolutionism." In *Creative Evolution,* translated by Arthur Mitchell, 272–370. New York: Henry Holt.

Caputo, Roland. 2003. "Five to *Ten:* Five Reflections on Abbas Kiarostami's *10.*" *Senses of Cinema* 29. http://sensesofcinema.com/2003/29/abbas-kiarostami/ten/.

Dabashi, Hamid. 2001. *Close-Up: Iranian Cinema Past, Present, and Future.* New York: Verso Books.

Deleuze, Gilles, and Felix Guattari. 2004. *A Thousand Plateaus: Capitalism and Schizophrenia.* Translated by Brian Massumi. London: Continuum Press. (First published 1988 by The Athlone Press.)

Deren, Maya. 1970. "Poetry and the Film: A Symposium." In *Film Culture Reader,* edited by P. Adams Sitney. New York: Praeger. (Reprint, New York: Cooper Square Press, 2000.)

Hauptman, Jodi. 2005. *Beyond the Visible: The Art of Odilon Redon.* New York: Museum of Modern Art.

Hayward, Susan. 2000. *Cinema Studies: The Key Concepts.* London: Routledge.

Moussavi, Granaz. 2000. *Barefoot Till Morning.* Tehran: Sali Publisher.

Pasolini, Pier Paolo. 1988. *Heretical Empiricism.* Translated by Ben Lawton and Louise K. Barnett. Edited by Louise K. Barnett. Bloomington: Indiana University Press.

Rumi, Jalaludin Mohammad (Balkhi). 2003. "Candlelight Becomes Moth." In *Rumi: The Book of Love: Poems of Ecstasy and Longing.* Translated by Coleman Barks, 65. Harper Collins. http://www.scribd.com/doc/24981522/Rumi-The-Book-of-Love-Poems-of-Ecstasy-and-Longing.

3 Maps and Movies
Talking with Deepa Mehta

Sukhmani Khorana

In December 2007 I met Deepa Mehta at a suburban mall in Brampton, a city in greater Toronto with a substantial Indian settlement. She was in the production phase of her forthcoming film, *Heaven on Earth* (Mehta 2008), which is about the spousal abuse rampant amongst Punjabi families living in Canada. Some of the scenes were being shot amidst the city's hustle and bustle, with regular shoppers stopping to see what the fuss was about, and Mehta's assistant, Dusty Mancinelli, graciously permitting me to film from a distance. Other scenes would take place in a makeshift Canadian classroom that had been created by Hamilton-Mehta Productions in a dilapidated part of the mall. While waiting for Mehta to get some free time, my aunt, a local, pointed out that Brampton isn't the most upscale part of Toronto, being notorious for ethnic ghettoes and substandard public health care. I figured Mehta's latest narrative, this time about diasporic Indians rather than those based in the homeland, fit right into the socioeconomic landscape of *desi*[1] Toronto. Would it get rave reviews from Western critics, like her elements film trilogy (comprising *Fire*, *Earth*, and the Oscar-nominated *Water* [Mehta 1996, 1998, 2005]), and receive the indifference or condemnation of the mother country? Did she care about these reviews? Was Deepa Mehta the pet hate figure of Hindu fundamentalists as fearless and formidable as Deepa Mehta the onset filmmaker? I couldn't wait to find out.

From my location in Australian academic and artistic institutions, I had been using Mehta's elements trilogy as a springboard for my doctoral thesis and documentary on diasporic creativity. This was an intellectual, emotional, and spiritual journey not unlike the conception, development, and distribution of Mehta's border-crossing cinema. She herself is a border crosser whose *Water*, despite being in India's national language (Hindi), was a Canadian nominee in the Best Foreign Film category of the 2006 Academy Awards. During a Canadian-Indian buffet lunch with the cast and crew of *Heaven on Earth*, I observed the transnational, hyphenated identity of every aspect of her cinema. When it finally came time to interview her, we were two Indian-born women of different generations sitting on a production set with a map of Canada in the background. It was a perfect frame, a much-needed one for containing our forthcoming conversation about old homes, new homes, and the in-between cinema that transcends national and generic boundaries.

THE BIRTH AND GROWTH OF THE TRILOGY

SK: You've said that you started thinking of the trilogy when you saw a widow in Varanasi during the shooting of George Lucas's (1992–1993) *The Young Indiana Jones Chronicles*. Is that when you thought about *Water*, or the entire trilogy?

DM: It didn't happen like that [thinking of the trilogy sequence]. I was shooting in Varanasi, and that's the first time. You know you read about widows—my grandmother is a widow—but I had never seen such institutionalization of widows until I went to Varanasi. There was a widow there called Gyanvati who was about 80 years old, and through her I got to know about ashrams and found it very moving. I thought that if I make a film, it would be about something surrounding widows; then I forgot about it. Then I wrote *Fire*.

SK: So you weren't thinking of a trilogy. Was it organic?

DM: Yes, it was very organic. I wrote *Fire* and shot it, and near the end of it, Shabana Azmi, who plays the lead character Radha, said "What's your next film about?" I told her that I was going to do a film about partition based on Bapsi Sidhwa's book, *Cracking India*. So she said, what's it called, and it just came out—I said *Earth*. It literally just happened like that because it is about the division of the earth, but it is also metaphoric—what does our *matrubhoomi*[2] mean to us? It made perfect sense, then, to make *Water* [discussed previously], and I knew *Water* again would be a metaphor for life, and the flow of life, and purity of water, stagnation of water.

SK: Just like tradition.

DM: Yes, like tradition. So I guess *Fire* became about the politics of sexuality, *Earth* about the politics of war and nation, and *Water* became about the politics of religion from a female point of view.

SK: You are saying it "became" about the politics of religion.

DM: Yeah, because I'm not going to say I'll sit and write a book or a film or a script about the politics of religion. What does that mean? Nothing. It becomes something while you are writing it. And while shooting it, it should go to another plane because if you just stick to the script page, it is very boring. So it was within the evolution of the film that it became something.

THE INFLUENCE OF HOME AND ABROAD

SK: I find it fascinating that you've said it was only when you were in Varanasi that you realized what was happening to the widows. This is true for me also to some extent. So do you think when you are overseas and you return to the homeland you look at your country from a different pair of eyes?

DM: I can't answer that because I haven't [looked at India differently after going overseas]. All I know is that even before I left India and got married and came to Toronto, the first short film I made was for the Ministry of Family Planning. It was about a girl who was a sweeper's daughter, and she was getting married at the age of fourteen. I was intrigued by her story. It wasn't a study or in any way an academic film. She was a frightened young girl, and yet she was so excited because she was going to get new clothes. It just caught my imagination, and I thought I would like to document it.

SK: Do you think going overseas influences you in terms of the directors you watch?

DM: When I was growing up in Delhi and I went to university in Delhi, I used to watch [Indian] films. I grew up with a very healthy dose of Indian commercial cinema. My father was a film distributor, so from a very young age I saw commercial Indian cinema. But once I went to university, or even my last year of school, I really started watching and enjoying Satyajit Ray and Ritwik Ghatak and had exposure to non-Hindi cinema and non-Hollywood cinema. At university, I was also exposed to directors like Truffaut and Godard. There was also intense exposure to Japanese cinema. So, Ozu, Mizoguchi.

SK: Do directors like Ray influence you more in terms of the content of your films or film technique? I see a certain humanitarianism in his films that is also present in yours. I'm sure it's not deliberate, but is there a certain kind of resonance there?

DM: I've said this often, and I continue to quote it. Again, a filmmaker that I really admire, Luis Bunuel, has said that "it's only when a film is specific does it become universal." I think it's much easier for me to tell a story that I'm familiar with, whether it's as a woman or whether it's about a subject that I would like to know more about. So, for me, while I'm writing the script, or researching the film, or even making the film, I'm still learning. So I never do a film where I think I know all about it because I think that's terribly boring. The process of exploration is what really intrigues me, and especially if it's on a subject that I really care about. For example, right now we are shooting *Heaven on Earth*, and it's very specific. It's about the Punjabi immigrant community in contemporary Toronto. That's a subject that has intrigued me for a long time. It's very difficult for people who come from Ludhiana, or Hoshiarpur, or small towns like the districts of Bhatinda to come here soon after marriage and start working in factories the next day. That's their life. Spousal abuse is enormous.

THE NEW HOME

SK: Is the Canadian government active in doing anything about it [spousal abuse]?

DM: I don't think they have a clue how to deal with it. That's the tragedy. Whether it's a Punjabi, Tamil, or Sikh [family], an Asian woman will never call 911. There is a question of losing one's dignity. It's shameful, so the government has no clue how to deal with them. But what we have in Canada right now is amazing. There is a Sikh gentleman here called Baldev Bhattal, and [the Sikhs] do an enormous amount of work with women who have suffered domestic violence or spousal abuse because they know how to talk to them. And they also do lot of work with the men themselves because they recognize that everybody is a victim because the dynamics of immigration really turn the values that felt right at home and were working back home upside down. So the dynamics of the household change, and you want to maintain them, but you can't. The stress of trying to maintain something that is nonexistent and doesn't work for you shows on a woman first, but that doesn't mean that men aren't victims as well.

SK: That's a very interesting way of looking at it because Indian culture is often depicted as parochial with the men in a dominant, chauvinistic position.

DM: I don't think so. I think that is naive and perhaps a bit outdated. Before *Heaven on Earth*, I did a documentary on the issue.

SK: Is that where you gave cameras to the children of these couples?

DM: Yeah. Being a Punjabi, born in Amritsar, speaking Punjabi, I could read *Gurmukhi*.[3] Everybody took French and German in school, but I said no, I will take *Gurmukhi*. I was the only one in my class. But it was good because now, years later, I can pick up a newspaper and read, and it's been fascinating to do that. So I couldn't have done a film like *Heaven on Earth* unless I was very specific. Once you stop being specific, it dilutes the subject.

THE AUDIENCE(S)

SK: Would you consider your film as appealing to the Punjabi immigrant community in Canada?

DM: I really don't think about such things. Somebody once asked me, "Who are your films for?" and I said intelligent people. It doesn't matter what color they are, what gender they are, or what race they are.

SK: But I wish some of these "nonintelligent" people would go to a film festival or an alternative cinema.

DM: But they don't.

SK: Then it's like preaching to the converted. With intelligent people, if you give them a film like yours, they might say, that makes sense and we see where she is coming from. But what about the people who are never going to see them?

DM: I consider myself an intelligent person, but there is still so much that I don't know about. So if I see a film like Kusturica's [1988] *Time of the Gypsies*, I would be exposed to something new as I can't be expected to know about everything. For me, that's interesting. So there are filmmakers whose work sometimes opens windows. It isn't necessary that all intelligent people see all films. I don't write a film and say it's for women, or colored women, or Punjabi women. You can't, because then you stop writing for yourself, which is the only reason that you write.

SK: I was talking to David Hamilton [the producer of the trilogy], and he said to me that *Water*, in some ways, could be considered a crossover film because many people who may not otherwise watch an art film did actually watch *Water*. So what do you think makes a film more accessible even though it may be in the art category? Is it the promotion, or the way it's made, or something else?

DM: I don't know. I have no idea. If we look at *Water*, when we finished the film, we didn't have distribution for it. It isn't that Fox read the script and said okay, go ahead and make it. We only had Canadian distribution. So who knows? I didn't know it would be picked up by Fox Searchlight.

THE CREATIVE PROCESS

SK: When you are writing a script, do you start with an image, or a story, or something else?

DM: For me, it always starts with a question. I remember very distinctly with *Fire* saying something about women and choices, about the lack of them, or the limitations on them, in Delhi. I asked my friend, "What do you think would happen if an Indian woman from a working, middle-class family made a choice that was an extreme choice?" It's difficult enough making little choices like today I'm not going to go to work, today I'm not feeling well, today I'm not going to cook dinner, or something like that. So the film came out of the question of extreme choice, and what is the fallout of that. I've always started out that way. When I wrote *Water*, the environment was rampant with questions about the place of religion. When I wrote *Heaven on Earth*, I was reading the papers every day in Toronto about spousal abuse in the Punjabi community. And just learning more about the issue by talking to Bhuttal, talking to the men, talking to the women, and realizing that it is not very clear who the victims are. So it's always a question that starts my scripts.

SK: You are probably the only filmmaker that I can think of, not just in Bollywood, but also amongst the diasporic directors like Mira Nair, who goes to the past of India. Do you think you have a particular fascination with India's history?

DM: I thought I'd go back in time. So *Fire* was contemporary India, *Earth* was during the time of partition, and *Water* was further back.

SK: Is there a reason why you wanted to go back to the past?

DM: I think one has to learn from the past or at least examine it because we are here because of where we were.

THE RELATIONSHIP WITH BOLLYWOOD

SK: I don't understand why Bollywood directors aren't interested in history.

DM: I'm not a Bollywood director. I'm really not.

SK: That's true. But would you say you are using Indian actors in some of your films? I remember reading in Devyani's book [see Saltzman 2006] about John Abraham arriving later than scheduled for some rehearsals. Do you think that the transition from Bollywood to your sort of cinema is easy for them?

DM: I worked with Aamir Khan, who is amazing. The talent [pool] of Indian actors in the West will grow with time but is sadly very limited. One is stuck with Navin Andrews and Jimi Mistry, and that's it. There aren't many roles, so the opportunities are extremely scarce. There is an incredible pool of talent in India, so I feel very fortunate to be able to tap into that. When I cast John, everybody thought I was nuts because he was known for his tight jeans, or abs or something, but I knew that he was just right. It's the same with Aamir Khan too. Both John and Aamir were extremely professional. We've got a Bollywood star, Preity Zinta, in *Heaven on Earth*, and she is delightful. She is professional, always on time, and also extremely talented and right for the role.

SK: So when you were growing up and your father was a film distributor, did he have any contacts in Bollywood? Did anyone influence you in the filmmaking direction?

DM: Because my father owned movie halls as well, we used to have these actors who came over all the time. He distributed Raj Kapoor films, so people like Raj Kapoor and Vyjanthimla would come over. When I was young, it wasn't very cool to like Indian films.

SK: So it developed over time?

DM: As I grew older, I started liking Indian films. I still do, and I find it's the best escapist cinema.

SK: I like the films of that period.

DM: Films like *Sujata* and others by Bimal Roy [1959]. They are lovely films not because they have the songs, but they actually are about something. Even Guru Dutt's films like *Pyaasa* [1957] and *Sautela Bhai* [1962] are wonderful films.

SK: I wonder why it has changed now.

DM: I'm not a Bollywood expert, but I think that, you've done economics as you said, and everything stems from that. There is a trend toward sales and who will follow it. Once it stops selling, another trend starts.

SK: Do you feel that a film like *Water* is about India and must have an impact there? Are you saddened that it was released later in India?

DM: I wish it could have been, maybe if I got lucky. But then Ravi Chopra, who is not a distributor, actually said, I will distribute it because I want every Indian to see it. It was so nice of him. So maybe even if twenty people saw it, that is good.

SK: Do you think *Heaven on Earth* is going to be released in India the same time as the rest of the world?

DM: I really don't think of that. I really don't know how a film is going to turn out. I don't say I'm doing a film and it's going to open this time. Every film has its own life. It's wonderful when it takes shape, and you can't always fit it in a certain direction. To make a film is so difficult, and it has a life of its own. To try and maneuver or manipulate it into what you want it to be, rather than what it is, is a big mistake.

SK: That certainly seems to have happened with *Water*.

DM: With all my films. Everyone said, *Water* will find its audience, and it did. It touched many people, and it offended the people that wanted to be offended by it.

THE FUTURE (AND THE PAST)

SK: Do you have other projects in India coming?

DM: Yeah, there is a project called "Stella" [released as *Cooking with Stella* (Mehta 2009)], which I'm codirecting with my brother. We'll start shooting at the end of February if I'm still alive. After that, a project that I'm really interested in is called "Land of the Morning

Calm." It's a film about an ordinary young woman in her forties who got married into a Korean royal family. Royalty really intrigues me.

SK: Is it based on something?

DM: It's a true story. I've written half the script.

SK: Do you usually take a while to write a script?

DM: I usually visualize my script and the scene, and then I write it. I already know the beginning, the middle, and the end, but as far as the scenes are concerned, I have to visualize them first. People go mad when they read my scripts because there is so much detail, whether it is color, set design, or lighting.

SK: That's why I can see the reds in *Fire*, the browns in *Earth*, and the blues in *Water*. I had to compliment Giles (the cinematographer of the trilogy).

DM: He is amazing; it is lovely to work with him.

INDIA TO CANADA AND BACK

SK: What about your identity?

DM: When my plane lands in Toronto, I feel totally Canadian, and when it lands in Delhi, I feel totally Indian. So I'm fine; I'm really happy that I can feel completely Indian and completely Canadian.

SK: But are there aspects of your Indianness in Canada, and of your Canadianness in India, or is it separate?

DM: It's not separate. I am who I am.

SK: Was it hard in the beginning when you came to Canada?

DM: It wasn't hard at all, and I felt I was lucky. Maybe it had something to do with the fact that at that point, I was married to a Canadian, and he had his whole family and his whole network here. So it was much easier for me.

SK: Were you working in the film industry then?

DM: Yeah.

SK: Has Canadian film become more supportive of people from other backgrounds now?

DM: They better be.

SK: They nominated *Water* as their official entry to the Oscars. That was amazing.

DM: That was pretty amazing. What it did was, I think *Water* changed the way Canadians looked at their own films.

SK: *Fire* is in English, and that wasn't allowed.

DM: It depends on the bureaucracy and who is in government.

SK: If you had to tell me something about filmmaking, or how to make a good film, what advice would you give?

DM: I think it's important to do it only if you are passionate about it and if you know why you are passionate about it. It's tough at all times, whether you are a man or a woman. I always tell people that if you have something to say, and you want to use this medium, the medium of cinema, ask yourself why before you start. Be very clear as to why you want to do this because it is going to be very tough. I think it's really important for you, or anybody who wants to be a filmmaker, to really be honest with yourself.

Deepa Mehta's *Heaven on Earth* was screened at various film festivals and received a limited theatrical release in Canada in 2008. She also cowrote *Cooking with Stella* with Dilip Mehta, and her latest release is *Midnight's Children* (Mehta 2012), based on Salman Rushdie's Booker Prize–winning book of the same title.

NOTES

This interview was first published in issue 63 of *Bright Lights Film Journal* (February 2009).

1. *Desi* is a Hindi word that literally means "belonging to the nation." It is used colloquially in India and the Indian diaspora to imply strong allegiance to an Indian cultural identity.
2. *Matrubhoomi* is Sanskrit for "motherland."
3. *Gurmukhi* is the script in which Punjabi, the official language of the Indian state of Punjab, is written.

REFERENCES

Dutt, Guru, dir. 1957. *Pyaasa*. Mumbai: Guru Dutt Films Pvt. Ltd.
———. 1962. *Sautela Bhai*. Mumbai: Guru Dutt Films Pvt. Ltd.
Kusturica, Emir, dir. 1988. *Time of the Gypsies*. Culver City, CA: Columbia.
Lucas, George, dir. 1992–1993. *The Young Indiana Jones Chronicles*. TV series. Los Angeles: CBS Television.
Mehta, Deepa, dir. 1996. *Fire*. 1996. New York: Zeitgeist Films.
———. 1998. *Earth*. Anne Masson.
———. 2005. *Water*. Toronto: Mongrel Media.
———. 2008. *Heaven on Earth*. Toronto: Hamilton-Mehta Productions.
———. 2012. *Midnight's Children*. Los Angeles: 20th Century Fox.
Mehta, Dilip, dir. 2009. *Cooking with Stella*. Toronto: Mongrel Media.
Roy, Bimal, dir. 1959. *Sujata*. Mumbai: Bimal Roy Productions.
Saltzman, Devyani. 2006. *Shooting Water: A Mother-Daughter Journey and the Making of a Film*. New Delhi: Penguin Books.

4 *Los Libertadores* as Crossover Cinema

Noah Zweig

> [T]here is a growing awareness that popular encodings of history—rather than those created for professional historians or film scholars—are powerful materials in building a consensus on what constitutes history, and on what kind of history shall be constituted. To an extent, the memory of history many of us carry—if there be such a portable item as collective memory—is a mediated one. Thus, both the coverage of history, and its selective recovery, through textbooks, film, and other media, is an important one.
>
> —George F. Custen

The present chapter argues that a salient iteration of crossover cinema can be traced in recent filmmaking trends emerging out of Latin America and the Caribbean in the current era of the region's "pink tide," or its election of various left-of-center populist governments. This hemispheric move to the left—consisting not only of heads of state but also society actors—is associated principally with the petroleum-rich Venezuela, which in many respects jumpstarted the leftward trend by choosing the socialist-democratic Hugo Chávez administration (1998–). A core component of Chávez's "new socialism" is inter-American solidarity via bilateral barter agreements such as the multistate Bolivarian Alliance for the Americas (ALBA), designed to confront the hegemony of unilateral financial institutions such as the International Monetary Fund. While maintaining ties to the world economic system, largely through oil rents, the Chavista regime attempts to challenge Global Northern domination not by overthrowing neoliberal capitalism, but by accommodating it. The Bolivarian experiment's inherent paradox—the fact that Chávez talks about conquering capitalism, while further neoliberalizing the country—results in a situation in which these contradictions must be obscured in order for the administration to execute successful statecraft. One of the ways the Chávez government does this is by turning to the past—particularly the cinematic past, assisted by his state-run film studio Villa del Cine—in order to reinvent itself in the present.

Not surprisingly, early twenty-first-century cinema in Venezuela and other "Bolivarian" countries—Cuba, Argentina, Uruguay—and elsewhere in Latin

America has been characterized by an upsurge in biopics of eighteenth- and nineteenth-century revolutionaries associated with that region's independence, concurrent with their heads of state proclaiming their liberation from the yoke of neoliberal world powers, mainly the United States and Europe. Because the interconnected world economy of global capitalism makes true independence impossible, though, such declarations become more discursive than literal; and the films under discussion here are seen as examples of that discourse. Consequently, hagiographic works of cinema celebrating past leaders become convenient distractions for obviating these contradictions. It is not the argument of this chapter that these filmmakers are deliberately carrying the water for pink-tide governments; rather, like many symptomatic cultural productions, they comprise a cluster of larger synchronicities that happen to serve the interests of the state.

Although not all Venezuelan productions, the eight-part made-for-television biographical film series *Los Libertadores* (Liberators), under discussion here, is related to this conjuncture; these larger-than-life productions are symptomatic of the recourse to pastness necessitated by "neo-neoliberal" contradictoriness. In 2009, Spain's public service broadcaster Televisión Española (TVE) announced it would produce *Los Libertadores* in collaboration with the production and distribution company Wanda Films, founded by vice president of the the Ibero-American Federation of Film and Audiovisual Producers José María Morales and Lusa Films, the production company of the late Spanish actor Sancho Gracia (1936–2012). The biopics deal with the lives of eight leaders, all of them instrumental in the independence of Latin America and the Caribbean: *José Martí: el ojo del canario* (José Martí: The Eye of the Canary) (Pérez 2009), about Cuban national hero José Julián Martí Pérez (1853–1895); *Miguel Hidalgo—La historia jamás contada* (Miguel Hidalgo: The Untold Story) (Serrano 2010), a biopic of the Mexican priest and leader of the Mexican War of Independence (1810–1821), Miguel Hidalgo y Costilla (1753–1811); *Simón Bolívar* (Arvelo 2013), a cinematic rendering of the eponymous military and political hero's (1783–1830) life story; *Túpac Amaru* (2013), about José Gabriel Túpac Amaru (1742–1781), leader of an indigenous Peruvian people's uprising against Spanish rule; *Tiradentes* (Gomes 2013), a biofilm of the military adventures of Brazilian Joaquim Jose da Silva Xavier, or "Tiradentes" (1746–1792), leader of the republican and liberal movement Conjuración Mineira of 1789, which rose up against Portuguese rule; *El niño rojo* (The Red Boy) (Larraín 2013), about Bernardo O'Higgins Riquelme (1778–1842), a Chilean-Irish independence leader; *La Redota, una historia de Artigas* (Charlone 2009), a telling of José Gervasio Artigas Arnal's (1764–1850) story, "the father of Uruguayan nationhood"; and *Revolución, el cruce de los Andes* (Revolution: The Crossing of the Andes) (Ipiña 2009), about José Francisco de San Martín (1778–1850), the Argentine general who, together with O'Higgins, led the South American struggle for independence against Spain, resulting in the liberation of Chile. Because at the time of this writing only four out of eight of these films have been completed, the present chapter situates the following works in the context of crossover cinema: *José Martí*; *Revolución, el cruce de los Andes*; *La Redota, una historia de Artigas*; and *Miguel Hidalgo*.[1] A unifying theme of each story is the integrative idea of the *patria grande* (great homeland), based on two key concepts: the fraternity of Latin American and Caribbean peoples and their post-Independence open relationship with the rest of the world, founded on material, political, social, and cultural progress ("TVE redescubre a los 'Libertadores'" 2011). These characteristics—the films' specificity yet universality and the ameliorating effects they have on neo-neoliberalism—make them accordant with crossover cinema.

Likewise, to the extent that pink-tide governments have established multilateral relations among themselves through ALBA and other agreements,[2] "crossover" becomes a propitious category for illuminating the valences of such filmmaking. While early uses of crossover cinema referred to films from the Indian subcontinent, which were aimed primarily at Western audiences, the aim of this chapter is to reconfigure the concept in the context of Latin America and the Caribbean. In short, *Los Libertadores* provides a snapshot of Latin America's neo-neoliberal moment, which results in its recourse to pastness. As Cuban film critic Pérez Betancourt (2011, 123) explains, not a few wondered why Fernando Pérez bet on making a film as much poetic and experimental as controversial and accepted the task of bringing Martí to the screen as a coproduction with Spain, the empire. Though he does not use the term *neo-neoliberal*, Pérez Betancourt alludes to the contradictoriness of the political economy.

Los Libertadores portrays the accounts of revolutionary leaders, who, as TVE president Alberto Oliart puts it, "fought and who have now become admirable parts of our history" ("La faceta más humana" 2012). Likewise, in the eyes of the official Ibero-American bodies, *Los Libertadores* films are legitimate historical documents. As former Spanish prime minister (1982–1996) and current ambassador plenipotentiary Felipe González stated, "[The films are] their own view, a reflection of themselves" ("'Libertadores'" 2011).[3] In March 2011, the Organization of Ibero-American States announced its stamp of approval of the eight-part film series ("Noticias" 2011).

Sukhmani Khorana writes in the introduction to the present volume that crossover cinema is characterized by "its ability to transgress genre, audience and cultural, borders . . . [and] the personal/poetic and political border crossings being constantly undertaken and negotiated by filmmakers with cross-cultural affiliations and influences, and thereby performed by the hybrid content and form, as well as the distribution and reception, of the films themselves." Appropriately, the eight films do not have conventional exhibition patterns; such unique exhibition modes are congruent with the fluidity of crossover cinema's distribution. In Spain, they only air on television, while in Latin America they premiered in cinemas and were picked up by major American and Pan-American broadcasters.

CROSSOVER CINEMA AND LATIN AMERICA'S "THE POPULAR"

Los Libertadores films are being released in the context of ongoing uncertainty as to where these continental socialist-democratic populist projects are headed. While Chávez is critical of Soviet-style, twentieth-century socialism, he is less clear about what that "new socialism," or "Bolivarianism," entails. Indeed, two contradictory forces characterize Latin America's so-called pink tide. On the one hand, its socialist-democratic governments want to realize societies that are more egalitarian than the neoliberalized regimes that preceded them. On the other hand, they remain constrained by external factors, namely, global capitalism, so omnipresent that it blocks the implementation of these changes. Writing on the Bolivarian Revolution, anthropologist Fernando Coronil (2011) notes, "From the fissure between these worlds there emanate contradictory dispositions and incentives that stretch the present forward and push the desired future toward an uncertain horizon. The Left pursues a just future, but its particular content eludes it. It has a sense of direction but no clear destination" (234). Amidst the prospect of an uncertain future, the heads of states' knee-jerk impulses have been to repeatedly ground themselves in the past for short-term cultural solutions for long-term structural problems. Just as Bolivarian Venezuela has not broken from neoliberal economics—for example, its government remains mired in the paradoxical situation of selling oil to the United States—these films are coproduced with funding from Spain's TVE network.

In many respects, Latin America's twenty-first-century turn to the left—and its cultural productions—is navigated by what anthropologist Claudio Lomnitz terms *foundationalism*, a wish to return to an origin or founding moment, in this case a second chance at achieving a utopian project previously derailed. Foundationalism, in this context, is predicated on the view that the unpopular structural adjustment policies were undemocratically implemented; it is almost as if these mistakes can be rectified by looking backward (Lomnitz 2006). Lomnitz (2006) writes, "The 'lost moments' that are being symbolically recuperated all draw on specific national traditions and images of autonomy and self-governance: the grandeur of the Incas, the cult of towering figures like Bolívar or Juárez, the frustrated avant-garde experiments of modern socialism in Uruguay and Chile, the robust national power of Brazil's Estado Novo or of Argentine Peronism, the grassroots vindication of the Mexican Revolution." By the same token, in the case of Venezuela, Chávez has created a teleological narrative in which his presidency becomes the apotheosis of previous populist figures such as Venezuelan president Cipriano Castro (1899–1908), who famously stood up to foreign investors and campaigned against European powers that had blockaded Venezuelan ports (Ellner and Tinker Salas 2006, 48).

The Bolivarian program, and the policies of its allied governments, would be unrealizable without a cultural transformation. Culture here is understood in the Gramscian sense, namely, the sphere through which ideologies are disseminated and organized, the realm through which one can work with hegemony, constructing it or contesting and ultimately abolishing it to construct a new one (Forgacs 1984, 91). Out of this new popular culture emerges a new common sense. Social reproduction in any revolution requires the support of the popular classes and hence the need for a new ideology. The ideology of the pink tide is rooted in the past.

Argentine sociologist Néstor García Canclini (1982) writes, "The 'popular' nature of anything or phenomenon can only be established by the manner in which it is used or experienced, not by where it originates" (53). One of the Chávez government's priorities has been to build a "popular" revolutionary culture. But how can a state whose revolutionary ambitions are hemispheric construct a palatable culture for a region composed of heterogeneous peoples? This project becomes even more formidable in that what distinguishes the Bolivarian experiment as a cultural counterhegemonic project is that it is a top-down process. Unlike earlier socialist-democratic programs, though, Bolivarian Venezuela is a hyper-state-crafting "civil society" in its own image. For Gramsci, a precondition for realizing a revolutionary workers state is the construction of a counterhegemonic culture, outside of the state, unlike what is the case in Bolivarian Venezuela. For many cultural studies scholars, popular culture is understood as a series of disparate spaces in which popular subjects, in contrast to members of the dominant group, are formed (Rowe and Schelling 1991, 15). Stuart Hall (1980) writes that culture necessitates "both the meanings and values which arise amongst distinctive social groups and classes . . . [and] the lived traditions and practices through which those 'understandings' are exposed and in which they are embodied" (6). Importantly, Hall defines culture not as a homogenizing force, unlike earlier conceptions, but as a multiplicity of social agents and classes. This chapter shares such a nonessentializing grasp of culture for understanding crossover cinema in the context of the neo-neoliberalized Americas: while the present analysis is top down, what the people of the Americas do with the films is up to them.

LOS LIBERTADORES AND THE BIOPIC'S IMPORTANCE TO CROSSOVER CINEMA

Situating *Los Libertadores* in the context of the biopic helps shed light on their significance as crossover films. First, defining the biopic, one of cinema's most understudied genres, remains a difficult task. But the genre becomes an important articulation of the present in terms of crossover cinema. Drawing on Roland Barthes, film critic Ronald Bergan (1983) describes the biopic as "a fiction that dare not speak its name . . . [it takes] people's real lives and transforms them into the realms of myth" (22). However, while myths are an important component of the biopic, as film historian Marcia Landy (1996) points out, there is an important distinction between Barthesian myths and Gramscian folklore:

> Common sense as folklore is Gramsci's instrument for examining the persistence of the past and its rejuvenation of new forms. In contrast to a conception of folklore as primitive, pre-historical, and hence antihistorical, he describes it in more dynamic terms: Folklore is "tied to the culture of the dominant class, and in its own way, [folklore] has drawn from it the motifs which have become inserted into combinations with the previous traditions." (4)

In constructing counterhegemony, the popular classes are to claim folklore on their own terms. Indeed, unlike Barthes's mythologies, Gramsci's commonsensical folklore is not binary and is rooted in a series of contradictory threads (Landy 1996, 5). The multivalent transmission of these biopics is best understood as crossing over.

The biopic offers a particularly constructive articulation of crossover cinema in that it dialectically straddles the categories of national and international cinema; while such films are made for national audiences, at the same time, they want to be universal stories. According to historian Robert Rosenstone, the film biopic can be divided into four categories: the "classical" biopic of the Hollywood studio era, such as *Young Mr. Lincoln* (Ford 1939); the "serious" or "artistic" international biofilm, such as *Frida* (Taymor 2002), in which the filmmaker often works with historical consultants; the documentary biography, such as most of the TV films on the History Channel, which often serve a pedagogical purpose; and the experimental bio, such as *Thirty-Two Short Films about Glenn Gould* (Girard 1993), which call attention to themselves as productions, foregrounding formal disunity of their subjects (Rosenstone 2007, 15). Frequently, postmodern biopics present their subjects' lives in fragments, defying final conclusion or coherence (Bingham 2010, 133). If the goal of the previous three forms of the biopic is to grant their subjects transcendence, the postmodern biofilm denies such transcendence; the point of such films is the impossibility of replicating the life of its subject (Bingham 2010, 133). As spiritual journeys, the *Libertadores* series is congruent with the conventional dictates of the classical biopic. The *Libertadores* films are notably emphatic in delivering their subjects. Such narratives seem palatable amidst the messy realities of post-neoliberal Latin America. Postmodern biofilms, which connote open-endedness and fragmentation, would be an inappropriate form for *Los Libertadores*, whose objective is to provide teleological narratives for their polities.

As a manifestation of crossover cinema, then, the *Libertadores* series provides a means by which one can negotiate the contradictions of post-neoliberal Latin American integration. According to film historian Marcia Landy (1996):

> In writings on postmodernism, the past appears as a Disneyland, as tourist attraction, spectacle, and nostalgia. In neoliberalism as in fascism, familiar events and images from the past are invoked as rallying points, as forces for cohesion and consensus in the interests of national solidarity. Memory has also been invoked by postcolonial theorists and filmmakers in the interest of subaltern groups and as a critical weapon against reductive forms of identity politics. (2)

The same is the case with "post-neoliberal" Latin America, where the past becomes a tool on which postmodern populist regimes can draw to divert attention from the contradictions of their policies.

THE BIOPIC'S RELATION TO CROSSOVER CINEMA

Historically, biopics serve a functional role. In his groundbreaking study of the Hollywood biopic, film historian George Custen draws on Frankfurt School sociologist Leo Lowenthal's analysis of biographies from 1948, which the latter divides into two categories: "idols of consumption" and "idols of production." According to Custen, because the majority of biographical films in the post–World War II period featured entertainers as subjects—rather than films about scientists, inventors, and medical researchers, which had characterized pre–World War II biopics—these midcentury films can be considered idol-of-consumption biopics in that their role was to legitimate the new consumer economy.

Custen argues that there are no hard-and-fast rules to the biopic, inasmuch as its definition changes afresh with each cinematic generation. Notions of fame do not change as much as different types of people become the prime focus of interest in each era (Custen 1992, 7). Biopics from the 1930s can be characterized by noncommodification, in that they deal with creators, which, as film scholar Dennis Bingham (2010) puts it, are "ensconced in a myth of helpless destiny, of a natural drive to create, a myth about creativity that dies hard" (52). Thus, Hollywood biopics of post–World War II era were slow to reflect American culture of the 1950s and 1960s epitomized by the advent of nuclear power, the suburbanization of major segments of the population, and the rise of second-wave feminism (Custen 1992, 29).

For Lowenethal, the traditional role of literary biography is largely a practical one in that it has helped prepare the masses to accept their places in the social hierarchy of early industrial capitalism; books such as the late-nineteenth-century *The Lives of the Saints* legitimate a remote series of admirable lives, which people in turn could emulate. Lowenthal was particularly critical of the plethora of entertainer biographies because they had the socializing effect of quiescence and acquiescence rather than activation and resistance (Custen 1992, 33). Custen (1992, 88–89) considers the preponderance of post–World War II performer biopics as a grand justification for the legitimation of popular entertainment. In other words, idol-of-consumption biopics serve the function of naturalizing the culture industry.

THE EIGHT *LIBERTADORES* FILMS IN DETAIL

In addition to the backdrop of the election of pink-tide regimes, *Los Libertadores*, which premiered in cinemas and on television in Spain, arrived in the early 2010s, in the context of multiple Latin American and Caribbean countries celebrating the bicentennials of their independence. Commenting on the relevance of *Los Libertadores*, ambassador plenipotentiary Felipe González noted that he hopes these lessons of 200 years ago can be instructive for the "Arab Spring," which at the time of writing is sweeping across the Middle East and North Africa ("La faceta más humana" 2012).

Jose Martí, a coproduction with the Cuban Institute of Cinematographic Art and Industry (ICAIC), was released at a time shortly after Fidel Castro stepped down from the presidency; the absence of a decades-long charismatic leader created an identity crisis in Cuba. The film also comes at a time when opposing political forces are claiming Martí (Pérez Betancourt 2011). By depicting Martí's formative years, including paying attention to the life changes he made to become an intellectual, the film deals not only with Martí (Daniel Romero Bildaín), the apostle of Cuban independence, but also Cuban identity (Machado 2010). By changing the formula of the biopic and focusing the action solely on Martí's youth, Pérez paints a bildungsroman that crosses over in terms of being both universal and very Cuban. Pérez links the paternalism of Martí's father Mariano Martí (Rolando Brito) with that of the colonial Spanish power, both of which the young man is rebelling against. One of the film's main points is that while Martí was a man of a very unique disposition, one that defined the history of Cuba, he was also an ordinary human being like any of us ("Felipe González apadrina a los 'Libertadores'" 2011). Like *The Motorcycle Diaries* (*Diarios de motocicleta*) (Salles 2004), *José Martí* "refers to the first experiences at the beginning of the path to moments of consecration and historical significance of the character biography" (Del Río 2010, 127). The film recounts Martí's formative years—as he was the son of a solider and a housewife—between the ages of nine and seventeen, at which point he was sent into exile for seditious activity. But for the screenwriters, this was a tall order since there is very little historical or biographical information on the leader's childhood. Fernando Pérez describes the film as "more subjective than biographical" (quoted in "Fernando Pérez presenta en el Festival de Huelva" 2010). The film delineates Martí's development as a thinker, focusing on his relationship with the director of the Boys' School of Havana, Don Rafael María de Mendive (Julio César Ramírez), who inspired him to join the growing independence movement. The film presents Spain as a society of masters and slaves. As Joel del Río explains, the film is appealing "to the eternal teenager in all of us that rebels, questions parents, [is] contradictory and uncertain" (Del Río 2010). *Jose Martí* humanizes the apostle by presenting him as a simple teenage schoolboy, who is almost prosaic but also exhibits a poetic temperament and is caught up in his indomitable love of freedom. Pérez was interested in making a film about growth, not so much as physical development, but in development as an interior journey. From an early age, Martí was unable to distinguish between his fate and that of others, the fate of Cuba.

Revolución, el cruce de los Andes, a coproduction between Argentina's TV Pública, the Encuentro Channel, and the National Institute of Cinema and Audiovisual Arts, reconstructs General José Francisco de San Martín's (Rodrigo de la Serna) (1778–1850) trans-Andean expedition in which San Martín led 5,000 men from Cuyo toward Chile, ultimately defeating Spanish forces. The film was shot in Buenos Aires and the town of Barreal, located in the southeast of the province of San Juan in the valley of Calingasta (Gonzales Chaves 2012). When *Revolución* was released in 2011, it attracted more than 300,000 viewers ("La película 'Revolución. El cruce de los Andes'" 2012). The film opens in Buenos Aires in 1880, where a journalist (Lautaro Delgado) interviews San Martín's secretary Manuel Esteban de Corvalán, one of the last survivors of the Andean expedition, who was fifteen years old at the time of the crossing. Like *Citizen Kane* (Welles 1941), *Revolución* is interested in investigative, journalistic power and how reporters contribute to historiography (Lunardelli 2011). Corvalán, the film's narrator, describes principally the crossing and the battle of Chacabuco of 1817, when San Martín's army defeated the Spanish forces. Many compare the crossing to the journeys of Hannibal, Napoleon, and Bolívar himself (in Latin America, San Martín is often called "the other Liberator"), who would in 1819 traverse another series of Andean mountains.

La Redota begins in 1884, more than three decades after the death of Artigas. Dictator Máximo Santos (Franklin Rodríguez) (1847–1889) appoints Uruguayan painter Juan Manuel Blanes (Yamandú Cruz) to paint a heroic portrait of Artigas (Jorge Esmoris), whose struggle against the Portuguese prevented Uruguay from becoming a part of Brazil. What Blanes has to work with for his artwork is one extant drawing of Artiga's face and notes by the fictional Aníbal Guzmán Larra (Rodolfo Sancho), a former Spanish spy hired to assassinate Artigas. The latter became a hero during a critical moment of the Napoleonic Wars (1803–1815), when in 1808 the Portuguese king exiled himself to Brazil, while Montevideo became imperial Spain's last stronghold in South America. The tension began with the signing of the armistice between Buenos Aires and the Spanish governor of Montevideo

Francisco Javier de Elío in 1811, in which Uruguay's Banda Oriental ceded the Spanish crown. Paul Vierci (the film's cowriter) explained why the principal character is the fictional Guzmán Larra: "[Such a historical take] can take some licenses but not any license. The historical accuracy, in essence, can benefit from a freer handling of the characters and situations, whether these are functional or enrich the story. This is the role played by the character Guzmán Larra, a 'plausible fiction'" ("Cuando/Por Qué" 2011). Such an artistic license lends itself to structuring the film like Joseph Conrad's *Heart of Darkness*.

Before the European debacle, Guzmán Larra had betrayed his native Spain to stay in the Americas by stealing money. He was captured in Buenos Aires, and in exchange for his life, it was agreed that he murder Artigas, the rebel leader of the east, which had been not subject to the hegemony of Buenos Aires. As with Pérez's *José Martí*, Charlone has created an imaginary work. His film recounts what in Uruguay is called "the Redota," the Artigas-led eastward exodus of some 800 rebels, many of them gauchos to Salto Chico (present-day Concordia, Argentina). These rebels were responding to the colonial rule of Elío. Supposedly the term *Redota* comes from some of the gauchos' mispronunciation of *derrota*, the Spanish-language word for "defeat" (the historian Clemente Frigerio later started referring to it as "the Eastern Exodus"), referring to the exiles' sense of disappointment after a failed insurrection. On the exodus, the rebels pass through the region of Arrroyo Ayuí, where Guzmán Larra encounters a multicultural and multiracial society in which they all wait for the leader they hope will bring them salvation. But at the same time, everyone participates in this new world. There is a marked contrast between Montevideo and the country Ayuí, which is wild, barbaric, and primitive in appearance. It exploits blacks, American-Indians, and white Creoles, each with their own traditions and customs, the result of which was a new race and a mixed culture. *La Redota* thus becomes two diachronic searches after Artigas: that of Guzmán Larra and that of Blanes.

According to Charlone, both the radical left and the ultraright claim Artigas. The real story, he says, points to possible "strong evidence that there was an assassination attempt [on] Artigas." Current Uruguayan president José Mujica (2010–), accompanied by his wife Senator Lucia Topolansky, attended the premiere of the film, which was shot in Spain, Brazil, Paraguay, and Uruguay ("Película 'Artigas—La Redota'" 2011).

Miguel Hidalgo, la historia jamás contada, a coproduction with the Mexican Institute of Cinematography (IMCINE), recounts the story of the titular priest, one of the initiators of the Mexican War of Independence. In 1811, royalist forces arrest Hidalgo (Demián Bichir), expel him from the clergy for his revolutionary activities, and send him to a prison in Chihuahua. In his cell, Hidalgo recollects in flashbacks the times when he aspired to be an actor and playwright in the parish town of San Felipe de las Torres Mochas, where the priesthood sent Hidalgo as punishment for his progressive views. Before long, he becomes a thorn in the side among the town's conservatives, mainly on the pretext of the debts he owes the church, but really due to his politics, including his support for indigenous peoples. His stint at the parish implants larger ideas of liberation in his head. Hidalgo befriends local merchant José Quintana (Juan Ignacio Aranda), a businessman, who, like him, loves the theater. Together the two men come up with the idea of putting on a local production of Molière's *Tartuffe*, a play that Mexico had banned and that Hidalgo translated from French to Spanish. When Quintana's daughter Josefa (Ana de la Reguera) arrives in San Felipe de las Torres Mochas, Hidalgo becomes smitten. His sexual relationship with Josefa forces him to leave the clergy, which ultimately sets him on the course of becoming a prime agent in the War of Independence.

CONCLUSION

As Claudio Lomnitz (2006) indicates, to the extent that the current Latin American lefts exist amidst no current alternative to capitalism, the very categories of "left" and "right" have to be reconfigured. While such a recategorization is outside the realm of this discussion, the principal claim of this chapter is that *crossover* is a propitious term to describe some of the cinematic culture emerging out of Latin America. To the extent to which Latin American and Caribbean countries are unifying, not under Third Worldism, but under a host of neo-neoliberal policies, necessitates new prescriptive terms.

Los Libertadores seeks to recuperate common history and promote cultural links between Spain and Latin America ("El actor y productor Sancho Gracia" 2012). As Latin America and the Caribbean become increasingly integrated, in historically new ways, there is a need for new geocultural categories. Terms such as *transnational* and *world* have a great deal of baggage; moreover, a qualitatively new period of Latin American history requires new imaginaries. This chapter contends that "crossover" is a constructive indicator for the resulting culture from Latin America's paradoxical junction, namely, between neo-neoliberal capitalist and socialist rhetoric.

NOTES

1. Appropriately, the eight films do not have a conventional exhibition pattern; such unique exhibition patterns are congruent with crossover cinema. In Spain, they only air on television, while in Latin America they premiered in cinemas and were picked up by major American and Pan-American broadcasters.
2. By redirecting its circuits of accumulation to benefit the Global South and in doing so create an alterative and parallel globalization through various hemispheric barter economic systems such as the oil program Petrocaribe, the thirty-three-nation-strong regional bloc the Community of Latin American and Caribbean States (CELAC) and the Bolivarian Alliance for the Americas (ALBA), which began in 2004 when Venezuela started selling Cuba discounted

oil in exchange for Cuban doctors who were sent to Venezuela's poorest states. Since that year, ALBA has grown and now is composed of Antigua and Barbuda, Bolivia, Dominica, Saint Vincent and the Grenadines, Nicaragua, and Ecuador, and whose objective, Chávez claims, is to carry out South American independence leader Simón Bolívar's (1783–1830) dream of a united Latin America.
3. Throughout, all translations are the author's own.

REFERENCES

Arvelo, Alberto, dir. 2013. *Simón Bolivar*. Caracas, Venezuela: Producciones Insurgentes, San Mateo Films and WMG Film.
Bergan, Ronald. 1983. "What Ever Happened to the Biopic?" *Films and Filming* 326(July): 21–22.
Bingham, Dennis. 2010. *Whose Lives Are They Anyway? The Biopic as Contemporary Film Genre*. New Brunswick, NJ: Rutgers University Press.
Charlone, César, dir. 2009. *La Redota, una historia de Artigas*. Montevideo, Uruguay: Wanda Films, Lusa Films and TVE.
Coronil, Fernando. 2011. "The Future in Question: History and Utopia in Latin America (1989–2010)." In *Business as Usual: The Roots of the Global Financial Meltdown,* edited by Craig Calhoun and Georgi Derluguian, 231–64. New York: New York University Press.
"Cuando/Por Qué: César Cahrlone Conociendo al equipo detrás de Artigas—La Redota." 2011. *La Redota, la Película,* April 7. http://laredotalapelicula.com/2011/04/07/como-que-cuando-por-que-cesar-charlone-conociendo-al-equipo-detras-de-la-redota-una-historia-de-artigas/.
Custen, George F. 1992. *Bio/Pics: How Hollywood Constructed Public History*. New Brunswick, NJ: Rutgers University Press.
Del Río, Joel. 2010. "Con los ojos fijos en la altura (+Galería)." *Juventud rebelde,* April 3. http://www.juventudrebelde.cu/cultura/2010-04-03/jose-marti-con-los-ojos-fijos-en-la-altura-galeria/.
"El actor y productor Sancho Gracia consigue poner en marcha un proyecto de ocho películas sobre los heroes latinoamericanos." 2012. *AmericaEconomica.com*. http://www.americaeconomica.com/index.php?name = libertadores.
Ellner, Steve, and Miguel Tinker Salas. 2006. "The Venezuelan Exceptionalism Thesis: Separating Myth from Reality." In *Venezuela: Hugo Chávez and the Decline of an "Exceptional Democracy,"* edited by Steve Ellner and Miguel Tinker Salas, 3–15. Lanham, MD: Rowman & Littlefield.
"Felipe González apadrina a los 'Libertadores' de TVE." 2011. *Vertele!* March 10. http://www.vertele.com/noticias/felipe-gonzalez-estrella-en-la-presentacion-de-libertadores/.
"Fernando Pérez presenta en el Festival de Huelva 'José Martí, el ojo del canario.'" 2010. *Diario de Cuba*. November 16. http://www.diariodecuba.com/cultura/1753-fernando-perez-presenta-en-el-festival-de-huelva-jose-marti-el-ojo-del-canario.
Ford, John, dir. 1939. *Young Mr. Lincoln*. Los Angeles: Cosmopolitan Productions, Twentieth Century Fox Films.
Forgacs, David. 1984. "National-Popular: Genealogy of a Concept." In *Formations of Nation and People,* edited by the Formations Editorial Board, 83–98. London: Routledge.
García Canclini, Néstor. 1982. *Las culturas populares en el capitalismo*. Havana: Casa de las Américas.
Girard, Françoise, dir. 1993. *Thirty-two Short Films about Glenn Gould*. Lisbon, Portugal: CBC, Glen Gould.

Gomes, Marcelo, dir. 2013. *Tiradentes*. Rio de Janeiro: Wanda Films, TVE.
Gonzales Chaves, Adolfo. 2012. "Proyección de 'Revolución, el cruce de los Andres [sic]'." *La noticia1.com,* March 8. http://www.lanoticia1.com/noticia/gonzales-chaves-proyeccion-de-revolucion-el-cruce-de-los-andres-32969.html.
Hall, Stuart. 1980. "Cultural Studies: Two Paradigms." *Media, Culture, and Society* 2: 57–72.
Ipiña, Leandro, dir. 2009. *Revolución, el cruce de los Andes*. Buenos Aires: TV Pública.
"La faceta más humana de los libertadores de Latinoamérica en ocho películas." 2012. *Mascultura*. http://www.mascultura.com.mx/liberadores.
Landy, Marcia. 1996. *Cinematic Uses of the Past*. Minneapolis: University of Minnesota Press.
"La película 'Revolución. El cruce de los Andes' llega a la pantalla chica." 2012. *El Recado*. August 15. http://elrecado.net/cultura/10008-la-pelicula-qrevolucion-el-cruce-de-los-andesq-llega-a-la-pantalla-chica.
Larraín, Ricardo, dir. 2013. *El niño rojo*. Santiago, Chile: TVE.
"'Libertadores': ocho películas sobre los heroes de la independencia de América Latina (+ fotos)." 2011. *Noticias 24,* March 10. http://www.noticias24.com/gente/noticia/23029/libertadores-ocho-peliculas-sobre-los-heroes-de-la-independencia-de-america-latina.
Lomnitz, Claudio. 2006. "Latin America's Rebellion: Will the New Left Set a New Agenda?" *Boston Review,* September/October. http://bostonreview.net/BR31.5/lomnitz.php.
Lunardelli, Laura. 2011. "'Revolution: The Crossing of the Andes' Premieres in Argentina." Translated by Claudio Pairoba. *El blog de Claudio Pairoba,* April 5. http://planetciencia.blogspot.com/2011/04/revolution-crossing-of-andes-premieres.html.
Machado, Mabel. 2010. "Entrevista con Broselianda Hernández." *La jiribilla: revista de cultura Cubana,* April 17–23. http://www.lajiribilla.cu/2010/n467_04/467_11.html.
"Noticias: los libertadores de Latinoamericana, en ocho películas." 2011. *Secretaría General Iberoamericana* (SGI), March 14. http://segib.org/news/2011/03/los-libertadores-de-latinoamerica-en-ocho-peliculas/.
"Película 'Artigas—La Redota' de César Charlone." 2011. *Bicentario Uruguay 1811–2011.* April 8. http://www.bicentenariouruguay.com/novedades/artigas-la-redota-de-cesar-charlone.
Pérez, Fernando, dir. 2009. *José Martí, el ojo del canario*. Havana, Cuba: ICAIC, TVE and Lusa Films.
Pérez Betancourt, Rolando. 2011. "José Martí: el ojo del canario." In *José Martí, el ojo del canario, un film de Fernando Pérez,* edited by Carlos Velazco, 123–25. Havana: Ediciones ICAIC.
Rosenstone, Robert. 2007. "In Praise of the Biopic." In *Lights, Camera, History: Portraying the Past in Film*. Edited by Richard Francaviglia and Jerry Rodnitzky, 11–29. Arlington: Texas A&M University Press.
Rowe, William, and Vivian Schelling. 1991. *Memory and Modernity: Popular Culture in Latin America*. London: Verso.
Salles, Walter, dir. 2004. *The Motorcycle Diaries*. Buenos Aires: Film Four.
Serrano, Antonio, dir. 2010. *Miguel Hidalgo—la historia jamás contada*. Mexico City, Mexico: Astillero Films and IMCINE.
Taymor, Julia, dir. 2002. *Frida*. Los Angeles: Handprint Entertainment.
"TVE redescubre a los 'Libertadores', ocho líderes de la independencia latinoamericana en su faceta más humana." 2011. RTVE.es, October 3. http://www.rtve.es/rtve/20110310/tve-redescubre-libertadores-ocho-lideres-independencia-latinoamericana-su-faceta-mas-humana/415615.shtml.
Túpac Amaru. 2013. (Unknown director.) Lima, Peru: TVE.
Welles, Orson, dir. 1941. *Citizen Kane*. Los Angeles: RKO.

Part II
Reading outside the Canon

5 Hong Kong Film as Crossover Cinema
Maintaining the HK Aesthetic

Peter C. Pugsley

Contemporary Hong Kong (HK) films are often identified by their use of aesthetically determined urban landscapes based around an excess of neon lights and shop fronts adorned with traditional Chinese script. However, the idea that HK cinema is uniquely representative of local (Chinese-based) cultures suggests a naive view of the crossover nature of HK cinema that draws from extended, generational interaction with Japanese, European, and Hollywood cinematic styles. This chapter explores how HK cinema has emerged in line with Kavoori's (2009) definition of crossover cinema as a site that draws on the specifics of one locale to address more universalistic themes, and "where the specifics of ethnicity are recast within wider narrative concerns of a global kind" (260). While Chinese ethnicity and the diasporic cultures of China remain a vital element in HK cinema, the pressures associated with ensuring box-office returns for foreign investors and an emergent base of a cinema-savvy global audience means that HK films are no longer exclusively marked by their "Chineseness." The nexus of the HK cinema industry with regional and global production/distribution networks has nurtured an art-cinema aesthetic (and narrative style) employed by directors such as Wong Kar Wai and Fruit Chan and a corresponding genre aesthetic in popular mainstream crime dramas from Alan Mak or the comedies from Stephen Chow. The long-standing imprint of Japanese Yakuza and martial arts action films, for instance, clearly underpin the HK aesthetics found in the *Infernal Affairs* (*Wujian dao*) (Lau and Mak 2002) trilogy and replicated in recent films including *Accident* (*Yi ngoi*) (Cheang 2009), *Confession of Pain* (*Seung sing* or *Shang cheng*) (Lau and Mak 2006), and *Overheard* (*Sit yan fungwan*) (Mak and Chong 2009).

Added to these cinematic and cultural influences are the Hollywood distribution deals with Miramax, Sony Pictures, or Warner (Dombrowski 2008) that produce expectations that HK films will move beyond Cantonese-language and broader diasporic Chinese audiences. It is these external production factors that see HK directors adopt a more readily identifiable transnational aesthetic and narrative palette to attract foreign audiences, while trying to retain the core traits of HK cinema. Importantly, these films need to deliver an *aesthetic moment*, which Annette Kuhn (2005) sees as a function of cinema that is "characterized by a feeling of being, or becoming, at one with a work of art" and giving the sensation of "entering into another kind of reality" (404). For local audiences of HK films, this moment is rich in recognition of their culture being played out on-screen, including the overt use of identifiable cityscapes. For others, this moment triggers different modes of recognition, from an ontological questioning of one's Chineseness (in diasporic audiences) to a more distant "Othering" by foreign, non-Chinese audiences. For HK directors, the challenge is to maintain the specifics of HK ethnicity and produce a form of crossover cinema that continues to deliver a distinct HK aesthetic.

FILM AESTHETICS

So then, what is this HK aesthetic, and how does it perpetuate HK film as a form of crossover cinema? Jean Mitry (1997) suggests that the study of any film involves a crucial understanding of the "notions of language, structure and perception which *define* this image, its role, and its capabilities and which constitutes the *foundations* of any aesthetic of film" (3). Thus, while the latter part of Mitry's argument leans toward the existence of universality in the "foundations" of film, the former indicates a more fluid (and hence culturally more adaptable) approach to be found in the content, marked by the identifying factors such as language, structure, and perception. In relation to the post-1970s crime films that came to signify HK film, the foundational genre tropes were readily apparent, but there was something more distinct about these films. Stephen Teo (2010, 163) discusses the arrival of "Hong Kong noir" as the "topographic vision of hell" found in films that present HK as a "perennially dark or shadowy city," such as the Chow Yun Fat series of crime-action thrillers directed by John Woo, including *A Better Tomorrow* (*Yingxiong bense*) (1986) and *The Killer* (*Diexue shuangxiong*) (1989). David Bordwell (2000) notes that the cheap and grubby look of 1970s action films had given way to a "hard-edged style that compared favorably with Hollywood" (208). Vivian P. Y. Lee (2009, 87) tracks a later shift from the "crisis consciousness" of 1980s films that acutely reflected concerns over the impending return to the People's Republic of China, to the urbanized lawlessness found in the films of John Woo. Lee (2009) suggests that the action cinema that emerged, perhaps best exemplified by the work of Johnnie To, features a large helping of "self-reflexive parody" (88) of the earlier films. The HK aesthetic is one made identifiable by its postmodern skyline as emblematic of what Tan and Fernando (2007) see—using Singapore as their point of focus—as "technocratic nationalism," a patriotically driven concept found in a nation's desire to advance its image as:

> first and foremost a globally connected marketplace of ideas and commodities. In this regard, Singapore's legacy as an *entrepot* port is crucial,

and consequently, conceptions of film as merchandise for transnational transaction become dominant, while questions of culture, or of cinema as having cultural currency, have taken a back seat. (128)

Although Singapore was able to shake off the shackles of British colonialism for its own independence, it is also—like HK—bound by its reliance on transnational commercial concerns, and the ability to maintain a strong sense of local culture is increasingly under threat. Tan and Fernando (2007) expand on their argument by suggesting that films are, however, able to convey a sense of "cultural nationalism" found in "content that carries auras of cultural resonance and national distinction" (128). They give the example of the use of "Singlish" in Singaporean films, which performs a task similar to Cantonese in HK films because it is a culturally located indicator that "bears the irrevocable mark of local ingenuity and industry" found in the heart of the local society (Tan and Fernando 2007, 136).

Investigating the crossover elements of HK film requires an understanding of the unique characteristics of a constantly evolving cinematic environment. Crucial to this understanding is the complex integration of foreign and local influences. In terms of external sources, David Bordwell (2001) writes:

> The new-generation HK directors of the 1970s and 1980s, such as John Woo, Tsui Hark, Yuen Kuei, and others seem to have understood the emerging Hwood [sic] style very well. We know that they were watching the films of Scorsese, Spielberg, and other influential directors. So we find much of the same sort of features in their movies. (4)

Thus, we can see, as Khorana notes in the introduction to this volume, that the influences are embedded a priori at the "site of cross-cultural conceptualization and production," *before* the film is produced. However, as this chapter focuses on recent HK films of the crime genre, it is instructive to call on Lisa Dombrowski's (2008) explanation of the aesthetic elements that HK audiences have been exposed to via HK action films (in general) that:

> tend to be more vivid than coherent, sporting both universal and generic conventions and local cultural references, expressive physicality and extreme sentimentality, sophomoric silliness and brutal violence, bizarre plot twists and shamelessly politically incorrect humor. (8)

For Dombrowski, it is exactly for these reasons that HK films fail to impact U.S. markets and companies like Miramax must intervene—often through brutal reediting—to ensure that the films are able to resonate with foreign audiences.

One recent film to continue the crime-action genre is *Accident* (*Yi ngoi* in Cantonese, or *Yì wài* in Mandarin; Cheang 2009) starring Louis Koo as the somber Ho "Brain" Kwok-Fai. Koo's costars are all well-known actors in HK but also have cultural ties reaching beyond HK, including Taiwanese actor/musician Richie Ren/Jen as Chan Fong-chow and three mainland-born actors: Hangzhou-born, U.S.-schooled Michelle Ye as the Woman; Tianjin-born Lam Suet as Fatty; and Guangdong-born Stanley Fung as Uncle. Soi Cheang also directed the assassin tale *Dog Bite Dog* (*Gou yao gou*) (2006) and his own adaptation of the Japanese manga *Shamo* as an ultraviolent, live-action kickboxing film, released in 2007. *Accident* was produced by two HK-based companies, Milkyway Image and Media Asia Films. The latter company has firm distribution arrangements with mainland China and Taiwan, as well as Southeast Asian nations such as Singapore, Indonesia, and Malaysia. Milkyway Image is an independent film company formed by local directors Johnnie To and Wai Ka-Fai as a way of promoting their brand of gritty crime dramas that are heavily influenced by French and Hollywood noir.

Opening with an oddly surreal, but graphic image of a woman being ejected through the front windscreen of a car during a crash and a title card with the characters *yi ngoi* (and the English, lowercase translation "accident"), *Accident* cuts to several scenes shot from the interior of moving cars. The external view is a glimpse of HK street life: pedestrians, shopkeepers, and delivery trucks. A black Mercedes Benz pulls up in the middle of a narrow street, and the driver, a well-dressed young woman, gets out discovering a flat tire. Horns start honking as a minor traffic jam builds. An older man in a suit steps from his car to ask the woman to unblock the road, but she refuses until she has some help. He squeezes his late-model European car (a Volvo) past hers and continues on, only to encounter a string of seemingly inconsequential mishaps that eventually result in a bizarre "accident" that will ultimately claim his life. These opening scenes establish a banal view of everyday HK. Western decadence appears in the cars being driven, while the mundane activities of those on the street suggest small-time vendors and office workers going about their daily business. The theme of organized crime, and "Triad" gangs in particular, suggests a contemporary HK, but the film could easily have been set in one of the mainland's bigger cities, such as Guangzhou or Shanghai. Brain's air of paranoid detachment from those around him encapsulates the isolation of life in a big city and reflects a sense of Baudelaire's flaneur, in much the same way that Huang (2000) views Tony Leung's Cop 633 in a much earlier film, *Chungking Express* [*Chóngqìng Sēnlín*] (Wong 1994). As the protagonists (an unaligned group of seemingly altruistic mavericks) traverse the city, they utilize elevated stairways, public buses, trams, and trains in their setting up of crimes designed to appear as accidents, against the triads. The cityscape and its various modes of transport therefore become implicit in a plot that increasingly pushes the limits of credibility.

Accident does not present HK as a site of optimism and great wealth. It serves as a culturally significant backdrop that is globally recognized through crime-genre films. The use of Cantonese language throughout, together with the iconographic streetscapes, helps to locate it as a nonmainland film, yet provide an unmistakable Chineseness to the audience. The arrival of Richie Ren as the target, Chan, in the latter half of the film also provides a link for audiences across not only the mainland but also Taiwan through Ren's prior successes as an actor and as a popular music star of some significance across the region. Cheang maintains the steely blue-gray aesthetic palette of earlier HK action films, most notably used in the crisp, clinical visual tropes in the *Infernal Affairs* trilogy. This provides a more subdued tone than that of many contemporary mainland films, such as those of Feng Xiaogang or Zhang Yimou, and perhaps better reflects the stark realism found in films by Jia Zhangke and Li Yu. It also reflects the tone of earlier Japanese cop films, such as Beat Takeshi's *Hana-bi* (1997).

While *Accident* presents an aesthetic firmly marked by technocratic nationalism, *Confession of Pain* (Lau and Mak 2006) is imbued with an image of HK that is interspersed with a strong sense of cultural nationalism. Like *Accident*, *Confession of Pain* was coproduced by Media Asia Films, but it also called on a much stronger international base for funding, including Polybona Films from mainland China and Avex Entertainment from Japan. Avex Entertainment had long been recognized for its music catalogue and strong distribution links across the region, including into Thailand and Singapore. Moving into film scores and then to production itself, Avex's entry into film production proved short lived, as the company later decided to reconcentrate its efforts directly on the music industry.

Confession of Pain features two icons of the HK film industry: Tony Leung Chiu-Wai (*Hard Boiled* [*Làshou shéntàn*], *In the Mood for Love* [*Huāyàng niánhuá*]) as the increasingly mysterious Detective Hei; and Takeshi Kaneshiro (a Japanese citizen, born in Taiwan) as the widowed Bong, Hei's colleague who has quit the force to drown his loss in whiskey. *Confession of Pain* is an ultimately tragic tale of infidelity that opens with a sweeping aerial view of a glittering HK by night. A soul-gospel song begins playing, which is soon recognizable as the Christmas carol "Silent Night" (sung in English, this song also appears at the end of the film where it is followed by a song in Mandarin). One other song, "Remember," is also in English. However, in moments of high drama in the nondiegetic soundtrack, there is an emphasis on traditional Chinese music, such as the use of the stringed *huqin* (Chinese violin) and an instrument credited as the "Chinese drum." A large neon sign indicates that it is 2003, and the Christmas theme is heightened as we sweep down to a street party complete with tinsel, baubles, and Santa Claus hats. Shots of the glittering skyline are interspersed throughout the film, as either establishing shots or as a highly visible background to interior shots through apartment windows. There is a crisp, clean look to the film—the (post) modern city is on show here in the first half of the film, apart from the odd grimy crime scene. A progression of time is indicated by a "Three years later 2006" slide superimposed over another aerial view, this time from the top of the architecturally striking Tsing Ma

Bridge that connects HK with its airport on Lantau Island, reflecting a brief concession to technocratic nationalism. Later scenes feature street-level HK including markets and building sites—an indication that HK is never really "finished" but is an ongoing project. One flashback scene related by Hei to Bong features a contrastive black and white as the scene is recreated while Bong remains in color (physically present as well as temporally located in the present) and stands watching the scene unfold around him.

Like Johnnie To's (2005, 2006) *Election* films, Lau and Mak have also done away (mostly) with guns—their violence is primal, featuring knives and bashings with heavy objects including a candlestick holder, a brick, a hammer, and a decorative Buddhist statue. In terms of regional influence, these are tropes of savagery found in the work of Korean director Park Chan-wook (*Old Boy* [*Oldeuboi*] 2004, *Sympathy for Lady Vengeance* [*Chinjeolhan geumjassi*]) and Japan's Takeshi Miike (*Ichi, The Killer* [*Koroshiya Ichi*] 2002). Indeed, Bordwell (2000) had noted that "following the precedent of Japan (which since the 1920s has offered up the most gruesome films in the world) HK filmmakers have pushed the boundaries of taste" (200), but obviously boundaries were to be pushed further.

Vivian P. Y. Lee (2009) suggests that *Confession of Pain* "frequently refers to familiar images of the city as if to encode its filmic space within the local cinematic convention" (152), but also to distance itself from the "nonplace" of *Infernal Affairs*. HK culture is made complex according to Lee (2009) because "a particular brand of nostalgic consumerism still holds sway, as popular products and images carrying an aura of 'old Hong Kong' run in parallel with the cult of 'old Shanghai'" (13). Although there are no overt references to the mainland, several scenes take place in Macau utilizing its colonial architecture and neon strips as iconographic indicators of the location change. Kavoori's notion of crossover cinema is replicated here in that the desire to present a cosmopolitan view of HK as a transnational city is dependent on its ability to reflect an awareness of global trends. In this sense, HK cinema has proved itself quite adept to the point that "like the Cantopop song which mixes Eastern scales with American four-bar structure and Latin instrumentation, the [HK] action movie has creatively reworked international conventions of film style" (Bordwell 2000, 200). As Lee (2009) notes in her introduction, the "trademark" qualities of HK cinema will remain "subject to pragmatic adjustments and structural re-engineering that respond to not only the vicissitudes of the global market, but also the newly important 'national domestic' market in mainland China" (7).

Directors Alan Mak and Felix Chong (the writers of the *Infernal Affairs* series) returned to the crime genre with the surveillance film *Overheard* in 2009. *Overheard* was produced by Sil-Metropole Organisation, essentially a state-owned studio controlled by Beijing that arose out of a merger of four production companies that had converged around HK during the mid-twentieth century. Featuring a trio of undercover cops, each troubled with their own personal problems, *Overheard* is a tense high-tech thriller in which everyone seems to be planting bugs, phone tapping, and generally listening to each other's private conversations trying to work out who is double-crossing whom. *Overheard* is a film that all but ignores the cultural nationalism of HK's Chinese connections (apart from the brief glimpses of Chinese text on computer and mobile phone screens, and some fleeting vision of Buddhist charms and texts) to denote both visually and through its score that it is a contemporary film. Its sense of technological nationalism is heightened by a subplot involving the ill child of Gene Yeung (Louis Koo) who requires constant high-tech medical treatment. Links to the global stock market also feature heavily, as the team becomes caught up in trading through listening to the conversations of leading stockbrokers. Koo as the highly strung Gene is particularly vulnerable because he needs money to pay for his son's medical expenses. Once again, as in the iconic images from the original *Infernal Affairs*, swooping rooftop scenes feature heavily, integrated into the story as both a commentary on HK society (where people have to go outside to smoke) and because cigarette lighters are handy places to conceal listening devices.

Overheard continues the long history of utilizing actors from beyond HK, starring American-born and raised Daniel Wu; mainland actress Zhang Jingchu; Macau-born Lam Ka-Wah; and another Chinese-American, New York–born Michael Wong as the brash American Willie Ma, alongside local actors Lau Ching-Wan, Alex Fong Chung-Sun, and Waise Lee. The main cast returned in the 2011 sequel, *Overheard 2*, also directed by Mak and Chong.

THE HK-MOTHERLAND RELATIONSHIP

In trying to create cinema that literally provides a crossover for audiences from HK and the mainland (although often called the "inland," as parts of the HK Special Administrative Region (SAR) are physically/geographically connected to the mainland), stronger industrial links have formed. Laikwan Pang (2010) sees this as creating two options for the film industry: official coproductions with China (including concessions to strict political censorship and to the use of Mandarin) or the production of regional films for Cantonese (and foreign) audiences. The first of these options—utilizing China as a financial and physical base for coproductions—offers the lure of inexpensive location shoots, a cheaper-to-employ cast and crew, and an almost guaranteed share of a much larger audience. The result is an increasing marginalization of the domestic HK market (although with significant compensation through new agreements with neighboring Guangdong Province that expand the "local" audience from seven million to more than ninety million). Pang (2010) argues that this move "might imply a new cultural identity for this regional cinema" (141). And linguistically, the formalizing of film policy between Guangdong Province and HK could be, in Pang's (2010) view, "a first step toward China's acceptance of an alternative cultural industry, an indirect recognition of a cultural alterity within the national self, as Cantonese is largely incomprehensible to most Chinese citizens" (143).

This use of language in HK film has taken on a new significance over the past two decades: prior to, and post, the 1997 Handover. As Emily Tsz Yan Fong (2010) points out, the code switching between languages (especially Cantonese/English or Cantonese/Mandarin) is increasingly showing a "possible change in the power dynamics of group relations between Hong Konger and mainland Chinese" (32). The most notable aspect of this change, according to Fong (2010), has been a diminution of "Hong Kong culture-specific slang and more use of 'plain' language and Mandarin" (36) in HK films. Fong's study looks at a series of misunderstandings between Cantonese speakers and their Mandarin counterparts, with the mistakes generally pointing to a failure on the part of the Cantonese speakers (the HK "natives") to understand Mandarin. The result is a subordination of Cantonese to Mandarin, an almost direct reversal of earlier filmic representations where Mandarin was merely an "outsider language" (Fong 2010, 48). Fong (2010) suggests that the use of Mandarin in HK films is both strategically efficient in terms of procuring support (and exploiting advantages of the Closer Economic Partnership Arrangement between the mainland and HK) and in terms of acknowledging China's "rise as a world power" and Mandarin's climb "as a local and global form of linguistic capital" (49).

Pang's second option proposes a maintaining of the status quo, but perhaps with an optimistic view where more HK films will be dubbed into Mandarin (Putonghua) for official release in the mainland. This model builds on not only the strong diasporic base for Cantonese cinema but also the valued international reputation of this cinema in particular genres, most notably in the action and kung fu genres but also through the art cinema of directors such as Wong Kar Wai and Fruit Chan. Such options also highlight the temporality of the predicament in which HK's once enviable film industry finds itself, with shrinking box-office takings, a drying up of investment, an "exodus of talents," and an ongoing, losing battle with piracy, which leads Chan and Fung (2010) to surmise that "it is only natural for their practitioners to seek to exploit the rich potential of the China market" (78). For Chan and Fung (2010), there has been a resultant hybridization of HK film (and television) with Chinese film, at not only the cultural level but also the structural, impacting on "the operation and organization of audiovisual production" (78). What becomes interesting is the way in which the HK film industry so eagerly grasps coproductions even though these mean "dwelling in the Chinese social context without getting politically entangled" (Chan and Fung 2010, 80). As Davis (2010) contends, China's move toward a more liberalized market has created a "'Chinawood' aspiring to match Hollywood internationally while continuing to serve the Party at the national level" (124). According to Teo (2010), HK film has had to integrate action scenes into "virtually every film in every genre" (155) to maintain a high level of employment for the array of professional stunt actors, choreographers, and directors that find themselves limited in their skills to adapt to other kinds of filmmaking.

Some major changes to the mainland's regulations in the early 2000s saw a lifting of the protectionist quota system that tied HK to twenty "foreign" films per year, which so incensed Hollywood. There was a corresponding loosening of demands that at least 50 percent of personnel on a coproduction were from the mainland, and story lines no longer had to be strictly set in the mainland (Chan and Fung 2010, 81). Results were almost immediate, with coproductions like Zhang Yimou's *Hero* (*Yingxiong* 2002) quickly racing to the top of the box office and consistently holding top-grossing places (e.g., John Woo's *Red Cliff* [*Chi bi*] 2008) across the mainland (Chan and Fung 2010, 82). One of the nationalistic outcomes of such coproductions is the ability to claim all of these films as "Chinese films," regardless of their origins or those of their actors or crew. The creation of the China Film Group creates the illusion of an arm's-length organization supporting the development of film; however, its allegiances (and funding) are controlled by the Beijing-based State Administration of Radio, Film and Television (Davis 2010, 124).

This shift exposes the long-standing dilemma faced by those in HK where they endured a "love-hate relationship with China, a simultaneously alluring and forbidding love-object that was also *zuguo jiaxing*, their motherland and home" (Tan 2001, 1). Tan's historical contextualization places China's golden age of filmmaking in the 1930s within a sphere of intense movements governed by the push toward commensurate drives for nationalism and modernism. The result was a Sinification of Chinese film marked by social realism, creating a genre that "was already a hybrid, incorporating traditional Chinese art forms and assimilating foreign cultural influences" (Tan 2001, 2).

However, the previously described hybrid was inherently fraught with the unresolvable difference between the two regions. Ackbar Abbas (2000) tracks the rise of both Shanghai and HK as occupying different spaces on what could be seen as a continuum of cosmopolitanism, with HK lurching ahead as a result of increased capital following the mainland's Communist Revolution in 1949 and exacerbated by the impending sense of change following the 1984 Joint Declaration ceding HK back to China in 1997. For many years, HK was viewed as a cosmopolitan gateway between East and West. Abbas (2000) questions Ulf Hannerz's (1990) ideal of cosmopolitanism as one encapsulated by a desire to engage with the Other, suggesting a flaw in this reasoning. The problem, it seems, is that such a view discounts the hegemonic variations encountered when one culture is forced on another. While Abbas cites colonialism as one such example, surely the fractious relationship between HK and the mainland would see the latter holding all the power. However, HK's early exposure to the West (and Japan), and its hybrid adaptability, sees it become the desirable Other, the savvy cosmopole to an awakening mainland. What film allows is for audiences to see a quotidian HK where "the picture perfect global space lies outside of the everyday reality" (Huang 2000, 395).

However, while Shanghai's rapid development from the 1990s has reinvigorated that city (as Beijing was reinvigorated in the lead-up to the 2008 Olympic Games), not all of China has been able to grasp the mantle of cosmopolitanism. Thus, the gap between HK and the mainland remains (even though all are now provisionally "one country"), hence the need for cultural texts such as film to traverse the cultural landscape in order to resonate with audiences in both territories.

One further complicating element in the China-HK relationship is the birthplace of directors and actors. The complex nature of citizenship is reflected in key personnel: Jackie Chan (born in HK but schooled in Beijing), Jet Li (born in Beijing but came to prominence as a HK actor), John Woo (born in Guangzhou but raised in HK), Fay Wong (born in Beijing and joined her father in HK in her late teens), and Wong Kar Wai (born in Shanghai but raised in HK from the age of five). Claims for "authenticity" in a Chinese film are therefore perhaps easier to justify. The marketability of HK stars in the mainland (often in tandem with their careers as Cantopop singing stars, where they generally concede to include a few songs in Mandarin on each album) also aids in the promotion of films in China and into the global diaspora. Others have even more complex links reflective of HK's position as a cultural hub in Asia, as exemplified by noted director Tsui Hark (*Once Upon a Time in China* [*Wu Zhuangyuan huang feihong*] I-V 1991–1995, *The Blade* [*Dao*] 1995), a Vietnamese-born émigré who arrived in HK when he was thirteen and later moved to the United States, or acclaimed Taiwanese/Japanese star of *Confession of Pain* Takeshi Kaneshiro (*Chungking Express* 1994; *House of Flying Daggers* [*Shi mian maifu*] 2004; and Sato Shimako's Japanese noir thriller *K-20: Legend of the Mask* [*Ketuenti: Kaijin niju menso den*] 2008). Thus, we see the performance of transnational selves (as elaborated by Khorana in the introductory chapter) enacted through not only the actors but also by the directors themselves.

EXTERNAL INFLUENCES

All these links to various forms of Chineseness in HK films take place within an undeniably globalized environment marked by a long history of ties with the cinemas of Japan, Europe, and Hollywood. This is perhaps an opportune moment to (briefly) examine how these foreign cultures have interacted and helped to shape the crossover elements of HK cinema. I would like to expand on Meaghan Morris's introduction to her coedited collection on HK action films where she sees action cinema (her genre of focus) as providing a site in which there is a series of "cross-cultural logics of contact and connection (audio-visual and sociocultural as well as bodily and technological)" (Morris, Li, and Chan 2005, 13). I suggest that this extends across the cinematic realm of contemporary HK film, a notion supported by Vivian Lee's (2009) investigation of Johnnie To's 1999 Triad thriller *The Mission*

(*Qianghuo*, literally "Gunfire") openly acknowledged as being inspired by Kurosawa's *Seven Samurai* by experimenting with "a kind of 'motion in stillness'" (90) as found in the "controlled and stylized choreography of the shooting scenes" (91). Lee (2009) feels that To exhibits:

> a high degree of self-awareness in adapting the visual language of Kurosawa to reenvision a specific local terrain, the *jianghu* (underworld), reworking the themes of brotherhood and loyalty within a patriarchal hierarchy in a contemporary urban setting where male bonds are more defined by team spirit rather than pre-determined by some higher moral or social order. (91)

Therefore, while this logic is easily delineated in a genre-specific study, it also carries particular universal values applicable to other HK cinema genres, such as comedy. For Lee (2009), Stephen Chow's regionally successful *Shaolin Soccer* (*Shaolin zuqiu* 2001) represents a:

> "new localism" in contemporary East Asian cinema, through which the "local" is recoded in a film language amenable to a wider audience in the region. My reading of Chow's films attends to the creative deployment of conventional themes, visual vocabulary, and subject matter alongside mixed references to Hollywood classics to obtain a postmodern "remix" of style and imagery. (16)

But what is it that drives these filmmakers to seek influence from beyond the region and their Chinese roots? Gina Marchetti (2011) suggests that along with other East Asian filmmakers, HK new wave directors such as Allen Fong (*Father and Son* 1981), and more recently Fruit Chan, "reacted against [. . .] earlier types of cinematic realism by evoking Italian Neo-Realism. They pursued (as the French New Wave had) a modernist aesthetic while maintaining many important links to earlier realist forms" (63). Citing Paul Shrader's view of "transcendental style," Marchetti (2011) notes how iconic filmmakers such as Bresson, Ozu, and Dreyer "achieve the transcendent through a style that favours stasis over action, quietude over drama, the repetition of the details of quotidian life over the celebration of the spectacle of the extraordinary" (65). This is certainly at odds with the general Western view of HK cinema as marked by its various forms of action cinema. Indeed, Wong Kar Wai's vision of the HK aesthetic differs markedly from that of the crime genre. Wong's assuredness of place permits him to do away with clichéd skyline images. For Wong, the intersection of cultures and ethnicities (especially in *Chungking Express*) proves a valuable site for exploration. His knowledge of European film aesthetics (ably supported by Australian cinematographer Christopher Doyle and art director William Chang Suk Ping) counters the steely blue grays of Mak et al. and draws from a combination owing more to Krzysztof Kieślowski (*The Double Life of Véronique*

1991, and his trilogy of *Three Colors Red, White, Blue* 1993–1994) and Zhang Yimou (*Red Sorghum* [*Hóng gāoliáng*] 1988, *Raise the Red Lantern* [*Dà hóng dēnglóng gāogāo guà*] 1991), two directors whose color palettes were more openly flamboyant than those of his fellow HK filmmakers.

Stylistically, performances and movements in many HK films owe a debt to Japanese cinema, especially the considered, often melancholy, approach of Ozu or Kurosawa. The influence of Japanese cinema in HK films is difficult to ignore, especially given the overt attempts to replicate Japanese cinematic styles, as Bordwell (2000) notes:

> Kurosawa and his colleagues featured lightning swordplay, bodies crashing through screens, amputations, and geysers of blood. Hong Kong filmmakers had ample opportunity to study the films featuring the blind masseur-swordsman *Zatoichi,* a series that Shaws (Shaw Brothers) distributed locally. Shaws sent staff members to Japan to study production methods and began to hire Japanese directors and cameramen. Run Run Shaw and his manager Raymond Chow would screen a Japanese film for directors and decide how to borrow its plot. (206)

These influences move beyond the images that ultimately appear on the screen. The multilayered hybridization in the HK cinema industry is inclusive in its reach through funding, locations, and "the crossing of boundaries at various levels, including the transnational, international, regional, municipal and local" (Chan and Fung 2010, 86). The international delegation of duties is now seen as essential in HK filmmaking, exemplified by the astute allocation of tasks exhibited with the release of *Hero* (Zhang Yimou 2002), which saw its internationally connected HK producers deal with distribution matters, and its Chinese producers deal with the location and technical production side of things. A similar structure assisted in the distribution of *Confession of Pain*, *Accident*, and *Overheard*, and the films of Stephen Chow (especially *Kung-fu Hustle* [*Gōngfū*] 2004, and *CJ7* [*Cháng Jiāng qī hào*] 2008) have utilized strong ties between HK, Beijing, Japan, and Hollywood to ensure their success. Li (2011) sees a development of this hybridization in more recent films set in Shanghai, which "employed transnational or trans-regional capital and creative talents" (103) such as Zhang Yibai's *The Longest Night in Shanghai* (*Ye: Shanghai*) (2007), a film that not only drew from HK, Taiwanese, and Japanese actors but also relied on local investment and finance from Japan. The result is a film that depicts Shanghai as "a trans-linguistic and trans-cultural space welcoming and accessible to anyone, regardless of cultural origin or social status" (Li 2011, 105), a depiction that could not have been seen until recently as this new Shanghai evokes HK because it "affirms and glorifies China's economic development and embraces a modernized city space, high technology, advanced transportation and consumerism" (Li 2011, 105). Li also notes how Ann Hui's (2006) *The Postmodern Life of My Aunt* (*Yima de houxiandai shenghuo*) contains one character who persistently claims that her daughter has relocated to Los Angeles (even though she actually works in a small restaurant in rural China). In Li's (2011) view, this "satirizes the impact that China's integration into the global economy has had on the mentality of the Chinese people" (108) through the desire to be seen as part of this global network. This reiterates the idea that one can "escape" from China, a strongly apparent (and remarked on) motif in HK films of the 1990s in the lead-up to the 1997 Handover.

The idea of crossover cinema can also be read in a global-marketing sense in terms of HK films, by absorbing foreign influences, therefore being more accessible for foreign audiences. Lisa Dombrowski (2008) points to the approach of giant U.S. distributor Miramax in adapting films for non-HK audiences:

> Miramax's editors typically cut Hong Kong releases to address issues related to content, pacing and style, thereby bring the films into closer alignment with Hollywood storytelling conventions that value efficiency, cohesion and verisimilitude. (4)

Thus, what foreign audiences receive is a U.S.-based interpretation of the HK aesthetic that "cites diverse idioms, repackages codes, and combines genres that are thought to be culturally, aesthetically, or cinematically incompatible" (Yau 2001, 7), about as far removed from Hollywood as one could get.

CONCLUSION

Stephen Teo (2010) refers to the aestheticized violence that is a major feature of contemporary HK film, a violence that is both "choreographic and stylized" (156). Teo's claim is that the portrayal of violence in this manner (including Stephen Chow's attempts to show violence humorously) creates a site for it to be critiqued. Interestingly, Teo points to Johnnie To's (2005) *Election* (*He shehui*, literally "Black society") and *Election 2* (To 2006) as rare examples of HK gangster films where violence is not represented by guns but by the *absence* of guns; registering as a code-of-ethics response to the sense of honor among the gangs involved. The resulting violence, including the sudden, savage bashing of Big D (played by the ever-popular Tony Leung Ka-fei) is made the more potent because of its brutal, "primal" nature (Teo 2010, 164), taking place on the banks of a river (or reservoir), a much more contrastive setting than the mean streets of downtown HK. Teo (2010) concludes by asking how HK's:

> critique of violence will be affected by the film industry's survival within a larger market network in the Chinese mainland, as the industry must observe stricter censorship to become more and more integrated into the mainland market. (165)

This view has salience in some respects; there is a need for HK to tread lightly when it comes to crossing over into the mainland. Will HK be able to maintain these particular aesthetic traits, like Teo's aesthetics of violence? On the other hand, censorship concerns are more likely to be raised by Beijing for images that are politically sensitive or perhaps overly sexual in nature.

Despite the previously mentioned issues, HK cinema has retained much of its strength. Perhaps this is surprising in light of Stephen Teo's (1997) comments made around the time of the 1997 Handover when he posed:

> The challenge of the future is how this generation, and the intermediate one, will adapt to integration with China and still assert the separate identity that was, briefly, theirs. In the long term, it is not even certain whether Hong Kong will be able to continue making movies in Cantonese, the dialect that has made Hong Kong cinema unique and given it its identity. (254)

So while Teo's dire prediction of the (possible) eradication of one of the key cultural indicators of HK cinema is yet to be realized, HK cinema carefully negotiates the terrain of internationalization that befalls all national cinemas in the twenty-first century (with the possible exception of North Korea). The universality of recent films is tempered by the adherence to the technological and cultural nationalism proudly exhibited on-screen in films such as *Accident* and *Confession of Pain*. What emerges in HK cinema is a transnational aesthetic infused with local culture, indicative of local traditions and language, and a sign of the continued crossover nature of HK cinema.

REFERENCES

Abbas, Ackbar. 2000. "Cosmopolitan Descriptions: Shanghai and Hong Kong." *Public Culture* 12(3): 769–86.

Bordwell, David. 2000. *Planet Hong Kong: Popular Cinema and the Art of Entertainment*. Cambridge, MA: Harvard University Press.

———. 2001. "Technology and Technique: Hollywood, Hong Kong, and the Emergence of Contemporary Film Style." Sir Edward Youde Memorial Fund Lecture, Hong Kong, November 24. www.sfaa.gov.hk/doc/en/scholar/seym/11_Bordwell.doc.

Chan, Joseph M., and Anthony Y. H. Fung. 2010. "Structural Hybridization in Film and Television Production in Hong Kong." *Visual Anthropology* 24(1): 77–89.

Cheang, Soi, dir. 2009. *Accident* [*Yi ngoi*]. Hong Kong: Milky Way Image and Media Asia Films.

Davis, Darrell William. 2010. "Market and Marketization in the China Film Business." *Cinema Journal* 49(3): 121–25.

Dombrowski, Lisa. 2008. "Miramax's Asian Experiment: Creating a Model for Crossover Hits." *Scope* 10. http://www.scope.nottingham.ac.uk/article.php?issue = 10&id = 988.

Fong, Emily Tsz Yan. 2010. "Changing Intergroup Relations with Mainland Chinese: An Analysis of Changes in Hong Kong Movies as a Popular Cultural Discourse."

Multilingua: Journal of Cross-Cultural and Interlanguage Communication 29(1): 29–53.
Hannerz, Ulf. 1990. "Cosmopolitans and Locals in World Culture." In *Global Culture*, edited by Mike Featherstone, 237–52. London: Sage.
Huang, Tsung-yi. 2000. "Hong Kong Blue: *Flaneurie* with the Camera's Eye in a Phantasmagoric Global City." *Journal of Narrative Theory* 30(3): 385–402.
Hui, Ann, dir. 2006. *The Postmodern Life of My Aunt* [*Yima de houxiandai shenghuo*]. Hong Kong: Polybona Film.
Kavoori, Anandam. 2009. "Film Review: Why the Sun Shines on Slum Dog." *Global Media and Communication* 5(2): 259–62.
Kuhn, Annette. 2005. "Thresholds: Film as Film and the Aesthetic Experience." *Screen* 46(4): 401–14.
Lau, Andrew, and Alan Mak, dir. 2002. *Infernal Affairs* [*Wujian dao*]. Hong Kong: Media Asia Films and Basic Pictures.
———. 2006. *Confession of Pain* [*Seung sing*]. Hong Kong: Media Asia Films, Polybona Films and Avex Entertainment.
Lee, Vivian PY. 2009. *Hong Kong Cinema Since 1997: The Post-Nostalgia Imagination*. London: Palgrave Macmillan.
Li, Zeng. 2011. "Living for the City: Cinematic Imaginary of the Cityscape in China's Transnational Films." *Critical Arts: South-North Cultural and Media Studies* 25(1): 102–17.
Mak, Alan, and Felix Chong, dir. 2009. *Overheard* [*Qieting fengyun*]. Hong Kong: Sil-Metropole Organisation.
Marchetti, Gina. 2011. "Bicycle Thieves and Pickpockets in the 'Desert of the Real': Transnational Chinese Cinema, Postmodernism, and the Transcendental Style." In *East Asian Cinemas: Regional Flows and Global Transformations*, edited by Vivian P. Y. Lee, 61–86. New York: Palgrave Macmillan.
Mitry, Jean. 1997. *The Aesthetics and Psychology of the Cinema*. Translated by Christopher King. Bloomington: Indiana University Press. (Translated from *Esthétique et Psychologie du Cinéma*, abridged ed., 1990. Original French edition published in 1963, Paris, France: Groupe Mame.)
Morris, Meaghan, Siu Leung Li, and Stephen Ching-kiu Chan, eds. 2005. *Hong Kong Connections: Transnational Imagination in Action Cinema*. Durham, NC: Duke University Press.
Pang, Laikwan. 2010. "Hong Kong Cinema as a Dialect Cinema?" *Cinema Journal* 49(3): 140–43.
Tan, See Kam. 2001. "Chinese Diasporic Imaginations in Hong Kong Films: Sinicist Belligerence and Melancholia." *Screen* 42(1): 1–20.
Tan, See Kam, and Jeremy Fernando. 2007. "Singapore." In *The Cinema of Small Nations*, edited by Mette Hjort and Duncan Petrie, 127–43. Bloomington: Indiana University Press.
Teo, Stephen. 1997. *Hong Kong Cinema: The Extra Dimensions*. London: BFI Publishing.
———. 2010. "The Aesthetics of Mythical Violence in Hong Kong Action Films." *New Cinemas: Journal of Contemporary Film* 8(3): 155–67.
To, Johnnie, dir. 2005. *Election* [*He shehui*]. Hong Kong. Milky Way Image and One Hundred Years of Film.
———. 2006. *Election 2*. Hong Kong. Milky Way Image and One Hundred Years of Film.
Wong, Kar-wai, dir. 1994. *Chungking Express* [*Chóngqìng Sēnlín*]. Hong Kong: Jet Tone Production.
Yau, Esther C. M., ed. 2001. *At Full Speed: Hong Kong Cinema in a Borderless World*. Minneapolis: University of Minnesota Press.

6 On No Longer Speaking Chinese
Crossover Stardom and the Performance of Accented English

Olivia Khoo

The much anticipated film version of Arthur Golden's best-selling novel *Memoirs of a Geisha* arrived tailing a flurry of controversy. Critics and viewers in Japan, China, and the United States criticized director Rob Marshall and producer Steven Spielberg's decision to shoot the film in English and furthermore to have three Chinese actresses play the lead roles of geisha. The official response to these criticisms, voiced by the film's Japanese stars themselves, is that Japan does not have any female actresses with the star power or international box-office pull of any of the film's three Chinese lead actresses: Gong Li, Zhang Ziyi, and Michelle Yeoh. As to shooting the film in English, this seemed not so much a choice as an expectation, in return for the film's US$80 million budget. This chapter aims to focus these criticisms and expectations on the wider phenomenon of female stars who previously worked solely in Chinese-language cinemas now taking on English-speaking roles in America. While the employment of foreign actresses in Hollywood is nothing new, it is arguable that the recent crossover of Chinese actresses into English-language cinematic industries represents a new period of modernity for representations of Chinese femininity. Chinese femininity in the period of the 1990s and beyond is being redefined cinematically. But what is at stake in these new visual manifestations enabled by the crossover? How can we read this "translingual stardom," to adapt a term of Lydia Liu's, to regard its wider implications for cross-cultural politics?

Liu's notion of "translingual practice" provides a useful conceptual framework through which to engage the issues involved in the crossover between Mandarin-language cinematic industries and Hollywood, and the forms of mediation (linguistic and otherwise) involved in the translation across these two sites. Liu (1995) defines translingual practice as "the process by which new words, meanings, discourses, and modes of representation arise, circulate, and acquire legitimacy within the host language due to, or in spite of, the latter's contact/collision with the guest language" (26). In the context of crossover cinema, translingual stardom represents the practice of casting actors likely to appeal beyond cultural borders with the aim of accessing new markets and audiences. As a practice that engages cross-cultural or "crossover" reception, translingual stardom functions as a mode of translation that can enable new modes of representation, in this case for Chinese femininity, to "arise, circulate, and acquire legitimacy" (Liu 1995, 26). What emerges, in the confrontation of these crossover actresses with the "language" of Hollywood, is a new kind of representation that I will call the "reverse Butterfly" narrative. The translingual stardom exemplified by the crossover roles of Chinese actresses in recent years provides a break from, through a reversal of, the predominant cross-cultural paradigm involving Asian women and Western men; namely, the story of Madame Butterfly. Although originally placed within a Japanese context in Puccini's famous opera of the same name, the narrative of the callous white man and the self-sacrificing Asian woman who waits for him has been applied to a variety of different national contexts within Asia, for example, as retold in the musical *Miss Saigon*.

Throughout the long history of Western (cinematic) representation of the exotic Asian woman, the story of Madame Butterfly is a narrative that has been repeated time and again. The eventual abandonment of the Asian woman when the white man returns "home" is, to a large degree, attributable to the fact that she represents a certain primitivism; naive and dependent, she could never be brought to live in a Western urban center. On the situation of Chinese women on screen brought "home" to the West (through the international film festival circuit, among other means), Rey Chow has analyzed how primitivism operates as a specific mode of representation characterizing Fifth Generation mainland Chinese cinema. For the first time since the Cultural Revolution, Chinese cinema became available to Euro-American film markets, and Fifth Generation directors were inevitably viewed as their country's ethnographers (Chow 1995, 171). What they chose to represent were women and the subalterns, the rural and peasant classes. Yet this particular representation proved phenomenally popular with Western audiences. In the situation where Chinese actresses have literally *arrived* in Hollywood, the discourse of primitivism becomes less applicable, and the role of "Butterfly" is no longer a comfortable fit. What emerges in their place is a new type of representation in the form of the "reverse Butterfly" narrative. Instead of the long-suffering Asian woman dying or pining away for her callous lover, it is the white man who sacrifices himself for the Asian woman as a sign of her new agency. These "reverse Butterfly" films display Chinese femininity on the screen in a newly exoticized form, "modernized" precisely through their use of English.

This new period of modernity for Chinese femininity has not, however, come without resistance. In spite of, or perhaps because of, the representation of Chinese femininity as modern and exotic, audience reception of these crossover roles has largely been negative. The unintended effect (or affect) attached to translingual stardom is a sense of disappointment felt by spectators over a loss of authenticity when actors are "removed" from the national cinema contexts they are usually associated with. This loss of authenticity manifests the assumption that English is still regarded by many as the language of the West, despite its rapid global spread accompanied by its transformation and indigenization in the non-Western world. In *English as a Global Language*, sociolinguist David Crystal (1997) argues that while the spread of English was initially a product of the expansion of the British colonial empire, it is now American capitalism—in the form of films, the Internet, and international tourism—that is bringing about the rapid global dissemination of the English language today. The use of the term *global* as a way of prefixing the English language makes it appear unmarked, without accent, yet this is not in fact the case. English is still regarded in many parts of the world as the language of the elite, and different accents of English have always carried different ideological meanings, signifying class stratification for example. English-language usage is *not* neutral. It is inseparable both from a historical legacy of colonialism and from the internationalization of capitalism (Holborow 1999, 191). Its status and usage in Asian diasporic contexts in the West is also worthy of mention.

ACCENTED CINEMA, ACCENTED ENGLISH

The title of this chapter is a play on the title of Ien Ang's (2001) seminal essay (and book collection) *On Not Speaking Chinese*, which has become a foundational text in Chinese diaspora studies. Ang's essay was inspired by her first trip to China where, automatically interpellated as "Chinese," she had to constantly defend herself from the fact that she could not speak Mandarin. Others regarded her inability to speak the language as a lack, a sign of loss of authenticity, since the possession of Chinese-language skills, in particular Mandarin, is taken as a marker of "authentic" Chineseness. For Ang, the guilt attached to this linguistic "shortcoming" developed into an urge to apologize for writing about her experiences to an academic audience in English. Ang uses this situation to establish a foundation for a diasporic politics. She writes:

> "Not speaking Chinese" . . . has become a personal political issue to me, an existential condition which goes beyond the particularities of an arbitrary personal history. It is a condition that has been hegemonically constructed as a lack, a sign of loss of authenticity. This, then, is the reason why I felt compelled to apologize that I have written this text in English–the global *lingua franca* which is one of the clearest expressions of the pervasiveness of Western hegemony. Yet it is precisely this urge to apologize which I would now like to question and counter as well. (Ang 2001, 31–32)

Ang directs attention to the problematic nature of English as a globally hegemonic language in answer to the suggestion that *not* speaking Chinese can be regarded as a lack or a loss. But what kinds of issues arise when

Chinese actresses choose not to speak Chinese even when they clearly can? From the point of view of Western reception to these crossover actresses, "no longer speaking Chinese" is also regarded as a loss of authenticity. To suggest a "crossover" of these stars is to imply borders or boundaries that have been traversed, with the consequences that this entails. The issues involved in policing the boundaries of language are more than simply about protecting language ownership; they also concern the denial of particular kinds of subjectivities that are deemed visible and acceptable because "speakable."

There are political and ideological implications to English-language usage that also pertain to what becomes *visible* both on- and offscreen. These implications are foregrounded in the split between the audible and the visible for audiences unaccustomed to seeing Chinese actresses performing in contemporary Hollywood films in English. The use of English by these Chinese actresses, their translingualism, and the crossing of borders that this entails, implies on the one hand appropriation, subversion, and/or resistance against Hollywood's hegemony, and, on the other, a form of "progress" or "acceptance" within it. Yet speaking English does not necessarily mean either full participation in or resistance against the existing power structure (here, Hollywood), unless resistance is rethought as "a negotiation or process of *contested transaction* rather than a simple refusal" (Berry and Farquhar 2006, 208). What is transacted, through the appearance of Chinese actresses in Hollywood, is the negotiated representation of the "reverse Butterfly" story. However, what tempers the power of this story is the accented nature of the English spoken by these actresses. Accented English, I will argue, functions simultaneously as a kind of resistance and submission, and in this way, a "contested transaction," that makes the telling of the "reverse Butterfly" story possible. The crossover role of Chinese actresses into English-speaking roles in Hollywood is therefore accented both literally and figuratively.

I would suggest, following Hamid Naficy (2001, 25), that the inclusion of vocal accents in Hollywood cinema "transforms the act of spectatorship" (as it is usually attributed to the classical Hollywood spectator), and hence the kinds of assumptions we as spectators make, just as *not* speaking Chinese is based on certain assumptions of a loss of authenticity. In one of the most articulate discussions of how circumstances of diaspora can inflect cinematic production and experience, Naficy's *An Accented Cinema: Exilic and Diasporic Filmmaking* analyzes cinematic works that are marked by experiences of mobility, in particular exile and diaspora. Naficy suggests that these experiences can influence a film's style, which he calls an "accented style," although the gender politics of these conditions are not explicitly examined. Naficy argues that the dominant cinema, meaning Hollywood—both classical and new—is considered universal and unmarked, that is, without accent, since it is free from overt ideology and intended for entertainment only. By comparison, all alternative cinemas, including those by exilic and diasporic filmmakers, are accented. Naficy does not take the concept of "accent" literally—as part of the speech or pronunciation of the characters—but as something that is inscribed in the style of the film or in its mode of production. Thus the entire "grammar" and "vocabulary" of the film text itself (its narrative, visual style, characters, and plot for example) are alternate to the dominant Hollywood paradigm:

> If the dominant cinema is considered universal and without accent, the films that diasporic and exilic subjects make are accented.... The accent emanates not so much from the accented speech of diegetic characters as from the displacement of the filmmakers and their artisanal production modes. (Naficy 2001, 4)

By confining my observations to (literally) accented speech within the dominant cinema, however, it is possible to observe more specific developments in visual signification and reception as represented by these translingual Chinese stars. As Lydia Liu (1995) notes, language practice and use is "a site of manifested historical relationships where the meanings of Western domination and the anti-imperial struggle may be reopened and interrogated in a new light" (xvi). By examining the relationship between "no longer speaking Chinese" and the creation of new forms of visuality manifested by these crossover actresses on-screen, it is clear that language itself, and in particular accented English, can destabilize spectatorial assumptions about identity—in particular the visual signs representing traditional "Chinese femininity."[1] If an accent suggests displacement (of not belonging, because "marked" as different), then it also suggests another (authentic) place of origin. Hence, an accent signifies an individual as being displaced, no matter how hard that individual tries to fit in. It is arguable, then, that diasporic existence is always "accented." However, if we take the introduction of crossover stars as the introduction of a "foreign" element that can disrupt otherwise unmarked dominant cinema, albeit momentarily, it is also possible to open up a space for constructing new modes of visuality that are only just emerging. Stars are, of course, visual representations par excellence.

TRANSLINGUAL STARDOM

The chapter will only focus on crossovers from Mandarin-speaking cinema institutions (namely, mainland Chinese cinema) into Hollywood—by stars such as Joan Chen, Gong Li, Luo Yan, and most recently and spectacularly, Zhang Ziyi—and not Cantonese-dominated industries; namely, Hong Kong.[2] Given the history of British occupation in the former colony, Hong Kong stars such as Michelle Yeoh and Maggie Cheung signify very differently to their Mandarin-speaking counterparts. The resignification of Chinese masculinity also falls outside the scope of this chapter since most of the significant male crossover stars—such as Jackie Chan, Chow Yun-Fat, and Jet Li—were previously working in the Hong Kong film industry. The question of why there are no prominent male crossover stars in Hollywood from the People's Republic of China (PRC) is, however, an interesting line to pursue and requires at least a mention in order to highlight the conservative gender politics of globalization.[3]

In terms of the crossover of Chinese female stars into English-speaking roles, there have been at least two distinct periods of this. Both are preceded by the brief and ill-fated crossover of the actress Li Lihua. Born on August 17, 1924, in Hebei, China, Li began her movie career in Shanghai in 1940 and moved to Hong Kong after the Sino-Japanese war. She starred in some of the colony's first Mandarin-language films. In 1957, at the height of her career, Li went to Hollywood at the invitation of Cecil B. de Mille and played a war bride in the film *China Doll* (1958) opposite Victor Mature. This film, and her role in it, was very poorly received by her fans. As a result, Li returned to Hong Kong in 1960 to resurrect her Chinese-language film career. She worked with the Shaw Brothers and starred in films such as *Yang Guifei* (1962) and *Empress Wu* (1963), both directed by Li Hanxiang, and in King Hu's *The Fate of Lee Khan* (1973). Li moved to New York in 1972 but has now resettled permanently in Hong Kong.

Appearing in Hollywood in a period more accepting of difference, Joan Chen is one of the earliest examples of a crossover star from mainland China to America who is still working today. Chen immigrated to the United States in 1981 at the age of 19. She made her Hollywood debut in Daryl Duke's *Taipan* in 1986. Of the same generation as Chen, Vivian Wu's English-language films include Wayne Wang's *The Joy Luck Club* (1993), Peter Greenaway's *The Pillow Book* (1996), the John Woo-produced *Red Skies* (Larry Carroll and Robert Lieberman 2002), *Eve and the Fire Horse* (Julia Kwan 2005), *Shanghai Red* (Oscar L. Costo 2006), and most recently, *Snow Flower and the Secret Fan* (Wayne Wang 2011). Both Chen and Wu adopted English names, married Americans, and immigrated to the United States.[4] These factors mark a divide between the actresses of this period (from the 1980s and early to mid-1990s) and those of the period following (from the late 1990s to the present day).

Although popular to Western audiences for her roles in Fifth Generation Chinese cinema, Gong Li's arrival in America appears relatively "late" after these successes. She first appeared in Wayne Wang's *Chinese Box* in 1997 but did not star in another Hollywood film for a further seven years. However, despite or perhaps because of the controversy surrounding *Memoirs of a Geisha*, more roles have been offered to Gong Li in Hollywood, and she has recently completed three other English-language films, *Miami Vice* (Michael Mann 2006), *Hannibal Rising* (Peter Webber 2007), and *Shanghai* (Mikael Håfström 2010). Other actresses have only just begun their crossover: Luo Yan produced and starred in Yim Ho's *Pavilion of Women* in 2001 and in Kevin Connor's TV movie *Marco Polo* in 2007, and Zhang Ziyi made her Hollywood debut with a small part in Brett Ratner's *Rush Hour 2* (2001). Following her lead role in *Memoirs of a Geisha* (with several nominations for best actress awards in British and American awards ceremonies), Zhang has already received several offers of work in the United States. She appeared in Jonas Akerlund's *The Horsemen* (2009) and voiced the character of Karai in the film version of the *Teenage Mutant Ninja Turtles* (Kevin Munroe 2007). Other famous Chinese actresses have also expressed an interest in crossing over.[5] This recent exodus of Chinese actresses into American productions has reconfigured Hollywood's cinematic landscape, albeit on a small scale.

FIRST-GENERATION CROSSOVER STARS: MIMICRY AS RESISTANCE

As one of the first contemporary crossover actresses from the mainland, Joan Chen has had to take on many of the stereotypical "China doll" (prostitute) or "Dragon Lady" (villainess) roles, with many of her early films set safely, and conveniently, in the distant past. Chen's first major role in a Hollywood film was in *Taipan* (1986), released a year before Bernardo Bertolucci's epic *The Last Emperor* (1987), the film that brought Chen to wider exposure in America. Although cinematically unremarkable, *Taipan* is useful as an indicator of the early roles available for Chinese crossover actresses in the 1980s.

Taipan is set in Macau in 1839 and stars Bryan Brown as the leading British merchant ruler of Portuguese Macau (the "Taipan"). Joan Chen plays his mistress, Mei Mei, whom he keeps hidden away from European high society. Mei Mei spends most of her time in her room draped in revealing negligees, except during one significant scene in which the Taipan holds a ball for the island's elite. Mei Mei, who is not invited, dons a colorful, billowing gown and summons the Taipan to her room. He is shocked and displeased by her attempt at emulation, and Mei Mei is devastated. The scene turns from comical to serious, and from syntax rendered in deliberately "bad" English to perfect English, as she tries to stab herself and threatens to die in stereotypical "Madame Butterfly" style. Of the films from the first crossover period, there is a heavy and deliberate use of "bad" English (in the form of short, broken sentences) to build a comic rapport with the Western audience and also to suggest authenticity, in addition to using "accented" English. After a miscarriage, Mei Mei says to the Taipan, "I want your son terrifical bad" and "Mei Mei more gorgeous after tragedy. Going to make you fantastical happy." The performance of accented English (combined with grammatical and syntactical errors) is used here for comedic effect and underwrites Mei Mei's failed act of mimicry.

While mimicry can be viewed as a form of resistance, as Chris Berry and Mary Farquhar (2006, 222) so astutely observe in their book *China on Screen*, the question, for many non-Western film talents is no longer how to reject or resist the colonizing powers of Hollywood and global filmmaking, but rather how to *join* them. Marking this aspiration, mimicry operates as a

On No Longer Speaking Chinese   73

Figure 6.1   Joan Chen as Mei Mei in *Taipan*.
Source: *Taipan* (Daryl Duke, 1986), De Laurentiis Entertainment Group.

form of resistance that is tempered by the desire for emulation and participation. As the authors observe, drawing from Homi Bhabha's (1994) notion of colonial mimicry in the context of Chinese cinema:

> Although colonial mimicry demonstrates a certain submission to the colonial order, its inherent ambivalence can simultaneously constitute resistance. The colonial order encourages the colonized to aspire to be like the colonizer. But it rests upon the requirement that this aspiration can never quite be realized. . . . Resistance starts when, as a result of following the imperative to mimic, the colonized demands the things the colonizer would deny him or her, such as political sovereignty. (Berry and Farquhar 2006, 222)

With age and experience, at least in Joan Chen's case, the roles she now plays have diversified away from this reflexive requirement toward mimicry. Chen recently starred in a predominantly Chinese-language role in an Asian-American film, playing an accidentally pregnant older woman with a lesbian daughter in Alice Wu's *Saving Face* (2004). In the vein of Ang Lee's *The Wedding Banquet* (1993), Chen's character pretends not to understand English even though she can. This is not, however, another role of emulation, but one that allows Chen greater creative freedom. It is also, importantly, a role set in contemporary times. While the roles available to crossover actresses may not yet have caught up (in terms of their temporal location—preferring to view Chinese femininity not in its modern form but rather as timeless, ancient, traditional, and "primitive"), the desire to have them speak English has all but become a necessity; hence, the performance of accented English appears especially disconcerting. Other aspects of their roles are, however, slowly evolving, especially in their reconfigured relations with white male costars. This "reverse Butterfly" narrative can be seen across a number of recent films featuring crossover actresses of the second generation such as Gong Li.

SECOND GENERATION: "REVERSE BUTTERFLY" FILMS

Representing the second period of crossover actresses from China, it seemed that Gong Li's American debut was a long time coming, especially for a star already well known to Western audiences. Indeed, it was almost a decade between her role in the Hollywood blockbuster *Memoirs of a Geisha* and her first English-speaking role in *Chinese Box*. In Wang's film, Gong Li plays Vivian, a recent immigrant from the PRC to Hong Kong. *Chinese Box* also stars Jeremy Irons as a British financial journalist who has lived in Hong Kong for the past fifteen years. He is in love with Vivian, although he later becomes fascinated with a street hustler named Jean (Maggie Cheung) whom he wants to interview. The plot of *Chinese Box* is overtly allegorical. John represents the retreating British colonial power. He has a rare form of leukemia, with only a few months to live, and dies with the changing of the guard. Within this broadly allegorical structure, Gong Li represents the mainland's presence in Hong Kong, and correspondingly, Maggie Cheung signifies a new "modern" Hong Kong. This is not a reductionist reading; the film invites such an understanding and depends on the forms of intertextuality that the stars bring to their roles.

There are competing visions of Chinese femininity offered in *Chinese Box*, with the cultural representation of mainland Chinese femininity presented very differently from its Hong Kong counterpart. Yiman Wang (2000) makes the astute observation that Jean is associated with the documentary mode of representation, whereas Vivian is coded according to classical Hollywood film conventions. As Laura Mulvey's (1989) analysis of classical Hollywood film suggests, women are objects "to-be-looked-at," while the active gaze is male. The stylistic and formal devices of classical narrative cinema support this basic structure by facilitating spectators' identification with the point of view of the male protagonist. Yet, I would argue, there is a reconfiguration of this seemingly straightforward model of spectatorship determined by the accented nature of the English spoken by Gong Li. While visually Vivian may be coded according to classical Hollywood conventions, the disjuncture between what we expect to see and what we in fact hear precipitates a transformation of the dominant "Butterfly" paradigm into a "reverse Butterfly" narrative. In *Chinese Box*, the visions or ideals of Chinese femininity are again collapsed onto a white male body, but this time according to a "reverse Butterfly" narrative as the new, exotic way to tell stories of the East-West encounter.

Because "reverse Butterfly" films continue to be directed by white male directors, they are still located within the realm of a white (heterosexist) male fantasy. However, the films are now being used to explore white male disempowerment, and in the case of *Chinese Box*, as a response to the loss of British colonial power over Hong Kong. The fact that the director of *Chinese Box* is an Asian-American is complicated by the fact that Wayne Wang identifies with his white male protagonist played by Jeremy Irons. In an interview with Sam Adams (1998), Wang recalls:

> I grew up in Hong Kong [as part of the] first Chinese generation to really want to be more Westernized. I was a colonial subject, and as much as I don't want to admit to it, I'm very influenced by [English culture]. I went to English private schools and was influenced by their TV, their food. Because I've left Hong Kong, even though I know [the city], I'm an outsider now, and I feel like I have a different perspective. Because of those two reasons, I felt that an English journalist who is an insider/outsider would be a more appropriate alter ego.

The camera establishes the action of the film from John's perspective, that is, from the perspective of a British expatriate, since many of the shots are directed from John's video camera. In another interview with *Salon* magazine, Wang says, "I really wanted to make the main character a bit of my own alter ego. The English journalist is probably closer to who I am" (Bear 1998). When asked how he related to the character of John Chang, a Chinese entrepreneur in Hong Kong whom Gong Li's character is in love with, Wang replied, "I have no interest or relationship with that kind of person, except as an outsider. I'm not a Hong Kong person anymore. I'm much more American now, and I don't pretend that I could completely understand Hong Kong" (Bear 1998).[6] Although America's relationship to Hong Kong is very different from that of Britain's, Wang conflates the Westerners' "outside"—that is, non-Chinese—experience.

With this "outside" perspective in mind, the film's portrayal of mainland Chinese femininity is significant, particularly in terms of how Gong Li's performance is constructed and has been read. Gong Li has been described as "luminous" and "glittering," one of the most beautiful and iconic film actresses on the planet (Susman 1998; Urban 1998). Protesting against Gong Li's English-speaking role when her command of the language was so poor, Edward Guthmann (1998) suggests, "What Wang doesn't seem to realize is that Gong Li's primary skills as an actress are visual—she has one of the most subtly expressive faces in the movies." Rather than using dialogue or speech, the "imaginary" qualities of cinema are conjured to elicit the effects of a visual "primitivism" in Gong Li's case.

Although Wayne Wang suggests that he wanted to bring Gong Li into the "modern age," this does not seem to have worked: "People didn't want to see her smoking! They don't want to see her in shades and jeans. But that's very much part of a modern woman in Hong Kong or China, for that matter" (Pride 1998). There is a spectatorial disappointment (to borrow Ackbar Abbas's term) based on the accented nature of Gong Li's English-language performance, whereby spectators are unwilling or unable to make the shift from seeing Gong Li as a sign of primitivism to a sign of a modern exoticism. Abbas (1997) defines disappointment as "the perception that every origin that we want to believe is unique and individual is already a repetition, like an old song that returns" (55). Although writing specifically on Wong Kar-Wai's filmic aesthetics as they relate to the issue of speed, there is arguably a similar operation of disappointment at work regarding the spectatorship of crossover stars, particularly if we regard the erotics of disappointment as where "the image deliberately raises expectations that are not met" (Abbas 1997, 54). Disappointment emerges when spectators recognize the "reverse Butterfly" story as a repetition of a foundational tale of cross-cultural romance, but one that no longer carries a unique cultural essence attached to the pure, self-sacrificing figure of "Butterfly."

Without occupying the role of "Butterfly," Gong Li's Vivian is given no choice but to mime roles for Western women, in particular a Western woman who is herself exoticized and who speaks an accented English—Marlene Dietrich. In a mise en abyme effect, we watch John watch Vivian watching

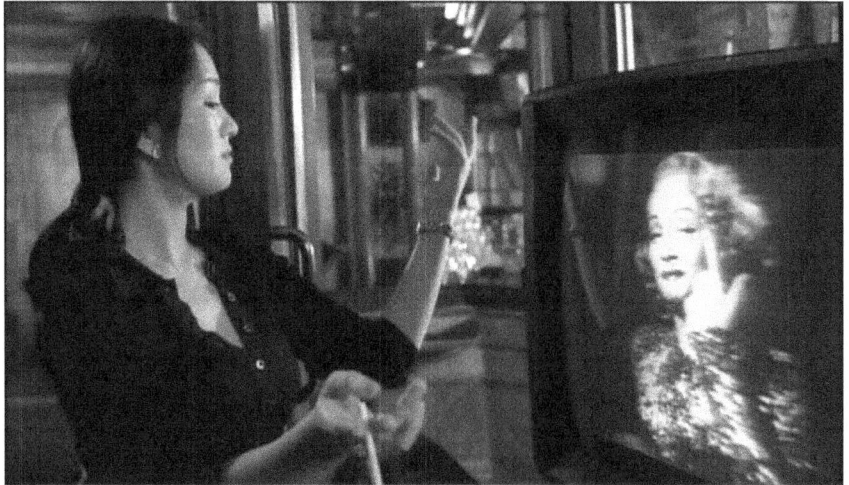

Figure 6.2 Gong Li emulates Dietrich.
Source: *Chinese Box* (Wayne Wang, 1997), Canal+, NDF International, and WW Productions.

Marlene Dietrich in the Billy Wilder film *A Foreign Affair* (1948). The film tells the story of a U.S. army captain in wartime Berlin who is torn between a café singer and ex-mistress of a prominent Nazi official (played by Marlene Dietrich), and the U.S. congresswoman investigating her. Vivian is emulating Dietrich's voice and mannerisms when John enters the room. He interrupts her by recounting an anecdote whereby whenever Dietrich saw an actor she desired, she would say to her producer friend at Paramount Studios: "Ooh Daddy, will you get me him?"

The mise en abyme structure within this Hollywood narrative facilitates a spectatorial identification with Jeremy Irons's character as he watches Gong Li perform and speak Dietrich's accented English. The suggestion seems to be that there is a "correct" image for Hollywood's "ethnic specimens"—in this case, as exotic seductress (Chow 1993, 29). Indeed, what is significant to this analysis is the very established tradition of European female stars who have crossed over successfully into Hollywood speaking an accented English (in addition to Dietrich, there is Greta Garbo, Ingrid Bergman, and Hedy Lamarr, for example). The cult following of these stars in the West can be contrasted to the poor reception of films featuring crossover stars from China. Whereas European accents (e.g., French or Latin) are considered "sexy" or "charming" or "sophisticated," the Chinese accent (speaking English) is often regarded as "primitive" or "crude." An interesting example of a "reverse crossover" involves the famous Chinese-American actress Anna May Wong's career in British and German films from the late 1920s to the early 1940s. Wong is known to have hired a tutor to rid her of her American accent and to teach her to speak with an upper-class British accent ("New Pictures" 1934).[7] Thus, there is a cultural politics involved in the privileging of certain types of accents, ethnicities, and identities over others.

Diane Negra's study of ethnic female stardom is useful for its examination of the politics of gender and ethnicity that underscore Hollywood's myths of assimilation. In *Off-White Hollywood: American Culture and Ethnic Female Stardom*, Negra (2001) is primarily concerned with Euro-American constructions of whiteness, which she argues makes the Hollywood industry "accented"—or "off-white." Negra does not use the term *accented*, although she implies similar acts of displacement and accommodation occurring within the Hollywood film industry. Negra examines how Hollywood utilizes certain ethnicities in order to perpetuate its myths of assimilation and, in doing so, incorporates and commodifies a range of different images of ethnic women. However, she suggests that Hollywood can really only do this for "white" ethnics, that is, those who can "pass." The accented English of Chinese actresses functions instead to highlight their irreducible difference, and the fact that they are speaking English is something that critics commentate on negatively, as though it detracts from their "authenticity."

Chinese Box was very poorly received by both Chinese and Western audiences. Gong Li is reported in the Chinese press as having said that the negative comments on the film were so humiliating that she said she would never again make another English-language film. Indeed, it took her almost a decade to recover from these criticisms to make her reappearance in Hollywood cinema as the fiery Hatsumomo in *Memoirs of a Geisha*. However, with three English-speaking roles since (in *Miami Vice*, *Hannibal Rising*, and *Shanghai*, a U.S.-China coproduction), Gong Li seems poised for her American renaissance. In the *China Daily* she is reported as saying, "At present, the scripts I have received are all from Hollywood and I probably don't have time for any others . . . But if time permits, then I will be happy to cooperate with domestic directors" ("Quality Actress" 2005). Her "return" to China after *Memoirs of a Geisha* in the films *Curse of the Golden Flower* (Zhang Yimou 2006) and *What Women Want* (Daming Chen 2011) is unlike Li Lihua's "failed" return; rather, Gong Li is now afforded even greater agency in her film roles. It is possible that the second period of crossover stars is substantively different from the first generation of Joan Chen and Vivian Wu precisely because of the success (and hence, cultural and symbolic capital) that actresses such as Gong Li and Zhang Ziyi have already achieved in Mandarin-language films that have been popular in the West. This has proved an important indicator for their later crossover success into English-language cinema. Luo Yan, for instance, does not hold the same kind of cultural cache.

As with Wayne Wang's *Chinese Box*, Yim Ho's *Pavilion of Women*, starring Luo Yan, was also very poorly received in America. The film is based on Pearl S. Buck's 1946 novel of the same name and is the first major American (Universal) and Chinese (Silver Dream) coproduction in film. Luo Yan, who moved from China to the United States in 1993, also produces, directs, writes, and performs, although this was her first, and to date only her second, English-language role.

All of the main characters in *Pavilion of Women* speak English, although the story is set in Suzhou in 1938. Luo Yan plays a wealthy Chinese woman, Madame Wu, who arranges a concubine for her husband for his fortieth birthday so that she can free herself of his sexual advances. She meets an American missionary, Father Andre, played by Willem Dafoe, who eventually becomes the tutor for her son. At first covertly, Madame Wu attends her son's lessons, and eventually, she and Father Andre fall in love. Their feelings for each other are brought to the surface during a performance of Chinese opera to celebrate the arrival of electricity to the town. The traditional arts are combined with the crowd's jubilation over the appearance of technology marking the settlement's first steps toward modernization. Father Andre asks Madame Wu to translate the opera for him and she explains the significance of butterflies in the performance. Without her having to complete the story, he supplies its last line, explaining that he knows how it ends because it is a love story that crosses cultural boundaries. Directly after this moment of cross-cultural understanding, there is a cut to the next scene, another lesson in which Father Andre plays his favorite opera to his students—not surprisingly, Puccini's *Madame Butterfly* (he plays the music from the climactic scene in which Cio Cio San commits suicide). The climax of this film is mirrored—or rather, refracted—when Father Andre sacrifices himself to save Madame Wu. He runs to distract Japanese soldiers during the breakout of war so that Madame Wu can escape but is shot in the back.

Critics have made scathing remarks on the use of English in this film, but far more interesting are the comments made on the film's temporality (relating to its use of English) that underscore how Chinese femininity becomes portrayed within the "reverse Butterfly" story as the sign of a (reluctantly conceded) modernity. On the film's paradoxical temporality (of being both "modern" and "ancient" at the same time), Arthur Lazere (2000) writes: "despite first-rate production values and cinematography . . . [*Pavilion of Women*] is an anomaly, a brand new film that plays like a relic from fifty years ago." In a review for the *New York Times*, chief critic A. O. Scott (2001) conjoins: "Watching *Pavilion of Women* is a curiously anachronistic experience, like encountering an old Bette Davis picture redone in color and at high volume." Michael Atkinson (2001) for the *Village Voice* adds: "Yim Ho's *Pavilion of Women* starts out like a dated musical: bloated orchestral overture, bustling peasant crowds, grand-mannered crane shots. That it never ripens and rots with song is a blessing, but what's left is nearly as difficult to love." Typically, the Chinese language is taken to represent authenticity and antiquity and is furthermore viewed as a sign of essential Chineseness. Rather than making the actresses *less* obviously different or ethnic, the fact that they are speaking in English in fact *accentuates* their difference since they are no longer acting in a "foreign" film, but in a Hollywood film predicated on their exotic difference.

MODERN-DAY BUTTERFLIES

Arguments about language competency aside, what is the basis of these unsettling effects of seeing Chinese actresses speaking in English? Why does the experience of watching these actresses appear anachronistic? What kind of femininity or sexuality is this English-speaking usage being associated with? I argue that it correlates with a new sign of modernity (a capitalist modernity) for China and a particular kind of Chinese femininity that inverts the old story of exoticism—precisely the traditional Madame Butterfly story—in order to speak of white male disempowerment. It is for this reason that the effects are both startling and unsettling. The accented nature of the English both undercuts and, at the same time, supports the dominant Hollywood structure, by being "alike, but not quite," and hence representing both submission and resistance, if resistance can be defined as "the effort to achieve agency of some sort" (Berry and Farquhar 2006, 209).

Other examples of the "reverse Butterfly" story performing this simultaneous play of resistance and submission characterizing translingual stardom include David Cronenberg's *M. Butterfly* (1993) and Peter Greenaway's *The*

Pillow Book. *M. Butterfly* also stars Jeremy Irons in a structurally similar role to that played in *Chinese Box*. Based on David Henry Hwang's play of the same name, Cronenberg's film shows a literal collapse of (an ideal of) a Chinese "woman" (who is really a male spy for the PRC masking as a woman), onto the body of the white man, through the character's reenactment of the Puccini opera in which he commits suicide.

Peter Greenaway's *The Pillow Book* provides a British example that also fantasizes the relationship between whiteness and exoticism. The plot involves a love triangle between Nagiko (Vivian Wu), Jerome, an English translator (Ewan McGregor), and a Japanese publisher (Yoshi Oida). Jerome is having an affair with both Nagiko and the publisher. When Nagiko ends her relationship with him because of this, he commits suicide. Like the sacrificial death in *M. Butterfly*, it is the white man who ends his life, inverting the outcome of the original story of Madame Butterfly. Jerome's skin is flayed by the publisher and made into a folded pillow book—literally rendering the body of the white man into a fetish object. The male stars of the "reverse Butterfly" films that have hitherto been discussed are very prominent European or American stars and are thus likely to draw large audiences to their films. This is a story in circulation with high visibility and a considerable amount of cultural sanction.

As to whether it is possible to shake loose from this old colonial paradigm in a way that more than merely "reverses," or inverts it, remains to be seen, as younger actresses such as Zhang Ziyi join the global arena of Hollywood films and regard mastering English as their next step to greater stardom. Despite the criticisms leveled against it, *Memoirs of a Geisha* stands as a landmark film in that it is the first time a major Hollywood film has cast Asian actors in all the main roles. Although the director Rob Marshall had decided on a "uniform" speech—a "lightly Japanese-accented English"—the film remains a jumble of accents, even after editing tricks (Horn 2005). However, it is the film's profusion and sheer irreducibility, despite its pursuit of a common "accented English," that is both its asset and a major point of contention. It is, at least, a film set in the not-so-distant past—from the period 1927 to just after World War II. Future prospects are also looking promising in terms of allowing modern images of Chinese femininity to circulate on the screen—if Gong Li's recent roles are any indication. In media appearances outside the cinema, concessions are already being made to place translingual stars in a contemporary setting. After her role in *Crouching Tiger, Hidden Dragon* (2000), Zhang Ziyi starred in a "Dining Out" advertisement for Visa credit cards in which she reenacts the tavern scene from the film, this time inside a modern French restaurant (and updated with action scenes modeled from *The Matrix*). She says (in English), "This soup is too salty," after which she indignantly fights all of the staff, destroying much of the restaurant before paying for the damages with her Visa card. The French accent of the restaurant chefs is trumped by Zhang Ziyi's Chinese-accented English—as the new exotic accent in the global arena of international tourism?

Indeed, *Crouching Tiger, Hidden Dragon*'s phenomenal success brought an "ancient" China, and the Chinese language, to a Western audience as a globally exotic product. What is interesting about the film for the purposes of this chapter is that Michelle Yeoh, who cannot speak Mandarin, had to learn her dialogue line by line in pinyin, with the help of a language tutor. "Speaking Chinese" therefore becomes something that can be "faked," or performed (with an element of fantasy or exoticism already surrounding Chinese femininity in the West). What these examples show is that it is impossible to assume that there is a "'true' voice [for the native] 'behind' her 'false' image" (Chow 1993, 29). Furthermore, the belief that the "native" must be a *silent* object is necessarily, and severely, called into question by these examples of translingual stardom. Hopefully, as we take into account these newly formed transnational subjectivities, we will begin to acknowledge that Hollywood cinema is no longer "unmarked," free from accent, despite its attempts to silence its other voices.

NOTES

1. I use the phrase "language *choice*" to allude to the final line of Ien Ang's (2001) essay *On Not Speaking Chinese*: "If I am inescapably Chinese by *descent*, I am only sometimes Chinese by *consent*. When and how is a matter of politics" (36).
2. Since Hong Kong's reversion to Chinese control in 1997, there have been an increasing number of Hong Kong films (including coproductions) made in Mandarin, or a mix of Mandarin and Cantonese, particularly in the past ten years. However, the local industry is still dominated by Cantonese-language productions.
3. Jet Li was born in Beijing, although the films he is most famous for are Hong Kong (Cantonese-language) films such as the *Once Upon a Time in China* series.
4. Gong Li and Zhang Ziyi have not immigrated to the United States and are therefore not "diasporic" in that sense, although their crossover appearance in Hollywood films raises issues of (diasporic) displacement. Vivian Wu has returned to Shanghai to live, and Gong Li took up Singaporean citizenship in 2008.
5. Liu Shaoqing, who starred in Xie Jin's *Hibiscus Town* (1988) and as the Empress Dowager Cixi in *Li Lianying, the Imperial Eunuch* (Tian Zhuangzhuang 1991), was arrested for tax evasion on July 24, 2002. She reportedly said to a friend, in a kind of preemptive statement as to what she would do if she were ever put in prison: "I will learn English first. My English won't be worse than my performing skills after I am released" ("China through a Lens" 2002).
6. It is important to note that Wong is not an immigrant to the United States, unlike the other crossover stars discussed, but was born and raised in America.
7. I thank Ackbar Abbas for bringing this advertisement to my attention.

REFERENCES

Abbas, Ackbar. 1997. "The Erotics of Disappointment." In *Wong Kar-wai*, edited by Jean-Marc Lalanne, David Martinez, Ackbar Abbas, and Jimmy Ngai, 39–82. Paris: Dis Voir.

Adams, Sam. 1998. "La Colonial: Interview with Wayne Wang." *Philadelphia City Paper,* April 30–May 7. http://archives.citypaper.net/articles/043098/movies.iview.wang.shtml. Accessed May 18, 2012.

Ang, Ien. 2001. *On Not Speaking Chinese.* London: Routledge.

Atkinson, Michael. 2001. "All Excess." *The Village Voice,* April 27. http://www.villagevoice.com/2001–05–01/film/all-excess/. Accessed May 18, 2012.

Bear, Lisa. 1998. "Thinking Outside the Chinese Box: An Interview with Wayne Wang." *Salon,* April 17. http://www.salon.com/1998/04/17/17int_3/. Accessed May 18, 2012.

Berry, Chris, and Mary Farquhar. 2006. *China on Screen: Cinema and Nation.* New York: Columbia University Press.

Bhabha, Homi. 1994. *The Location of Culture.* London: Routledge.

"China through a Lens." 2002. *Shanghai Star,* August 1. http://www.china.org.cn/english/NM-e/39599.htm. Accessed May 18, 2012.

Chow, Rey. 1993. *Writing Diaspora: Tactics of Intervention in Contemporary Cultural Studies.* Bloomington: Indiana University Press.

———. 1995. *Primitive Passions: Visuality, Sexuality, Ethnography, and Contemporary Chinese Cinema.* New York: Columbia University Press.

Crystal, David. 1997. *English as a Global Language.* Cambridge: Cambridge University Press.

Guthmann, Edward. 1998. "Too Many Pieces in 'Chinese Box': Wang Over-ambitious in Story of Hong Kong Changeover." *San Francisco Chronicle,* May 8. http://www.sfgate.com/cgi-bin/article.cgi?f = /c/a/1998/05/08/DD89908.DTL. Accessed May 18, 2012.

Holborow, Marnie. 1999. *The Politics of English: A Marxist View of Language.* London: Sage Publications.

Horn, John. 2005. "Uniformity, So to Speak." *Los Angeles Times,* November 27. http://articles.latimes.com/2005/nov/27/entertainment/ca-geisha27. Accessed May 18, 2012.

Lazere, Arthur. 2000. "*Pavilion of Women.*" *Culture Vulture.* http://www.culturevulture.net/Movies/PavilionofWomen.htm. Accessed May 18, 2012.

Liu, Lydia. 1995. *Translingual Practice: Literature, National Culture, and Translated Modernity—China, 1900–1937.* Stanford, CA: Stanford University Press.

Mulvey, Laura. 1989. *Visual and Other Pleasures.* London: Macmillan.

Naficy, Hamid. 2001. *An Accented Cinema: Exilic and Diasporic Filmmaking.* Princeton, NJ: Princeton University Press.

Negra, Diane. 2001. *Off-White Hollywood.* London: Routledge.

"New Pictures, The." 1934. *Time,* October 1. http://www.time.com/time/magazine/article/0,9171,930542,00.html. Accessed May 18, 2012.

Pride, Ray. 1998. "Chinese Box." *Boston Phoenix,* May 3. http://www.filmvault.com/filmvault/boston/c/chinesebox1.html. Accessed May 18, 2012.

"Quality Actress Gong Li Busy in Hollywood." 2005. *China Daily,* March 30. http://www.chinadaily.com.cn/english/doc/2005–03/30/content_429398.htm. Accessed May 18, 2012.

Scott, A. O. 2001. "Review of *Pavilion of Women.*" *New York Times,* May 4. http://movies.nytimes.com/movie/review?res = 950CEED61338F937A35756C0A9679C8B63. Accessed May 18, 2012.

Susman, Gary. 1998. "Chinese Box." *Rough Cut Reviews.* http://www.roughcut.com/reviews/movies/vault/chinese_box.html. Accessed August 24, 2007.

Urban, Andrew L. 1998. "Chinese Box." *Urban Cinefile.* http://www.urbancinefile.com.au/home/view.asp?a = 2048&s = Video_files. Accessed May 18, 2012.

Wang, Yiman. 2000. "Chinese Box-Camera Box." *Intersections: Gender, History and Culture in the Asian Context* 3 (January). http://intersections.anu.edu.au/issue3/wang2.html. Accessed May 18, 2012.

7 Bridging Pop Culture and Identity Politics
Fatih Akin's Road Movie *In July*

Aisha Jamal

As the European Council debated Turkey's entry into the European Union (EU) in 1999, German-Turkish director Fatih Akin produced his second feature, *In July* (2000), which is as much concerned with German and Turkish identity in the EU as with that of other immigrant groups. In his much-awaited follow-up to his crime-genre debut success *Short Sharp Shock* (1998), Akin—himself a child of Turkish immigrants to Germany and a very successful practitioner of crossover cinematic practices—decided to playfully revert the expectations put on him by the critical community. With the summer romance film *In July*, he changed milieus while pursuing his interest in genre cinema but surprised many with his unusual choice of characters and the film's mix of comedy, romance, and road movie genres. The film garnered a lukewarm reception upon release and was written off by most critics as a kitschy, yet sweet, romance. Unlike *Short Sharp Shock,* popular press coverage of *In July* did not address any of the political and social issues in the film, particularly when they concerned the topic of Turkish-German relations; this is perhaps due to Akin's choice of "German" protagonists and the predominance of comedy in the film. However, the film is anything but ahistorical, and placed in its sociopolitical context, it can be understood as a film that responds to what most Europeans see as one of the main concerns in contemporary Europe—the populations that flow across their borders. Despite its lighthearted tone, Akin's film is very much concerned with the shifting representation and meaning of borders in a globalized world that is so often characterized by economic, political, and social integration.

Within the context of a "New Europe" that includes diverse member states, Akin's film travels multinational roads to explore the EU's cultural intersections between East and West and visits Europe's so-called periphery. By focusing on the depiction of various borders while investigating the formation of new personal, national and transnational identities, the film contributes to the current debate on the shape of a German national identity in the face of an expanding EU and widening European transnational impulses. Akin suggests that one can think of cultural identities, most specifically a German European identity, in the context of intercultural relationships between people of diverse backgrounds. The film thus advocates an identity that includes a plurality of dynamic and diverse relationships instead of one that is monolithic and introverted.

In *In July,* Akin turns the narrative of German-Turkish encounters around: here, the frame of reference is not used to engage with immigrant issues, as is so often the case in German stories of migration. Instead, the frame is used to challenge the identity of the nonimmigrant German protagonists, Daniel and Juli, in their travels abroad. These two German characters are turned into migrants, crossing borders and traversing the roads of various countries—an adventure that runs against the grain of the kinds of migration stories that are commonly depicted in German films.[1] Because Daniel and Juli make their way from Germany through Bulgaria, Romania, and Hungary to Turkey, the film does not engage in the familiar scenario of the East-to-West migration described as the "new migration" or the "post-89 migration," where people from the countries east of Germany struggle to reach the Western nation as their final destination (Mazierksa and Rascaroli 2006). By reversing this narrative structure, the film not only investigates migratory identities but also looks at the impact of transnationalism on German national identity for both Germans and immigrants living in contemporary Europe.

Daniel tells the first half of the story in a flashback to Isa, a young Turkish-German man smuggling the body of his dead uncle from Germany into Turkey. Daniel is a young teacher who sets out with plans to stay in Hamburg for the summer. However, his plans are cut short when he meets the young German woman, Juli, at a colorful flea market, who in turn quickly becomes enamored with him. She sells him an old Mayan ring bearing the symbol of the sun and prophesies that Daniel will recognize "the one" for him through this symbol. Daniel fails to recognize that she is referring to herself; instead, that same evening he meets Melek, a young Turkish-German woman who is on her way to Istanbul for a presumably romantic meeting at the Bosporus Bridge. The very next day, Daniel decides to follow her. On the way to Istanbul, Daniel encounters Juli along the road. Juli, disappointed upon having seen him with Melek on the street, has decided to leave Hamburg and let fate dictate her travels. Daniel and Juli then embark on a road adventure together, driving through Eastern Europe to reach Turkey.

Akin depicts the port city of Hamburg as a city shaped and influenced by migrants from around the world. In turn, Daniel, himself of possible Jewish-French origin,[2] is changed in the process of traveling around Europe. His travels not only enable him to discover new landscapes and his personal identity but also transform him in the process: the European communities he visits on the road shape his newfound, shifting sense of self. As a narrative device framing this development, Akin uses bridges, roads, and various forms of transportation to serve as symbols of mobility and connection; they are thereby relevant not only to Daniel's inner quest but also to various roadside adventures. In this sense, it is no accident that Daniel's quest and self-discovery coincide with a time in which Germany looks for self-definition and its unique identity as part of a united Europe.

THE MEANING, REPRESENTATION, AND
SHIFTING BORDERS OF *IN JULY*

In their efforts to reach Istanbul, Daniel and Juli cross four European borders. From its outset, *In July* places emphasis on physical demarcations of boundaries and foregrounds not only their use and function but also their constructedness. Take, for example, a scene at the Hungarian-Bulgarian border, where the two travelers search for a river to cross into Bulgaria, naturally assuming that geographic features such as rivers would demarcate the borders between distinct national territories. Accordingly, throughout the film several borders indeed appear to follow the natural features of the landscape. Yet, in their introduction to a book on border theory, Ganster and Lorey (2005, viii) argue that while rivers are frequently used to distinguish boundaries between people, they often represent only the approximate middle of the vast watersheds that drain into them and thus extend beyond what is thought to be their border marking. Although the physical landscape may inform decisions regarding the separation of national territories, it is thus acknowledged that borders are unstable and approximate; *In July* foregrounds this and furthermore examines the human construction of these borders.

In another scene, as Daniel and Juli are looking for the border to Hungary, they assume the first river they encounter to be the "natural" divide between the two countries. Yet, after a comical failed attempt to jump across the river in their car, they discover that the Danube, the actual dividing river, lies behind it. Both Daniel and Juli realize the inaccuracy of their preconceived notions about physical boundaries and national borders; consequently, they gain an important understanding of the arbitrariness of dividing lines.

Akin has acknowledged, indeed, that some scenes set in Bulgaria were actually shot across the border in Turkey. This marking of borders by sociopolitical intent and "unnatural" boundaries is most apparent at the checkpoint of the Bulgarian-Romanian border. Akin himself plays the border officer who sits in front of a small wooden hut as he plays chess with the Bulgarian border guard. As Deniz Göktürk (2002, 255) notes, Akin's role here is to perform national identity with self-conscious irony, drawing attention to the absurdity of this border control. Akin visually draws out the arbitrariness of the territorial boundary between these two countries: a dirt road runs from the Bulgarian side by the crossing pole and on into Romania, while the countryside on both sides appears to be identical. A simple crossing pole indicates the border between the two countries. Without the makeshift border, it would be impossible to differentiate the two nations by physical landscape alone.

The fact that boundaries are human inventions and thus reflect human visions of the social and political world appears manifest in the film's checkpoints like the one between Bulgaria and Romania, which is designated to "protect" both the Romanian and the Bulgarian nation from unwanted migrants, be they travelers or immigrants, but which in fact is little more than a nuisance to all passersby. Thus, in *In July*, checkpoints obviously fulfill the function of delineating the contours of the various national territories, albeit rather unsuccessfully.

In Akin's DVD audio commentary on this scene, he notes that Turkey has many inhabitants of Bulgarian and Romanian heritage (and vice versa), further establishing his view that borders are not really the dividing line between people. He argues that many similar cultural groups have been divided by the establishment of international political boundaries. Indeed, national borders frequently fall in places unrelated to interethnic boundaries. Like Germany, for example, Turkey is home to many different ethnic groups. Moreover, migration has led to the creation of wider social networks of various diasporas in both countries, and these migratory networks span across geographic divides. In the film, Isa, the young Turkish-German man who first hits Daniel with his car and then gives him a ride across the Turkish border, is tasked to drive his uncle's corpse back to Turkey after his "illegal" death in Germany. In the case of Isa's uncle, no artificial imposition of borders can thus contain existing transnational social networks.

THE BORDER AS A "SPATIALIZATION OF DIFFERENCE"

When Daniel and Juli plan their route through Europe, they stop in front of a road map at a rest stop in Bavaria. Looking at the map, the contours of each country appear clear as maps are created to inscribe boundaries and define territory. However, the use of the map in the film also points to the volatility of maps generally and to the material histories of national borders. As Daniel and Juli chart their route, they point to the former Yugoslavia as an area to be avoided, since the war of Yugoslav secession rages throughout the area. This makes the viewer aware that national borders are always shifting and that nations are not immutably fixed in time but rather subject to radical, unplanned redrawing.

The repeated reference throughout the film to the former Yugoslavia hints at the function of borders as a "spatialization of difference," defined by the border theorist Barbara Morehouse (2004, 32) as a metaphorical or material association of a geographic space with a specific behavior, background, or look. In *In July*, Luna, who seduces Daniel and steals all his money, drives a van with the country sticker "YU" for the former Yugoslavia on it. This sticker is partially covered with a big red "EX," to signify the change that this country was undergoing at the time. In this particular case, a "spatialization of difference" divided the country into ethnically separate nations. Boundaries in the case of the former Yugoslavia, as Morehouse (2004, 23) suggest, can be viewed as an outcome of the conflict, and the new borders here are an expression of ethnic-based nationalism.

But while physical borders may dissolve over time, boundaries manifest themselves in a great variety of practices and discourses, be they social, cultural, or political. In the film, Daniel makes several comments that explain how these boundaries can also be constructed through social discourse. For example, Daniel clearly states his mistrust of Turks when he mimics the Bulgarian border police, wondering how much worse the Turkish border police will be. This fear of the Turkish border officers is likely based on mistrust guided by popular culture images of Turkey in Germany and by depictions of its legal system in films like Alan Parker's (1978) *Midnight Express*, where the cruel and unforgiving Turkish police imprison and torture a foreign traveler.

In fact, Daniel is acutely aware of the borders separating his German home from the peripheral lands he is now traveling. In a heated argument with Juli by a river in Romania, he yells at her, "I wouldn't be hanging around here at the end of the world [am Arsch der Welt] if it were not for you." His comment exposes how he perceives the relationship between the "center" of Europe (Germany) and its "margins" (Eastern Europe); his belief that Hungary, Romania, Bulgaria, and Turkey are the "end of the world" stems from his awareness of existing power relations within the EU, where undeniably major political and economic decisions are steered by key Western European members like Germany.

Ironically, and problematically, the moments during which *In July* indulges most obviously in national or regional stereotypes is in the depiction of Bavaria, a southern German province. Before we even see images of Bavaria, Marion, Juli's best friend, asks in exasperation if Juli is serious about letting a random driver determine her destination. She asks: "And what if the first car is on the way to Bavaria? Do you want to live in Bavaria or what?" suggesting that no one in their right mind would make such a move. In the popular German imagination, Bavarians are often stereotyped: many think of conservative, beer-guzzling people who wear traditional outfits and who speak with heavy accents. It is a region that provokes distaste not only in Marion but also in Daniel, who refuses to accept Juli's claim that the sky is blue everywhere, even in Bavaria. In *In July*, Akin works hard to avoid fixed national stereotypes; however, the few scenes that do take place at an inn in Bavaria reinforce the regional stereotypes associated with this area as an undesirable destination and a subject of humor.

Nevertheless, the film's exploration of boundaries and border crossings is timely. *In July* examines the various embodiments of borders and their functions within the European context, which is also a main concern of the EU. In the EU, much talk is focused on the diminishing conceptualization of boundaries as barriers and on their replacement by cooperation among member states. Despite this, the opening of borders within the EU has generated the phenomenon of fortress Europe, in which the barrier function of the boundaries between the EU and other countries has greater significance (see Welch 2004). Thus, as borders preoccupy much of Akin's film, they also consume a large part of contemporary European political debate. In his article on the changing conceptualization of borders in the EU, Michael Smith (1996) sees the situation as precarious:

> The EU and its members have had to learn a new politics of inclusion which focuses less on difference than on variety, and less on the maintenance of boundaries than on their continual drawing. Boundaries in this conception are for crossing rather than defending. (23)

Smith advocates a flexible conception of borders as ever changing and unfixed in time and place. *In July* suggests that borders can be culturally meaningful, differentiating various imagined communities on the basis of such characteristics as a common culture, signaled in the film by the changes in language in each country. Yet, such communities may be transterritorial, only coincidentally reflecting the "natural" borders such as rivers or political spaces of states. The film is thus not only about the manifestation and function of borders in the European context; it also examines the crossing of borders and the current transnational atmosphere of Europe.

CONNECTING ACROSS BORDERS AND BOUNDARIES: A EUROPEAN TRANSNATIONALISM

Akin acknowledges in an interview for the German newspaper *Die Zeit* that his aim was not only to make a German film but "at the same time to make a European film" (Geisenhanslüke 2001). His film reveals different spaces and cultures in Europe as connected through transnational ties as it follows Daniel and Juli's travels throughout Europe. Akin's Europe is a place linked through various modes of transportation such as cars, trains, and boats. In this highly motorized society, Daniel relies on the kindness of strangers to get around as his own car fails him early on in the trip. Through his interaction with these various strangers, a sense of a European community emerges and is most prominently symbolized through roads; the film opens with this pervasive symbol as Isa's car speeds down a two-lane road with golden fields and large power lines on the side of the road. The caption informs the viewer that this scene takes place "somewhere in Bulgaria." This opening image of the road crisscrossing the barren landscape "somewhere" in Bulgaria emphasizes the vastness of the European terrain, while at the same time it serves as a symbol of the connection between the wider zones of this community.

Another salient metaphor of transnational European community that repeatedly occurs in the film is that of the bridge, specifically the Bosporus Bridge in Istanbul. Daniel first encounters the bridge in a Döner-Sandwich café in Hamburg, and it soon becomes the holy grail of Daniel's journey. The first image of the bridge is revealing of the transnational connections that the film draws out: the camera slowly zooms out of a painted image of the bridge, which hangs on the wall of the food joint. In the background,

Turkish instrumental music is playing, while Melek, speaking German, talks about her meeting at the bridge on Friday. The bringing together of these two separate places—the Bosporus and the Hamburg eatery—points to the network that exists between them. The Bosporus River and its bridge represent a symbol of cultural exchange—that is, a channel for exchange and connection.

However, in geographic terms, as well as in the European popular imagination, the Bosporus is seen as the dividing line between Europe and Asia—West and East. Although a river may have been assigned the task of signifying the division between two continents, here it is even more obvious that it can do so only symbolically. Visual elements of what is assumed to be synonymous with the East and with Asia—such as Islam and its architecture (see Robins 1996)—already appear on the western side of the river. Ottoman culture, well known for its hybrid nature, also pervades the entire city. In one pertinent example of the ambivalence with which borders and other dividing lines are imbued in the film, Daniel and Juli meet in front of a large mosque that is located to the west of the Bosporus. The river as division between the two continents thus emerges as a historical, geopolitical, and cultural construct. On either side of the mosque, Istanbul is home to people both with head scarves and without and to a wide range of residents and travelers of vastly different backgrounds. The bridge, then, takes on the meaning not of a dividing line between Asia and Europe, Old Istanbul and New Istanbul, or East and West, but rather of a vehicle of cultural encounter and exchange. This reflects Akin's personal convictions about the nature of borders. In an interview, Akin states, "Europe and Asia, those are virtual borders, imaginary borders" (Buck 2005, 87).

The Bosporus Bridge also holds a wider symbolic significance in contemporary political debates on Germany, Turkey, and the EU community. In his essay on Turkish-European identity, Kevin Robins (1996) writes that major blockages exist to considering this part of Europe an actual part of the community: "Coming to terms with 'the Turk' is a crucial aspect of the cultural reordering and re-association that must be undertaken in the European space" (64). As a nation, Turkey is seeking to be admitted as a member of the EU and, by extension, as a member of the new European community. However, the country is often thought of as home to an un-European, traditional, and introverted society. The film challenges this image of Turkey by instead suggesting that it has been changed by globalization. Take, for example, the scene in which Daniel travels within Turkey on a highly large and modern bus, enabling the mobility of both locals and tourists like himself. Once at the bus depot, the camera rushes past people dressed in tight jeans or skirts and women with their heads covered or streaked blond. Akin challenges the uniform identity assumed of Turkish culture, which he also notes in an interview with Caroline M. Buck (2005): "The EU image of Turkey is not wrong but often just one-sided" (87). The bridge becomes the ultimate symbol of two sides connected, proposing a binding network between the geographically European and Asian sides of the city, the country, and the two continents. Similarly, in the film, the bridge provides a symbolic link between people of various backgrounds; in the end, it becomes the meeting place for various people who, independently of each other, find their way there. The film's last shot shows a car carrying Daniel, Juli, Melek, and Isa driving over the bridge. The bridge thus connects the narrative from Daniel's first meeting with Melek in Hamburg to his present meeting with her at his journey's destination.

Akin's road film exhibits strong marks of the current atmosphere of cultural globalization, crossing borders into an international cinematic and musical culture that is dominated by the United States but also includes other world inspirations. Akin acknowledges throughout his film that cinema, as an international form, draws on a large and complex repertoire of images and narratives. Arjun Appadurai (1996, 35) labels this wide network of images, narratives, and ethnoscapes "mediascapes," which cut across conventional political and social boundaries. These mediascapes, Appadurai argues, allow one to acknowledge that imagination is a kind of collective property and does not belong to the individual. Imagination in "mediascapes" draws on all kinds of inspiration and knows no boundaries. Indeed, throughout his entire film, Akin pays tribute to the works and influences of various international filmmakers and musicians.

However, most obviously, *In July* appropriates aspects of the road movie, with its generic themes of exploration, escape, discovery, and redefinition, to explore the tensions and relationships of home and travel, immobility and mobility, the individual and the state, Germany and Europe. In conversation with the film critic and academic Amin Farzanefar (2005), Akin says that while his film is a road movie—traditionally an American genre—his film "leans more towards Kusturica, the French adventure films of the sixties" (244). In *In July*, Akin acknowledges how both American and European film culture have influenced his road movie. The opening scene of the film, for example, can be read as part of the road movie ethos, with imagery reminiscent of the quintessential American road film *Easy Rider* (Hopper 1969); the scene's highly saturated colors and shots of wide open fields bathed in the sweltering heat of the golden sun conjure up landscapes of the American West. When Isa steps out of his slick black car, he is wearing tight blue jeans with a black T-shirt and snakeskin cowboy boots—an homage to the genre's roots in Western films. In an effort to pay tribute to various classic examples of European cinema, the film also includes a scene reminiscent of the infamous flying bus in Méliès's (1902) early silent classic, *A Trip to the Moon* (*Le voyage dans la lune*).[3] In the DVD version's audio commentary, Akin mentions various scenes throughout the film that draw on such widely varied inspirations as Bollywood cinema, the films of Spanish filmmaker Pedro Almodovar and Serbian filmmaker Emir Kusturica, and silent classics such as *The Thief of Baghdad* (Walsh 1924). Musically, too, the film uses influences from around the world like jazz, ska, oldies, and electronic music.

Akin's film breaks the boundaries of the national not only symbolically and metaphorically through its narrative and use of imagery and music, but also through its production. As a coproduction between various European nations, *In July* emerged from a European cinematic community, with actors such as Serbian Branka Katic and French cinematographer Jean-Marc Bouzou. Additionally, because of the wide range of nationalities involved in making the film, the production team had to work in English (Jones 2003, 86). This mix of national involvement reflects the contemporary state of filmmaking in Europe. Dimitri Eleftheoritis argues, "Co-production is emerging as an important strategy for the survival of European cinema" (in Mazierska and Rascaroli 2006, 200). In this era of globalization, individuals and the entertainment industry alike must develop strategies of working outside the constricted national framework. Indeed, the foundation of Akin's film is in principle aligned with crossover cinematic practices, transgressing genre and cultural borders already in the stage of conceptualization and production. Thus, *In July* is forged from Akin's own multiple personal, poetic, and political affiliations beyond the strictly German, Turkish, or indeed German-Turkish context.

CONCLUSION

In a Europe confronted with rapidly changing borders, Akin's film explores issues of borders, territory, belonging, and the image of modern Europe. Through Daniel, the film suggests that flexibility, mobility, and rootlessness are central features of the contemporary European situation—features that are not to be dreaded but perhaps to be celebrated. *In July* shows that contemporary mobile subjects are not only those part of the "new migration" from the former Eastern communist and Turkish states to the prosperous "West." Akin's film turns the pattern around and sends its protagonists on the quest to reach Europe's fictive "edge": Turkey. In the process, he changes the image of Turkey in the popular German and European imagination from that of a strictly Islamic, unchanged society to one that has been deeply affected by globalization through tourism, modern transport, and wider transnational ties.[4] Furthermore, Turkey is not only shown as a place to be escaped, as many cinematic narratives enact, such as the Swiss film *Journey of Hope* (Koller 1990), about a Turkish family's dangerous illegal path to Switzerland, and the German film *Winterblume* ([Winter flower] Sözen 1997), about an exiled German man who desperately tries to return to Germany. For the protagonists in *In July,* Turkey is a dynamic country that can also offer positivity, understanding, and the possibility of pleasurable and transformational experiences.

While Akin's film is concerned with traveling across boundaries and borders, it does not suggest an eradication of national borders; instead, Akin contemplates their function and further problematizes their existence.

However, he also focuses on the joy that can be derived from movement and flexibility. Only through contact with the wider European territory and people does Daniel achieve a sense of self as a modern German European citizen. His travels evoke a sense of wider European community, which affects his transformation and opens him to the world around him. Daniel forges new ties and friendships with people outside his own background, including the German-Turkish Isa and Melek. His transformation does not involve abandoning a "German" identity for a European one, and, in the end, Daniel's travels unite him with other German-speaking characters. In the last shot of the film, where Daniel drives across the Bosporus Bridge with Melek and Juli in Isa's car, the film suggests that he will continue his adventures with a new outlook across the symbolic gateway between Europe and Asia. Thus, Akin's film and its finale make an important argument for the rethinking of cultural identities, namely, the German and European identity in the context of intercultural relationships. In his film, identities are thought of in terms of the experience of dynamic relationships, which in turn offers an optimistic outlook for a German transnational identity in a Europe that is constructing new frontiers and boundaries.

NOTES

1. See, for example, *Russian Disco* (Ziegenbalg 2012), *Distant Lights* (Schmid 2003), *A Little Bit of Freedom* (Yavuz 2002), and *The Wound* (Arslan 1998).
2. His first name is of Hebrew origin, and his last name is a recognizably French surname. The film, however, does not mention or thematize his background or the origins of the name.
3. He does so with a scene in which Luna is the face of the moon, smiling as a bus flies across the night sky, taken right out of Méliès's classic.
4. Although Germans may have long visited Turkey as a popular vacation spot, the image of Turks in the popular German imagination remains one of a backward, traditional people.

REFERENCES

Akin, Faith, dir. 1998. *Short Sharp Shock*. New York: Universal.
———. 2000. *In July*. Port Washington, NY: Koch Lorber Films.
Appadurai, Arjun. 1996. *Modernity at Large: Cultural Dimensions of Globalization*. Minneapolis: University of Minnesota Press.
Arslan, Yilmaz, dir. 1998. *The Wound*. Paris, France: uniFrance Films.
Buck, Caroline M. 2005. "Gegen Grenzen, wie vom Lineal gezogen." *Neues Deutschland,* June 9, 87.
Farzanefar, Amin. 2005. *Kino des Orients*. Marburg, Germany: Schüren Publishers.
Ganster, Paul, and David E. Lorey. 2005. "Introduction." In *Borders and Border Politics in a Globalizing World*, edited by Paul Ganster and David E. Lorey, viii–xxiii. Lanham, UK: SR Books.
Geisenhanslüke, Ralph. 2001. "Das Gesicht der Woche: Fatih Akin: Bonsai Banditen." *Die Zeit,* January 25.

Göktürk, Deniz. 2002. "Beyond Paternalism: Turkish German Traffic in Cinema." In *The German Cinema Book,* edited by Tim Bergfelder, Erica Carter, and Deniz Göktürk, 248–56. London: BFI Publishing.

Hopper, Dennis, dir. 1969. *Easy Rider.* Culver City, CA: Columbia TriStar Home Video.

Jones, Stan. 2003. "Turkish-German Cinema Today: A Case Study of Fatih Akin's *Kurz und schmerzlos* (1998) and *Im Juli* (2000)." In *European Cinema, Inside Out: Images of the Self and Other in Postcolonial European Film,* edited by Guido Rings and Rikki Morgen-Tamosunas, 70–86. Heidelberg, Germany: University Publishers.

Koller, Xavier, dir. 1990. *Journey of Hope.* New York: HBO Video.

Mazierska, Ewa, and Laura Rascaroli. 2006. *Crossing New Europe: Postmodern Travel and the European Road Movie.* London: Wallflower Press.

Méliès, Georges, dir. 1902. *A Trip to the Moon (Le voyage dans la lune).* Landmarks of Early Film. New York: Film Preservation Associates.

Morehouse, Barbara J. 2004. "Theoretical Approaches to Border-Spaces and Identities." In *Challenged Borderlands: Transcending Political and Cultural Boundaries,* edited by Vera Pavlakovich-Kochi, Barbara J. Morehouse, and Doris Wastl-Walter, 19–41. Aldershot, UK: Ashgate.

Parker, Alan, dir. 1978. *Midnight Express.* Culver City, CA: Columbia TriStar Home Video.

Robins, Kevin. 1996. "Interrupting Identities: Turkey/Europe." In *Questions of Cultural Identity,* edited by Stuart Hall and Paul du Gay, 61–87. London: Sage.

Schmid, Hans-Christian, dir. 2003. *Distant Lights.* New York: Universal.

Smith, Michael. 1996. "The European Union and a Changing Europe: Establishing the Boundaries of Order." *Journal of Common Market Studies* 34(1): 5–28.

Sözen, Kadir, dir. 1997. *Winterblume* (Winter flower). Caldwell, NJ: Kinocom.

Walsh, Raoul, dir. 1924. *The Thief of Baghdad.* New York: Criterion Collection.

Welch, Richard. 2004. "From Iron Curtain to Fortress Europe and Beyond." In *Challenged Borderlands: Transcending Political and Cultural Boundaries,* edited by Vera Pavlakovich-Kochi, Barbara J. Morehouse, and Doris Wastl-Walter, 81–91. Aldershot, UK: Ashgate.

Yavuz, Yüksel, dir. 2002. *A Little Bit of Freedom.* Chicago: Facets Multi Media.

Ziegenbalg, Oliver, dir. 2012. *Russian Disco.* Unterfohring, Germany: Paramount Pictures Germany.

8 Film Policy and the Emergence of the Cross-Cultural

Exploring Crossover Cinema in Flanders (Belgium)

Gertjan Willems and Kevin Smets

I am rooted, but I flow.

—Virginia Woolf, *The Waves*

THE CROSSOVER TREND IN RECENT FLEMISH CINEMA

Since the very beginnings of Belgian film production, and especially since the emergence of the sound film, two largely separated film sectors developed within the framework of "Belgian cinema." This has primarily been due to the existence of two big language communities in Belgium (Dutch and French) but, since the 1960s, has also been stimulated by the film production policy, which is mainly situated at the community level. In this chapter, we focus on the cinema from Flanders.[1] Due to the smallness of the Flemish home market, it is almost impossible for a professionally made Flemish feature film to be profitable.[2] Obviously, this has always been a major obstacle for raising the necessary financial means to make a film in Flanders (Mosley 2001, 3). This caused a lack of continuity in the Flemish film sector: from the 1950s until the 1990s, on average only three to five majoritarian Flemish films were released per year. Moreover, leaving a few notable exceptions aside, the small number of films produced received little commercial or artistic recognition. Since the turn of the millennium, however, a remarkable growth can be observed. In spite of the economic disadvantage that inevitably had its permanent repercussions on the Flemish film sector, the number of films per year steadily rose to thirteen in 2011. This bigger continuity was mainly stimulated by the renewal of the film production policy during the first decade of the twenty-first century (Engelen and Vande Winkel 2010; Willems 2010). On an economic level, a new automatic support mechanism, the so-called tax shelter, was implemented.[3] On a cultural level, the former selective support system was thoroughly reformed with the long-anticipated inauguration of an autonomous film fund (the Flemish Audiovisual Fund [VAF]) and a significant increase in the available financial means. The new film policy framework not only caused a growth in the number of films but was also an essential stimulator for the new dynamics in Flemish cinema.

Flemish films can now rely on a larger audience and a more positive critical acclaim in the home market. At the same time, the international artistic recognition is growing as more and more Flemish films are receiving attention at prestigious film festivals.

Within this recent upswing of Flemish cinema, a certain crossover trend may be observed.[4] Indeed, until recently, cross-cultural aspects in Flemish films were a rather rare phenomenon, even though the quest for cultural identity has always taken a central place within Flemish cinema (Mosley 2001). The cross-cultural (textual and/or contextual) inferences were mostly limited to the francophone Belgian or the Dutch culture (with occasional colonial ties to Congo), which meant that the "Flemish crossover cinema" mainly stuck to a Low Countries framework. However, due to the cultural particularity of Belgium, it is tempting to consider this section of Belgian film history as a peculiar kind of "micro crossover cinema," requiring a study of its own. From the 1980s on, coproductions were heavily stimulated on a European level, leading in many cases to merely economically inspired alliances in which the cross-cultural aspect was rather artificially incorporated.[5] Meanwhile, with filmmakers such as Chantal Akerman, Marion Hänsel, and Michel Khleifi, the cinema of the francophone community in Belgium was building up a genuine "crossover tradition" that was largely responsible for the international artistic reputation of Belgian cinema (Spaas 2000, 9). Since its recent blooming, however, Flemish cinema seems to be trying to make up its crossover arrears.

On the one hand, there is a clear increase in the number of films that incorporate cross-cultural aspects, be it in a film's narrative and representations or in its industrial or reception context. Films such as *Cut Loose* ([*Los*] Jan Verheyen 2008) or *Mixed Kebab* (Guy Lee Thys 2012) have brought these aspects more to the center of the film. On the other hand, crossover films *pur sang* are emerging as well. As this volume illustrates, there is great diversity in the kind of films that are brought together under this concept. Regarding the Flemish case, two broad (and fluid) lines can be distinguished. First, the phenomenon of migrant and diasporic filmmakers is finally entering Flemish cinema. While from 2002 onward, some pioneering work has been done by the Turkish-Flemish amateur director R. Kan Albay and the "native" Flemish director Guy Lee Thys, it was not until Kadir Balci's (2010a) debut *Turquaze* that the first professional Flemish feature film by and about migrants was released. At the same time, there is an expanding group of films in which the story takes place in a predominantly non-Flemish (geographical) setting, and for which the relevance of the term *Flemish cinema* is mainly limited to the production and funding structure. Films such as *Khadak* (Peter Brosens and Jessica Woodworth 2006), situated in Mongolia, or *Beyond the Steppes* (Vanja d'Alcantara 2010), situated in Poland and central Asia, tell stories in which explicit links with Flanders or Belgium are absent. The remarkable film *Blue Bird* (Gust Van den Berghe 2011) is related to these cases, being entirely shot in Togo with a Togolese cast but loosely inspired by the 1908 play *L'Oiseau Bleu* by Maurice Maeterlinck, the Belgian French-language Nobel Prize winner from the Flemish city of Ghent. Also in the primarily Peruvian-situated but essentially cross-cultural *Altiplano* (Brosens and Woodworth 2009), the textual link with Flanders is (extremely) limited. Moreover, this link appears to be accidental rather than indispensable. To some extent, the same goes for films that Pisters (2011) calls "cultural-meeting-point film[s], usually set in a Western city, where people of all colors and origins share a contemporary urban space" (178), such as *The Invader* (Nicolas Provost 2011) or *Four Roses* (Kris De Meester 2010). What these films generally have in common is that they have an international film festival and art-house audience, rather than a domestic one. Also notable is the fact that the cross-cultural character of these films often runs parallel with their makers' personal backgrounds.

With this chapter, we want to further examine the two distinguished, yet by no means absolutely distinct strands of this new crossover trend in contemporary Flemish cinema by taking a closer look at *Turquaze* on the one hand and *Altiplano* on the other. We argue that the Flemish case is of great relevance as considerations about cinema and the crossover are usually made in reference to larger film industries such as the German, French, or British (e.g., the relatively large body of literature on diasporic filmmakers). Yet processes of globalization and migration undermine or at least complicate the primacy of (large) nation-states in the field of cultural production, so that the cinema of "smaller" (sub)nations becomes particularly interesting to study (Hjort and Petrie 2007). Next to offering a textual examination of the films, paying particular attention to narrative and audiovisual references to cultural particularity and cultural crossover processes, this chapter also focuses on the level of conceptualization/preproduction. Indeed, as Khorana argues in her introduction to this anthology, this is where the crossover originates. Regarding this, special attention is paid to the role of film policy for the emergence of crossover films, since this is a crucial factor for almost any Flemish film to be realized. This contextual research relies mainly on original archival research (mainly at the VAF), official policy documents, press articles, an interview conducted in 2010 with director Kadir Balci during the production of *Turquaze*, and additional sources such as the official websites of both *Turquaze* and *Altiplano* and the "making of" documentary on the *Altiplano* DVD (Possehl 2009).

TURQUAZE AS DIASPORIC FILMMAKING

Jäckel's (2010) study on French and British film policies shows how film policy can play a crucial role in creating opportunities for minority, migrant, or diasporic filmmakers. *Turquaze* illustrates that this is the case in Flanders as well. This Flemish-Turkish coproduction directed by Kadir Balci was branded in the press as the first film from and about immigrants in Flanders. The film's main story line focuses on the relationship between two young adults in Ghent, Timur (with Turkish roots, played by the director's brother Burak Balci) and Sarah (played by Charlotte Van der Meersch). Their respective backgrounds and families pose a challenge to their relationship: Timur clashes with his conservative and patriarchal older brother, while Sarah's parents are overly concerned about her relationship with Timur. Escaping the conflicts, Timur returns to his mother in Istanbul, where he is soon surprised by Sarah's appearance, leading to their happy end. Despite the accrual of conflicts that emerge from the confrontation of two cultures, the film mainly attempts to demonstrate the possibility of an equilibrated multicultural society. Though particularly visible toward the plot's ending, several elements illustrate this throughout the film, such as Timur's integration within the typically Flemish marching band and his dreamy gaze at a painting in the Flemish style of Pieter Breughel the Elder and Emile Claus, showing the Turkish village of Timur's father (as evoked by a voice-over of the latter). Most prominently, the film's musical score blends Flemish rock and pop with Turk pop and oriental musical influences.

Writing from a European perspective, Berghahn and Sternberg (2010) have provided a valuable and rather inclusive conceptualization, which we will use to discuss *Turquaze* as an instance of diasporic cinema in the Flemish context. The authors argue that migrant and diasporic cinema concerns a rapidly expanding corpus of films that is located at the heart of the world cinema turn in European cinema. A certain sense of novelty was indeed apparent when *Turquaze* was released; press reviews often commented that a symbolic border had been crossed for Flemish cinema (De Ruyck 2009; Naegels 2010; Werbrouck 2010). The heterogeneous body of films under the category of migrant and diasporic cinema challenges the notion of immobile and national cinemas, both textually and in terms of production and (potentially) distribution. *Turquaze* fits that description as it takes the unsettling of homogeneous national and ethnic identities as its main theme. Moreover, the national is surpassed by the importance of the local and the translocal: it is not so much Belgium, Flanders, or Turkey that forms the basis for the development of the plot as specific districts of the "home" cities of Ghent and Istanbul. In terms of production and distribution, the film had a Turkish coproducer and was partly shot in Istanbul, and attempts were made to distribute the film in Turkey.

Berghahn and Sternberg (2010, 16–17) emphasize the distinction between the first migratory and subsequent diasporic generations and its importance for the representation of diasporic memory. Born in Belgium in a family of Turkish origin, Kadir Balci is an example of a diasporic filmmaker, articulating a specific kind of diasporic memory through his vaguely biographical film: memories of the first generation (the protagonist's parents) are interwoven with contemporary reflections on cross-cultural encounters. Migrant and diasporic filmmakers like Balci are often presented as reflecting a "double consciousness" (Naficy 2001) or "diasporic optic" (Moorti 2003) in their films, expressed through a "distinctive aesthetic approach" (Berghahn and Sternberg 2010, 41). Illustrations of such a hybrid cinema in *Turquaze* are the blending of musical genres, languages, and cultural symbols. Another element is that diasporic films are oftentimes imbued with tropes of mobility and the expansion and/or confinement of space (Berghahn and Sternberg 2010, 29–32). This is clearly played out in *Turquaze* as it depicts not only the claustrophobic familial-spatial situation of minor characters (e.g., Timur's sister-in-law who seems forced to stay home all the time) but also the translocation of the story within the cities of Ghent and Istanbul.

Further, diasporic cinema is a cinema of identity politics (Rajgopal 2003), often raising political and societal inequalities and providing critique of hegemonic structures (Göktürk 2000; Berghahn and Sternberg 2010, 32–34; Malik 1996). Implicitly rather than explicitly, *Turquaze* does so by demonstrating that the "ideal multicultural society" has not yet been formed, but that it is within reach of the present Flemish society. A final characteristic of diasporic cinema is its agenda with regards to postcolonial critique and world cinema, that is, "the relocation of the margins to the centre, the valorisation and, ultimately, 'the redemption of the marginal'" (Stam 2003, 35; see also Berghahn and Sternberg 2010, 42). This is a rather general characteristic or effect of the diasporic shift within world cinema and European cinema. Elements of this agenda were echoed in several interviews where Kadir Balci rejected the label of migrant or diasporic filmmaker (compared to filmmakers elsewhere), despite the clear manifestation of a diasporic optic. He argued that *Turquaze* was in the first instance a romantic drama and that its cross-cultural aspects were ancillary representations of reality (Balci 2010b; Tollenaere 2011). At the same time, however, these elements were highlighted not only by the producer and other professionals involved in the production process but also by the director himself. By doing so, they hoped to acquire extra funding from different governments or institutes working in the field of migration and diversity. The producer also stated that he wanted to capitalize on mainstream Turkish films that are screened in Belgian theaters and that attract huge audiences among the Turkish diaspora (Smets et al. 2011). With this in mind, the director reduced the degree of sexually explicit content in the film (De Ruyck 2009). The diasporic element was also omnipresent in *Turquaze*'s exhibition as the Flemish Minister of Education and Equal Opportunities sponsored special screenings and advance premieres of the film for teachers (to use the film in classes on diversity) and for Turkish organizations. The latter gave rise to a fierce debate in the Flemish press and in the Parliament over the film's relation with the community and the necessity of special screenings (Schelstraete 2010; Spaas 2010; Balci 2010b; Maly 2010). In other words, the *Turquaze* case made clear that the debate on the multicultural society and its relation to film and culture is quite intense in Flanders.

While *Turquaze* is an example of a wider trend in European cinema, this film is particularly interesting within its Flemish context as the role of Flemish cultural and film policy is noticeable. Several political initiatives have aspired to diversify and "multiculturalize" the cultural sector, as intended in a plan of action by former minister of culture Bert Anciaux (2004–2009).

Among other things, it became obligatory for cultural institutions to have at least 10 percent of their boards composed of people with "ethnic and cultural[ly] diverse backgrounds" (Taghon, Yildirim, and Redig 2006). A former staff member of the ministry suggested that there was a link with Balci's feature film, as the measure facilitated his brief participation in the board of the VAF, the institution that manages Flemish film funding (Naegels 2010). This enabled Balci to expand his professional network and to become familiar with policy structures. Although Balci (2010b) himself downplays the importance of this effect, he acknowledges the importance of the minister's diversity policy. A multicultural motivation played a part not only in the broader cultural policy that affected the film but also in the concrete film production policy: the migrant theme seemed to be an advantageous element in the positive support recommendations of the fund's evaluation commission. The hope underlying such a multicultural policy is that a filmmaker like Balci might serve as a positive example for talented youth with Turkish or other roots as they are currently underrepresented as cultural producers.

CROSSING BORDERS: *ALTIPLANO*

The crossover cinema concept is not limited to the emerging body of diasporic films. Diverse forms of coproductions and films or filmmakers that engage with other (cinematic) cultures are also covered by this concept. For these cases as well, Flemish film (production) policy plays a major role as we can observe an evolution from a rather stringent emphasis on the "Flemish character" of a film (in both textual and industrial terms) toward a greater openness regarding "non-Flemishness." As a result, several film projects in which non-Flemish cultures and settings take a prominent place, like the films mentioned previously, have in recent years been able to obtain support from the VAF. Illustrative of this evolution in Flemish cinema are the two first feature films of the Flemish filmmaker Peter Brosens, an anthropologist and former documentarian, and his American wife Jessica Woodworth, a former journalist. The Mongolian-set *Khadak* and the mainly Peruvian-set *Altiplano* are part of a trilogy on the troubled relation between man and nature, which was concluded by *The Fifth Season* (*La Cinquième Saison* 2012), set in the directors' home region in Belgium. In the following paragraphs, we focus on the critically acclaimed *Altiplano*. This film is notable for its reflexive nature through the use of "the image" and the act of watching as central motifs throughout the film. Accordingly, the importance of "the image" is also reflected in the film's visual style, which is characterized by slow, well-considered camera work consisting of carefully aestheticized framing and many long takes. Apart from these artistic choices, *Altiplano* is also remarkable for its cross-cultural aspects.

Paying much attention to the ritual and spiritual aspects of the Quechua society, the largest part of *Altiplano* is situated in the Peruvian Andes, where a mountain village suffers a mercury spill from a local mine. The inspiration for this setting comes from a real-life incident that struck the Peruvian village Choropampa in 2000 when a motortruck leaked 150 kilos of mercury and the American mining company consistently shirked its responsibilities. By taking this incident as a starting point, the filmmakers remain faithful to the social and ecological engagement that fueled their preceding documentary projects.[6] One of the villagers in *Altiplano* is Saturnina (played by the Peruvian actress Magaly Solier), who loses her fiancé to the contamination and subsequently vents her grief through protests against the imposed violation of the village's people and environment. The other main character in the film is Grace (played by the German-Iranian actress Jasmin Tabatai), an Iranian (war) photographer who returns from Iraq to Belgium after a traumatic war experience. When Grace's French-speaking Belgian partner Max, a surgeon working in the Andes, is killed by Saturnina's fellow villagers, Grace travels to the Peruvian village as part of her mourning process.

By intertwining the lives of the two women, the filmmakers share *Turquaze*'s aim to put forward the analogies and links between diverse cultures. This is reflected in the film's title, *Altiplano*, which suggests a place without borders. It also explains the directors' often declared aversion to the concept of "exoticism" because this implies an emphasis on differences between cultures (Schelstraete 2009). The coherence between cultures is also emphasized in the prologue of the film, where a statue of the Virgin Mary is smashed on the ground during a religious procession (indirectly because of the destabilizing appearance of mercury in the village).[7] At the same moment, but in another part of the world, Grace's Iraqi guide is shot down. In the DVD extra "The Making of *Altiplano*," Woodworth explains that the connection between the two events "is also reflected in the music, as the Moroccan French singer sings the *Stabat Mater* in Arabic over the fall of the virgin."

It may be clear that on a textual level *Altiplano*'s link with Flanders is very limited. Only three short scenes are set in a nonspecified Belgian location where the language of the dialogue is French. In these scenes, there are no direct references to Flanders or Belgium, as is the case with two other occasions in the film. One is where Grace explains to a Peruvian soldier that she is from Belgium, after which the soldier links this to the saxophone (as its inventor was the francophone Belgian Adolphe Sax). On the second occasion, the film's only sentence in Dutch (with a clearly Flemish accent), the short greeting "Hoe is 't?" (How are you?), can be heard. The greeting comes from a Flemish aid worker and is addressed to Max, who answers in French. Other languages used in the film are mainly Spanish and Quechua, and to a lesser extent English and Farsi. This diversity of languages is another sign of *Altiplano*'s crossover character and consequently decreases the film's bond with Flanders. The Flemish aid worker, now continuing in French, mentions that it is the Belgian national holiday, and to celebrate this, he gives a bottle of Trappist beer, a typical Belgian product, to Max, who answers: "It's true, I forgot. Long live Belgium. Or what's left of it." With his last words, Max clearly refers to the community difficulties in

Belgium. His first words, however, can be seen as a metareflective comment on the official Flemish-Belgian "nationality" of the film. Indeed, when watching the film, *Altiplano*'s geographic production and funding structure can easily be forgotten (contrary to what is the case for *Turquaze*). Furthermore, the textual references to this production basis are, as we have seen, rather Belgian and francophone than particularly Flemish. In earlier days of Flemish film production policy, these elements would have constituted a major obstacle to obtaining support. However, for the VAF's evaluation commission, the textual absence of Flemish links was insignificant.[8]

Nevertheless, the commission did make a problem of the limited Flemish contextual contribution to the film, in particular in relation to the cast and artistic crew.[9] Together with a number of other factors, this caused a limitation to be imposed on the production support amount. One of the other factors was the ability of *Altiplano* to attract international financiers, thereby highlighting another (nonstringent) characteristic of the crossover film: multinational and supranational funding (see also Naficy 2001, 56). Indeed, European support schemes such as Eurimages (from the Council of Europe) and the MEDIA programme (Mesures pour Encourager le Développement de l'Industrie Audio-visuelle, from the European Union) assumed an important place in *Altiplano*'s financial framework. Also, support mechanisms and production companies from the Netherlands, Germany, and the French Community of Belgium were involved. The fact that the film's financial structure does not mirror its textual multiculturalism seems to be less relevant here. It should be noted that *Altiplano*'s international attractiveness was linked to the film's anticipated artistic qualities, which were in turn partly created by the international film festival success of Brosens and Woodworth's previous film *Khadak* (2006).[10] This is also reflected in the participation of two film festivals in producing *Altiplano*, thereby pointing to the growing importance of film festivals in the process of film production (Ross 2011; Steinhart 2006). Nevertheless, as was clear with *Altiplano*'s premiere at the *Semaine de la critique* in Cannes, the main function and importance of film festivals still lies in exhibition of, and bringing attention to, films that often cannot rely on a domestic audience that shows an interest in the represented subjects, like *Turquaze* could.

CONCEPTUALIZING THE FLEMISH CROSSOVER TREND

Within the complex Belgian context, Flemish cinema has always been characterized by a quest for cultural identity. In recent years, this quest has become even more complex, with several films taking on a more cross-cultural character. Apart from cross-cultural themes that find their way into an increasing number of films, two major but open strands within the recent crossover trend in Flemish cinema can be observed. On the one hand, migrant and diasporic filmmakers finally seem to be emerging. On the other, several Flemish filmmakers tend to cross the globe to make their films, thereby minimizing links with Flemish indigenous culture. We found it useful to take *Turquaze* and *Altiplano* as case studies to further investigate these two strands, as they are representative in so far as *Turquaze* is a dynamic reflection of Flanders as a multicultural society hosting diverse communities and *Altiplano* is an example of how Flanders can serve as a creative host region for cosmopolitan reflections on the transgression of cultural boundaries. The two films differ greatly in their treatment of the ideas of home and territoriality, which is also reflected in the different position of (target) audiences: while *Turquaze* invites local/regional audiences to contemplate the society in which they are participating, *Altiplano* seems to address a more global audience with references to cosmopolitan and deterritorialized identities. As we have seen, a film like *Turquaze* quite neatly fits into conceptual frameworks of migrant and diasporic cinema such as the one provided by Berghahn and Sternberg (2010). Films like *Altiplano*, however, are much harder to categorize into existing frameworks. Such films can be considered to be part of a certain strand within transnational cinema (see Higson 2000), but there is a need for a proper conceptualization for these kinds of border-crossing films and filmmakers. The previous account of one such film may serve as a step in this direction, and perhaps the crossover cinema concept may be of help in providing a larger cross-cultural framework here.

In our discussions of *Turquaze* and *Altiplano*, film policy aspects received particular attention because of their immanent importance for the development of the crossover trend in recent Flemish cinema. The two films, and more generally, the two strands within the Flemish crossover trend, are facilitated by the same film policy. However, the two strands can be linked to two different (film and broader cultural) policy objectives. First, *Turquaze* is (both textually and in terms of production) representative of policy objectives that are concerned with stimulating the contemporary multicultural society in Flanders. Second, *Altiplano* fits perfectly into the objective of acquiring international artistic recognition for Flemish cinema and culture. While we do not disagree with Andrew Higson's (2000, 69) statement that "at the level of policy, the concept of national cinema still has some meaning," our study has shown that a cross-cultural dimension is unmistakably growing (see Jäckel 2007).Finally, we want to underline the exploratory character of this chapter. In wanting to explore the different forms the crossover takes in Flemish cinema, we have focused on two particular films, each representing a distinct crossover dynamic and different film policy objectives. We wish to bring this trend in Flemish cinema—and presumably in other small cinema "(sub)nations" as well—to the attention of scholars and invite them to further observe and follow it in the years to come.

NOTES

1. "Flemish cinema" is understood here as the collection of feature films of which the major production company is situated in Flanders, the Dutch-language, northern region of Belgium.Because of its (still growing) regional

autonomy on cultural, political, and economic levels, Flanders is often considered a "subnation."
2. Flanders has 6.2 million inhabitants. Theoretically, the Netherlands could remedy this shortcoming because of the common language, but in practice, Flemish films rarely make their way to the Dutch public, and vice versa.
3. The "tax shelter" is a federal (Belgian) tax incentive, which makes private investments in films more attractive.
4. The term *crossover* is used here according to the conceptualization that Sukhmani Khorana provides in her introduction to this anthology.
5. These films are often referred to as "Europuddings" (De Vinck 2009).
6. As a proof of their engagement with the subject they are dealing with in *Altiplano*, a 2002 documentary (by Ernesto Cabellos and Stephanie Boyd) on the Choropampa incident accompanies the DVD version of *Altiplano*.
7. Because of its symbiosis between catholic and pre-Columbian spiritual elements (the so-called Catholic Andean syncretism), the religious procession itself also points at the merging of different cultures.
8. *Altiplano* applied, each time successfully, for script-writing support, development support, production support, and support toward promotion. One should be aware that for the first three types of support, the commission's decision process was based on a dossier that inevitably differs from the final film. However, at all stages of the project, the textual link with Flanders was minimal.
9. Apart from Peter Brosens and the mentioned actor in a small supporting role, only the editor (Nico Leunen) was Flemish.
10. In addition to numerous other distinctions and selections, *Khadak* was granted the "Lion of the Future" award at the Venice film festival in 2006.

REFERENCES

Balci, Kadir, dir. 2010a. *Turquaze*. Belgium: MMG Film & TV Production.
Balci, Kadir. 2010b. "Willen is kunnen: het multicul-misverstand." *De Standaard,* October 1, 26.
Berghahn, Daniela, and Claudia Sternberg. 2010. "Locating Migrant and Diasporic Cinema in Contemporary Europe." In *European Cinema in Motion: Migrant and Diasporic Film in Contemporary Europe,* edited by Daniela Berghahn and Claudia Sternberg, 12–49. Houndmills, Basingstoke, UK: Palgrave Macmillan.
Brosens, Peter, and Jessica Woodworth, dir. 2009. *Altiplano*. Belgium: Ma Ja De Filmproduktion, Bo Films.
De Ruyck, Jo. 2009. "Gent is het decor voor eerste Vlaams-Turkse film." *Het Nieuwsblad,* March 11, 91.
De Vinck, Sophie. 2009. "Europudding or Europaradise? A Performance Evaluation of the Eurimages Co-production Film Fund, Twenty Years after its Inception." *Communications* 34(3): 257–85.
Engelen, Leen, and Roel Vande Winkel. 2010. "Made in Flanders (redux): Film Production, Government Funding and Television Participation in Flanders, Belgium." *Film International* 8(6): 50–59.
Göktürk, Deniz. 2000. "Turkish Women on German Streets: Closure and Exposure in Transnational Cinema." In *Spaces in European Cinema,* edited by Myrto Konstantarakos, 64–76. Exeter: Intellect.
Higson, Andrew. 2000. "The Limiting Imagination of National Cinema." In *Cinema and Nation,* edited by Mette Hjort and Scott MacKenzie, 63–74. London: Routledge.
Hjort, Mette, and Duncan Petrie. 2007. *The Cinema of Small Nations*. Edinburgh: Edinburgh University Press.

Jäckel, Anne. 2007. "The Inter/nationalism of French Film Policy." *Modern and Contemporary France* 15(1): 21–36.

———. 2010. "State and Other Funding for Migrant, Diasporic and World Cinemas in Europe." In *European Cinema in Motion: Migrant and Diasporic Film in Contemporary Europe,* edited by Daniela Berghahn and Claudia Sternberg, 76–95. Houndmills, Basingstoke, UK: Palgrave Macmillan.

Malik, Sarita. 1996. "Beyond 'The Cinema of Duty?' The Pleasures of Hybridity: Black British Film of the 1980s and 1990s." In *Dissolving Views: Key Writings on British Cinema,* edited by Andrew Higson, 202–15. London: Cassell.

Maly, Ico. 2010. "De islammythe." *Kif Kif,* October 30. http://www.kifkif.be/actua/de-islammythe.

Moorti, Sujata. 2003. "Desperately Seeking an Identity: Diasporic Cinema and the Articulation of Transnational Kinship." *International Journal of Cultural Studies* 6(3): 355–76.

Mosley, Philip. 2001. *Split Screen: Belgian Cinema and Cultural Identity.* New York: State University of New York Press.

Naegels, Tom. 2010. "Migrantenfilm tegen wil en dank." *De Standaard,* September 29, D4–D5.

Naficy, Hamid. 2001. *An Accented Cinema: Exilic and Eiasporic Filmmaking.* Princeton, NJ: Princeton University Press.

Pisters, Patricia. 2011. "The Mosaic Film: Nomadic Style and Politics in Transnational Media Culture." *Thamyris/Intersecting: Place, Sex and Race* 23(1): 175–90.

Possehl, Roland, dir. 2009. *The Making of Altiplano.* Germany: LOOKS Film & TV.

Rajgopal, Shoba. 2003. "The Politics of Location: Ethnic Identity and Cultural Conflict in the Cinema of the South Asian Diaspora." *Journal of Communication Inquiry* 27(1): 49–66.

Ross, Miriam. 2011. "The Film Festival as Producer: Latin American Films and Rotterdam's Hubert Bals Fund." *Screen* 52(2): 261–67.

Schelstraete, Inge. 2009 "Cinema moet uit je ervaring komen." *De Standaard,* November 21.

———. 2010. "Hier slegs Turkes." *De Standaard,* September 28, 24.

Smets, Kevin, Philippe Meers, Roel Vande Winkel, and Sofie Van Bauwel. 2011. "A Semi-public Diasporic Space: Turkish Film Screenings in Belgium." *Communications: The European Journal of Communication Studies* 36(4): 395–414.

Spaas, Lieve. 2000. *The Francophone Film: A Struggle for Identity.* Manchester: Manchester University Press.

Spaas, Nele. 2010. "Segregatie in de bioscoop." *De Standaard,* September 29.

Stam, Robert. 2003. "Beyond Third Cinema: The Aesthetics of Hybridity." In *Rethinking Third Cinema,* edited by Anthony R. Guneratne and Wimal Dissanayake, 31–48. London: Routledge.

Steinhart, Daniel. 2006. "Fostering International Cinema: The Rotterdam Film Festival, CineMart, and the Hubert Bals Fund." *Mediascape* 2(Spring): 1–13.

Taghon, Sofie, Söhret Yildirim, and Guy Redig. 2006. *Vlaams actieplan interculturalisering.* Brussels: Flemish Ministry of Culture, Youth and Sport. http://www.interculturaliseren.be/fileadmin/user_upload/pdf/actieplan_interculturaliseren.pdf.

Tollenaere, Rudy. 2011. "Echt blij met DVD-versie van Turquaze." *Het Nieuwsblad,* April 16, 72.

Werbrouck, Stefaan. 2010. "Op een filmset staan is vakantie." *Knack,* December 15, 8.

Willems, Gertjan. 2010. "Filmbeleid in Vlaanderen en Denemarken: een comparatieve analyse." *Tijdschrift voor communicatiewetenschap* 38(2): 172–86.

Part III
Watching Other Worlds

9 Leaping the Demographic Barrier
Theoretical Challenges for the Crossover Audience

Adrian M. Athique

THE TRANSNATIONAL SHIFT

In recent years, some attention has been given to the dynamics of a distinctive form of transnational media consumption primarily oriented around the reworked menu of "world cinema" (Chaudhuri 2005). This is an emergent discourse, by which I mean that it is neither a radically new proposition nor one that can be easily contained within the ways of thinking that went before. For much of the twentieth century, there was a widespread, and quite remarkable, consensus concerning the practice of positioning the cinemas of the world as primarily national, indigenous institutions neatly arranged in a hub-and-spoke relationship with an "international" Hollywood industry. A distinguishing feature of academic studies in "national cinema" was their tendency to assert various "reflective" and "effective" attributes of feature films as social objects (Hayward 1993; Gittings 2002; Hake 2002). In the first instance, the "reflective" component of the national cinema paradigm rested on the claim that a film can *represent* the producing nation. In this light, films were seen as naturalistically indicative of a nationally specific aesthetic and, by extension, as presenting a literal framing of the cultural identity, behaviors, and beliefs of the producing society. The parallel claim of an "effective" component of national cinema related instead to the identification of the cinema as a *socializing* force with a degree of persuasive power. Here, the film medium was granted a role as a nation builder, with this claim resting specifically on the purported community-building effects they exerted on citizens watching "national" films (see Jarvie 2000).

Consequently, feature films have long been assumed to have a transformative impact on the cultural identity, behaviors, and beliefs of their "domestic" viewers. What they offer to "nondomestic" viewers has always been rather less clear and, indeed, has tended to be positioned negatively as a mechanism of counterindoctrination or "cultural imperialism" (Tomlinson 1991). This negative framing of transnational media reception is, almost needless to say, entirely discordant with the celebratory aspects of the international film festival circuit that forms the high table of world cinema. It also has very little relationship to the political economy of the cinema, which is scarcely national in any of its operations. These are both points that draw our attention to the shortcomings of the theoretical introspection of national cinema studies within an overtly international world system. In any case, it is important to recognize two things. First, that national cinema studies were overwhelmingly typified by this characteristic reflective/ effective dualism (by which cinema is both shaped by and shaping national identity and historiography). The second, and perhaps more critical point, is that the national cinema model rested almost entirely on a model of media reception that remained largely untested (a causal link between performance and patriotism).

The international scope of the film medium was at least given some formal recognition via the collected pantheon of nationally branded industries and their attendant aesthetics and commentaries. In the twenty-first century, however, national monopolies over cultural authenticity have been effectively challenged by the various phenomena associated with globalization, not least of which are the supranational ambits of other media forms such as satellite television and the Internet. Against this backdrop, Steven Vertovec (1999) has described "transnationalism" as broadly referring to the "multiple ties and interactions linking people or institutions across the borders of nation-states" (447). Vertovec (1999, 449–56) identifies six major strands of enquiry into transnationalism: as a social morphology, a type of consciousness, a mode of cultural reproduction, an avenue of capital, a site of political engagement, and a reconstruction of place and locality. Although the media, and telecommunications in particular, are seen as being crucial in all of these strands, narrative media are seen to be most influential in two instances: as a mode of cultural reproduction and as a reconstruction of place or locality. The critical question for reception studies, therefore, is how to relate these two functions in both theory and practice.

At present, I would argue that these functions are typically encountered within two different theoretical traditions. Cultural reproduction across national borders is being dealt with extensively in cultural studies, largely through ethnographic studies focused on the intrinsic identity of transnational subjects (see Cunningham and Sinclair 2000; Karim 2006). This work contributes to a human geography based primarily on locating ideal types within a multicultural demography. By contrast, the relationship between transnational media exchanges and locality tends to be figured via the interface of mass communications theory, market logic, and the inclination of area studies toward subnational and supranational regions. This work rests on a more explicit cultural geography, within which transnational media encounters are being extensively mapped (Curtin and Shah 2010; Fung 2008; Moran and Keane 2004; Straubhaar 2007). In film studies too, the critical focus appears to have been shifting away from national canons and toward documenting the fortunes of films that are consciously designed to blend cultures or to generate cross-cultural appeal (Durovicova and Newman 2009; Ezra and Rowden 2006). This is the broader context of the "transnational shift" in media studies, and, in some respects, we could understand this reorientation in terms of the inevitable tension between describing national histories and fostering transnational commerce in a globalized world.

CROSSING OVER

In the European case, the eclipse of the national paradigm was at least in part a recognition of the cultural diversity of contemporary populations in many of those nations, as well as the broader experiment with economic integration across the continent (see Higson 2000). In India, the national status of the cinema had never enjoyed the same hegemony as it had in Europe. Between the 1960s and the 1990s, there was a state-sponsored "quality" cinema along the lines of the European model, but these films were barely seen beyond the metropolitan intelligentsia (Bannerjee 1982). The popular Indian cinema was itself constituted by half a dozen major regional industries operating under the auspices of a relatively closed national market. As such, the national status of the cinema in India, considered in competition or in concert, was well defined economically (which it wasn't in Europe), but it nonetheless remained difficult to define in terms of a national media culture due to the extent of its regionalization. Since the Indian film industries already existed within a long-standing common market, and cultural diversity was hardly a novel discovery in the Indian context, the trigger for a transnational take on the cinema had to come from other imperatives. In actuality, the embrace of the transnational paradigm in the Indian case was primarily a response to economic liberalization during the late 1990s. As export and currency controls were loosened, there was a newfound awareness of the commercial potentials of export activity for an industry whose global reputation largely stemmed from the circulation of pirated films in the developing world (Athique 2008b).

Looking to a new horizon, both the importance of hard currency returns and the legacy of colonialism directed nascent export ambitions toward the West. Given the origins of Indian cinema in the colonial period, the notion of a "Western viewer" was itself as old as the study of Indian cinema. Since the days of Satyajit Ray and the Indian Film Society movements in the 1950s, there had been a consistent comparison between an Indian audience, typified by illiteracy and an enthusiasm for escapist fare, and an occidental viewer acculturated to a diet of realism rather than fantasy, drama rather than melodrama, and psychological motivation over musical excess (see Vasudevan 2000). Of course, aside from the music, this realist model of Western audiences rather contradicted the popular fare consumed in European, North American, and Australasian cinema halls. It did, perhaps, suit the kind of audiences addressed by art-house cinemas and film festivals, which in anglophone countries have traditionally been the most common environment for the screening of foreign-language films. Prior to the 1990s, the only Indian films to reach any significant Western audiences were art films operating in this niche market, described by Jigna Desai (2004) as:

> based on positioning "foreign" films as ethnographic documents of "other" (national) cultures and therefore as representatives of national cinemas. In particular, foreign Third World films that can be read as portraying the other through cultural difference (i.e., gender and sexual experiences or nativist renderings of rural village life). (39)

The art-house audience in the West represents a collection of consumers with various degrees of investment in an ethnocultural scheme of world cinema. This coalition of interests might include those with an academic or professional interest either in cinema or in the producing culture. It also encompasses viewers whose consumption of foreign films represents a mixture of autodidacticism and aesthetic pleasure seeking, gaining them a measure of cosmopolitan cultural capital. Art-house outlets often colocate a Third World "exotic" with European *auteur* cinema and with the alternative or independent sector of the host nation's local film culture. During the last decade, however, Indian films have begun to appear more widely in the popular imagination. Part of the reason for this is that migrant audiences resident in the West, and inhabiting the same metropoles as the old art-house audiences, have given *popular* Indian cinema a commercially viable presence in the new context of multiplex exhibition (Kerrigan and Ozbilgin 2002, 200). A further factor at play in the buzz surrounding Bollywood in the West has been the success of a number of Indian-themed crossover films produced by directors of Indian origin (such as Deepa Mehta, Gurinder Chadha, and Mira Nair) now working within various Western film industries (see Desai 2004). The success of these films with niche (largely middlebrow) audiences has encouraged the staging of various events designed to promote "regular" Indian films amongst a more "mainstream" audience over the past decade.

At the outset, the British Film Institute (BFI) organized an extensive showcase of Indian cinema, ImagineAsia, as part of a nationwide Indian Summer festival, which also included the use of Bollywood themes in department-store merchandise, visual art exhibitions, and theatrical productions. This celebration of Indian popular culture under the rubric of "multiculturalism" was consciously designed to promote Indo-British trade exchanges, emphasize official recognition of Britain's large South Asian population, and draw profits from providing a context for the consumption of Indian cultural products by the United Kingdom's majority white population. The BFI's ImagineAsia festival of Indian cinema was considered a success *primarily* since it drew almost a third of its audience from outside of Britain's South Asian population (White and Rughani 2003). Similar experiments were also undertaken in North America and Australia, with the Indian film industry also collaborating to take its own Bollywood spectacular on an annualized world tour. Various efforts were undertaken to build on the established commercial markets of South Asian migrants and to promote films that could gain critical acceptance and mainstream box-office success in Europe and America. Films like Santosh Sivan's *Asoka* (2001), Sanjay Leela Bhansali's *Devdas* remake (2002), and Ashutosh Gowariker's *Lagaan* (2001) were seen as the calling cards for India's ambition to become a premium global brand in the entertainment sector. This is the broader context within which *crossover* became a buzzword in the Indian film industries.

The term *crossover* naturally demands critical attention because, as Desai (2004, 66) has observed, its use remains synonymous with the quest for white audiences for "ethnic" media artifacts. The crossing described by the term is unidirectional in two registers: "niche to mainstream" and "ethnic to universal." Crossing over from a niche audience to a larger "mainstream" audience promises greater exposure and profits. Crossing over from an "ethnic" audience to a "universal" one also primarily indicates a market expansion, in this case, one that requires cultural barriers to be overcome. It remains highly significant that the term has not been used to describe the cross-cultural consumption of mainstream media by niche or ethnic audiences or to describe minority-to-minority media exchanges. Rather, the crossover audience is overwhelmingly positioned as an aspirational market arising from culturally literate and/or cosmopolitan members of the majority population who are willing to extend their consumption of media cultures (and media *as* culture). In everyday life, the crossover audience is encountered as the media constituency emerging from the reception of international productions (primarily feature films) promoted by multiplex cinemas, film festivals, playback media, and the various arts channels available through cable television (Athique 2008a; Desai 2004; Huffer 2013).

MEDIACULTURALISM AND MARKETS

Within the context of multiculturalism, a crossover event is defined by the success of a media artifact located in one ethnic culture with a majority audience located in the "dominant" culture. This is because, while the logic of multiculturalism challenges the idea of a culturally homogenous national audience, it continues to assume "that there are certain audiences that are commensurate with communities and demographic populations" (Desai 2004, 66). As such, "the emphasis on crossover success shifts discussion away from the issues associated with the burden of representation and the relations between cultural producers and black British communities to appealing to white demographic markets," with Indian films becoming "integrated into capitalist expansion through the logic and rhetoric of multiculturalism" (Desai 2004, 66). Multiculturalism is not only a rhetorical project, however, since it also constructs and naturalizes a market with both internal and external aspects. Within the host nation, the acquisition, possession, and display of products of foreign cultural provenance is facilitated by a range of leisure industries providing music, textiles, movies, literature, furniture, and food. The transnational exchanges of the multicultural industry facilitate this trade in commodities between the importing and exporting nation. Within this framework, the rebranding of commercial Indian films in the West as postmodern pop art, as exemplified by the trope of Bollywood, is very much part of the continuing cycle of post-1960s orientalism.

From the Western perspective, it is possible to discern a certain cultural ennui couched in this latest commercialization of liberal multiculturalism as cosmopolitan "ethnic chic," while in India the imagination on-screen of a transnationally orientated middle-class and its occupation and consumption of the West represents the symbolic counterweight of the orientalist binary. It is imperative, therefore, to recognize that any discussion of cultural consumption that juxtaposes East and West remains powerfully inflected by the historical exercise of power in the Indo-European encounter. Beyond the present geopolitical context, the recent Bollywood fad can also be seen as the latest manifestation of India's status as one of the most successful nations in the erstwhile Third World at having its cultural produce "appropriated" in Western markets. India has always been one of the heavyweights for multicultural products: from rustic tribal jewelry, oriental fabrics, 1960s-style spiritualism, ethnocultural and adventure tourism, new age music, exotic foodstuffs, ethnographic texts, and "new literatures." Indian films have now joined this considerable bankroll as another source of foreign exchange earnings and another form of cultural currency in the ongoing encounter between India and its highly significant "Western Other." As such, the machinery of Western appropriation clearly functions with the support of equally significant machinery in the Indian economy, which works to sell various versions of "India" abroad.

It is also worth pointing out that the promise of an off-the-peg experience of exotic authenticity is one of the primary strategies employed in the marketing of multiculturalism (and specifically media culturalism). This is, in each and almost every case, a fallacy convenient to all of those involved. As such, the dusting off of Indian popular cinema and its new life as the camp, glamorous, and low-context Bollywood is typical, rather than atypical, of marketing Asian cultures in the West. Nonetheless, the wider circulation of Indian films and the spin off of Bollywood club cultures and Bollywood dance schools emerging around the world are helping to make the Bollywood dance routine the acceptable, Western-friendly face of multiculturalism at a time when other markers of difference, such as the *hijab*, have become symbols of conflict and irrational fear. In that sense, it is possible to make a strong argument that Bollywood films represent an effective projection of soft power within the global imagination of the West. It remains to be seen, however, whether this recent flirtation with Bollywood is only a passing fashion or whether it will become an ongoing addition to the cultural repertoire of Western multiculturalism. Further, it remains a point of likely contention whether the crossover effect emerges from the particular aesthetics of the films themselves, or whether Bollywood has merely been signified as a convenient intangible brand whose "colorful" meanings can be easily appropriated by a cultural economy firmly anchored in the developed world.

In the case of cinema, the noisy celebration of the films of other cultures is also commonly related to furthering desires to extend economic opportunities for the national media industry in those markets. Certainly, Western media companies have come to view India as a potentially lucrative media market, and, with Indian production budgets also increasing dramatically, a number of national industries have been keen to court Indian producers and their appetite for offshore production and postproduction facilities (Hassam and Paranjape 2010). Thus, while we may describe films as being crossover in terms of genre, aesthetic, and intent (with reference to their deployment of "hybrid" cultural codes), the ultimate test of crossover status necessarily takes place at the box office (see Kumar 2011). To succeed, a crossover film must go well beyond the "home" audience with which it has been traditionally associated and appeal to sufficient proportion of the "mainstream" market. In the West, this continues to represent a major challenge for Indian filmmakers, since by comparison with their established audience base, there is little reliable indication of latent crossover potential within those audience sectors. Without any long-standing experience of competing in lucrative Western markets, Indian film producers have had to rely on their intuition (and preconceptions) concerning audience taste every bit as much as their creative imagination in conceiving projects that might appeal to this broad exotic constituency.

At the same time, Western filmmakers have been keen to draw on the Bollywood aesthetic for their own ends, from Baz Luhrmann's stylistic borrowings in *Moulin Rouge* (2001) to Danny Boyle's Oscar-winning *Slumdog Millionaire* (2008), which applied a Bollywood-inspired makeover to the previously successful formula of Mira Nair's *Salaam Bombay* (1988). Those who speculate in the cultural industries (for themselves or on behalf of others) generally do so on the basis of their own interpretation of a potential market conceptualized in the form of an audience. This notion of an audience as an inhabited market underscores the interdependency between media providers and consumers, and this commercial relationship attributes agency, albeit unequally, to both. Naturally, the obvious limitations of a market-based definition of audience arise from the restriction of this agency to choices based on consumption. An audience imagined in these terms will always attribute more weight to the decisive act of consumption than to the production of meanings or pleasures. Nonetheless, this is undeniably imaginative work that is social in nature. This is also important work, whether it is undertaken by children's entertainers, classical musicians, or film professionals focusing on the successful exploitation of public taste. It is the capacity for imagining large numbers of plausible—but fictitious and essentially unknowable—consumers on which commercial success often depends. It is significant then, perhaps, that the big crossover successes have originated in the West, despite the considerable efforts made by India's most talented producers to capitalize on the newly fashionable status of their own productions.

IMAGINING AUDIENCES

It is the articulation of a social imagination more broadly that underpins the most fundamental operation of media. Benedict Anderson (1991) famously postulated that it was the personalized mass address of the print media that fostered a deep sense of fraternity amongst its readership and produced the social imagination of the modern world. Other scholars have also taken up this idea of media encouraging abstracted social formations and applied it to the sociology of television and the Internet (Appadurai 1996; Castells 1996). While the intangible nature of subjective experience naturally escapes quantifiable observation, what is beyond doubt is that our engagement with the modern media is inherently a social practice. It is the imagination that both differentiates us from and links us to others. Generally speaking, it does so in symbolic rather than physical terms. If we agree that social identity exists in the imagination, it becomes necessary to investigate the actions and modes of expression that seek to return the imagination to the material realm from which it draws its inspiration. From this perspective, culture can be understood not as a figment, but rather as the product of social imagination. By extension, the sum of cultural production thereby constructs the order of social life. In this broad sense, culture is ultimately as vast and unknowable as the imagination. Nonetheless, if we position cultural practices as *manifest* imagination, it is logical that this manifestation can at least be observed in part. As such, there may well be some validity in the "reflective" casting of film analysis, although it is by no means clear that anything as large and heterogeneous as a nation or ethnicity can be captured in a single text.

At the same time, qualitative research consistently demonstrates that "exotic" media content is commonly understood by audiences as being a product of another culture and also, in the case of any "non-Western" content, as being ethnically marked (Athique 2008a). Similarly, the major theorists of globalization at the end of the twentieth century typically began with the more or less explicit observation that human society had been discontinuous and variable in its manifest forms, even as they argued that technological and economic change was rapidly redrawing cultural maps (Appadurai 1996; Giddens 2002; Robertson 1994; Tomlinson 1999). In the parlance of state policy, the recognition of cultural geography is primarily evidenced in the phrase "cultural diversity," which encapsulates the notion that human differences operate at the level of language, spiritual belief systems, socializing rituals, kinship structures, moral regulation, cultural performance, and formal political organization. With the important exception of the latter, these factors are all seen as contributing toward a sense of collective identity expressed through the notion of ethnicity. Like the nation, to which it has been inextricably linked in the past two centuries, ethnicity is seen as being both expressed and transmitted through an overlapping set of culturally distinctive processes. Thus, there is a common implicit assumption that human difference in its present form is to a certain degree determined by the stability of social communication. This is obviously at variance with the universal themes and cosmopolitan motivations that underpin the various crossover projects discussed in this book.

At the same time, the dispersal of media content across political boundaries is undoubtedly destabilizing the analytical framework laid down by these forms of nationalist logic. Therefore, the global dispersal of media content inevitably prompts us to rethink the basic terms by which culture is positioned by the United Nations and by national media institutions. At the end of the last century, Arjun Appadurai claimed that national formations of the media audience were giving way in favor of a patchwork of ethnically oriented performances that spilled across state borders and demarcated the global geography of multiculturalism. He adopted the following proposition: "that we regard as cultural only those differences that either express, or set the groundwork for, the mobilization of group identities" and that "we restrict the term culture as a marked term to the subset of these differences that has been mobilized to articulate the boundary of difference" (Appadurai 1996, 13). However, despite Appadurai's recognition of the increased scale and mobility of mass communication, his proposition continues to support the central notion that the performative traditions are essential components of ethnic socialization (see Smith 1999). Philip Schlesinger (2000, 24), however, believes that the longevity of this "inherently internalist" tendency is not so much a reflection of social reality as a legacy of the social communication theory which formed the basis of media studies. Thus, despite the laborious attention paid to the complexities of relationships within various national media industries and to cross-border trade in cultural works, there is still

> no general principle for analysing the interaction between communicative communities, for assessing cultural and communicative flows in a global system . . . because that is not where the theoretical interest lies. Social communication theory is therefore about how shared cultural and communicative practices strengthen the identity of a group by creating boundaries. (Schlesinger 2000, 21)

What Appadurai's approach primarily achieves, therefore, is the transference of the national media paradigm onto biological rather than physical terrain. We can also see this tendency at work in the widespread adoption of Anderson's (1991) concept of the "imagined community." Anderson famously posited that participation in the audiences facilitated by mass media encouraged individuals to imagine themselves as part of larger and more abstracted social formations (primarily, nations). For textual media research, it is this broad conceptualization of a *collective* symbolic imagination that allows for the "reflective" reading of cultural artifacts as allegorical renditions of identifiable societies or social groups. For audience researchers, these "imagined communities" also tend to be closely aligned with a priori social groups, whose collective subjectivity can subsequently be read off of a sample of responses to media content. This is problematic for a number of reasons, but for our purposes, it is obviously important that neither approach offers a compelling argument for why people should have any interest in media originating outside of their own ethnic address (see Athique 2008a). As such, understanding audiences solely in terms of community formation scarcely provides an explanation for media flows that cross over, and thereby connect, social groups.

PROXIMITY AND RESIDENCY

This theoretical mismatch is, of course, part of wider lack. A crossover between audiences in this particular case is actually a step from one unknown into another. In the first instance, after a century of filmmaking in the subcontinent, it is fair to say that our understanding of India's "domestic" cinema audiences has scarcely progressed beyond unreliable box-office profits and untested notions of the uncultured escapism and primitive religiosity of the masses. Scholars, film directors, journalists, and various cineastes have all offered various explanations of the appeal of Indian films, but the operating context of the "originating" film culture is poorly documented in empirical terms. At the other pole of the crossover lies another ill-defined social formation, although, being much less of a practical and methodological challenge, it is not immediately clear why this should be the case. For a long time, the art-house audience was the normative taste culture addressed by academic film studies. However, the turn toward the audience in film studies has been accompanied by a parallel shift toward the products of popular cinema as forming the object of study. Together these conjoined developments have had the curious effect of making the normative spectators of the previous epoch one of the least researched media audiences of all. There is scarcely any research on the art-house and film festival audiences that many of us frequent. This is a classic case, perhaps, of not seeing the forest for the trees. Thus, both Indian and art-house audiences are imagined communities at least in the very loose sense that they are understood and addressed instinctively, rather than empirically.

The next immediate question is, How do members of the crossover audience rationalize their own participation in cross-cultural consumption? To answer this, we need to go beyond tracing the relocation of the film itself in order to establish how the action of social imagination links viewers to other places via the technology of representation. Rather than Appadurai's closed circuit of communication, we can usefully turn to Joseph Straubhaar's (1991) more relativistic approach to the cultural geography of media, expressed in terms of a scale of affinity between cultures. Straubhaar (2007) concurs that "countries and cultures . . . prefer their own local or national productions" due to various factors, including the local appeal of celebrities, locally specific humor, locally relevant issues, culturally specific styles, and "the appeal of similar looking ethnic faces" (91). At the same time, he notes that "if countries, did not produce certain genres of television, then audiences tend to prefer those kind of programs from nearby or similar cultures and languages" (Straubhaar 2007, 91). The notion of "nearby" cultures thereby adds a new dimension to cultural exchanges because, although it also claims that cultures are distinctive formations, it simultaneously implies that cultural difference is incremental rather than absolute. That is, while media content may be foreign outside of its originating culture, it is less so in some cultures than in others because some cultures are more alike than others.

We could apply this idea, as Koichi Iwabuchi does, to the East Asian region where Chinese, Japanese, and Korean media products circulate widely across this broader territory (Iwabuchi 2003). We could therefore consider these to be proximate cultures, where there is enough similarity and/or mutual comprehension to support a transnational media sphere at a regional level. Of course, this approach would not encompass the desired East-to-West pairing of the crossover film. Indian filmmakers are scarcely excited about being popular in Nepal. The impetus of crossover films clearly resides much further along the spectrum of cultural proximity, and, equally clearly, it is not simply a "next best thing" situation of the kind described by Straubhaar. There is more going on here. In some instances, perhaps, it might be a perceived cultural proximity that makes media content appealing, enacting discourses of affinity, affirmation, or imagined comprehension. In other cases, the polar opposite prevails. That is, it is the degree of cultural distance that makes media appealing, mobilizing an aesthetics of exoticism. We can see instances of this throughout the history of the cinema, from the imperialist fantasies of *Tarzan* (1932) to the romance of *South Pacific* (1958). In the Indian case, there have been consistent attempts to cater to an occidental market since *The Light of Asia* in 1925. Generally, the Western fascination with the East is critically associated with Edward Said's (1978) famous treatise *Orientalism*. The surprise success of Tamil films in Japan, however, is scarcely less exotic, and I would argue that Shah Rukh Khan dancing through the streets of London, Sydney, and New York for the past two decades indicates the reversal of the same lens (Rajadhyaksha 2003; Kaur 2002).

Rather than being simply a Western preoccupation, visualizing the faraway and fantastic has always been a major function for any cinema of attractions. As such, I have commonly worked with a very basic distinction in terms of comparing diegesis with the social context of reception. I have done this by arguing that all media products have the potential to operate in "resident" and "nonresident" contexts. The term *resident* is, of course, a variable and contested term, a signifier shaped by the geographic and bureaucratic territories where it is deployed. Nonetheless, there continues to be a broad unifying context to the word, which implies *belonging* in not only a symbolic but also a physical sense. A media audience might therefore be considered "resident" under conditions where viewers perceive what is on-screen as somehow coterminous with the society in which they live. This is an allegorical function served effectively by both fantastic and realist narrative, and, certainly, this was the normative viewing position promoted during the heyday of national media systems. The "nonresident" mode of media consumption, by contrast, is more useful for describing conditions of reception that fall outside of this viewing position. Nonresident audiences engage with a media artifact in any context where the diegetic world cannot reasonably be claimed to be "about here and about us." In much of the world, where imports make up the bulk of media content and where media systems interface with a wide range of transnational territories, it is nonresident experiences of media consumption that are the most common. These are not mutually exclusive audiences, however, since nonresident media inevitably cohabit with "resident" media formations in our daily experience.

WHO, WHEN, OR WHERE?

This double life of feature films is also true of many other media products. Nonetheless, it draws our attention to a critical aspect of recent crossover projects: they were not made for export only. In practice, it is a combination of old and new (or home and away) audiences that is being pursued, and this underpins their ambitions as much as any drive for international recognition or predilection for code switching. My original motivation in employing the resident/nonresident distinction was to emphasize that films engender different readings in different places, and that these differences could not be reduced to the nationality of their audiences. At the same time, for audiences, the resident and nonresident experiences of reception are often understood in relative terms as a framing of "us and them" (much less so as "self and other," which is a more academic concern). In my wider research into transnational audiences, it has been obvious that the ethnic and cultural background of individual viewers also has a bearing within their present physical and social location (Athique 2005b, 2011). As such, since the same film can be read in many different ways, relating media to audiences in the twenty-first century is akin to the juxtaposition of two moving objects. In my Australian study from 2002 to 2005, it is fair to say that the crossover audience was characterized not so much by the straightforward matter of bilateral cultural exchange as by the heterogeneity of its makeup. The obvious lack of demographic coherence, or a mutual perception of fraternal similarity, set this crossover audience well apart from the predominant explanations for the sociology of media (Athique 2005a).

Arguably, if we restrict our definition of the crossover audience more narrowly than the art-house audience per se, that is, to only those white viewers of brown media favored in the imagination of India's film press and the BFI, then we might be able to establish something more akin to a social category (they were a bare majority at the various Asian film festivals I attended in the West). In general terms, we could say the Anglo-Saxon art-house audience congregates ritually around the cultural conventions of "quality cinema," a branding that is formally shaped by directors, distributors, exhibitors, and critics. This taste culture has been established over the longer term by maintaining a strong distinction between popular and bourgeois taste cultures. These visceral and literary idioms are often identified, respectively, with lower-class and middle-class constituencies, but in practice, art-house and popular audiences are neither class specific nor mutually exclusive. It has been noted, however, that this audience tends to include a large proportion of film professionals, students, and academics (Lewis 1990). Consequently, a significant portion of the art-house audience appears to consider itself as being literate and semiexpert in the medium. For non-Western filmmakers, finding favor with either art-house or general exhibition audiences would constitute a crossover audience and recent trends appear to indicate an interest (or even obsession) with moving from this smaller niche market to a more general audience.

In either case, the most critical theoretical point in all this is that the crossover audience is most probably not a community in the sociological sense. The most fundamental thing to bear in mind is that audiences are not, by their very nature, discrete social groups. Taking part in an audience is a time-limited and partial component of the social world, and of the social experience of any individual. Neither is likely to be defined by this single action. As such, media audiences are not communities in a form that is well suited to demographic analysis and the pursuit of ideal types. Even some very good pieces of audience research fall prey to the mistake of populating imagined affinities with "representative" samples. In a globalized world, it is equally critical to recognize that media reception cannot be theoretically normalized within any single instance of reception. A model for contemporary media reception must contend with the "channel multiplication" that is inherent to globalization. The crossover audience is a useful example in this respect because it is conceived almost entirely as an exception to any general rule that matches resident media with their audiences. As such, we have to approach it as a coalition of persons engaged in an exploratory activity, forming a niche within their own lives. Matching social identity to a single source of media content would make no sense at all in this context. Thus, for analytical purposes, the crossover audience is only a social formation in an entirely circumstantial sense. This points toward the alternative understanding of the audience as being an event rather than a community. At the same time, the proliferation of media formats in everyday life also means that this is increasingly a crowd without simultaneity in either time or place.

We could, of course, say many of these things about a wider range of transnational audiences in the contemporary world. This further highlights the growing disjuncture between accelerating media dispersal and academic approaches that still consistently seek to position audiences as knowable social groups. Given that crossover filmmakers are engaged in such overt attempts to break the conventional framing of cultural affinity, it is even less feasible than usual to align the crossover audience with an attendant cultural form that establishes a tidy demographic boundary of this kind. Even where we may find common tropes within films themselves, and in the multiple hybridities that now exist between officially sanctioned cultures, it is sensible to assume that the particular encounter in question is not the definitive reality of anyone's cultural life and, almost certainly, not the only thing they do. Therefore, any sociological enquiry into the crossover audience needs to pursue a theoretical explanation that does not revolve around *who* they are, but rather one that illustrates *when, where*, and *under what conditions* the crossover audience is constituted. We can then consider the terms by which participants become amenable to cross-cultural narratives and better determine the place of this activity within their broader social experience. In doing so, we may be able to get a more convincing sense of the presently vague role of film culture as a translator, tour guide, social reformer, and/or diplomat. To do this kind of work, we first need to find approaches to understanding media audiences that are, like the crossover film, amenable to leaping the demographic barrier.

REFERENCES

Anderson, Benedict. 1991. *Imagined Communities: Reflections on the Spread of Nationalism*. London: Verso.

Appadurai, Arjun. 1996. *Modernity At Large: The Cultural Dimensions of Globalization*. Minneapolis: University of Minnesota Press.

Athique, Adrian. 2005a. "Non-Resident Cinema: Transnational Audiences for Indian Films." PhD diss., University of Wollongong, New South Wales, Australia.

———. 2005b. "Watching Indian Movies in Australia: Media, Community and Consumption." *South Asian Popular Culture* 3(2): 117–33.

———. 2008a. "The 'Crossover' Audience: Mediated Multiculturalism and the Indian Film." *Continuum: Journal of Media and Cultural Studies* 22(3): 299–311.

———. 2008b. "The Global Dynamics of Indian Media Piracy: Export Markets, Playback Formats and the Informal Economy." *Media, Culture and Society* 30(5): 699–717.

———. 2011. "Diasporic Audiences and Non-Resident Media: The Case of Indian Films." *Participations: Journal of Audience and Reception Studies* 8(2): 1–23.

Bannerjee, Shampa, ed. 1982. *New Indian Cinema*. New Delhi: National Film Development Council.

Castells, Manuel. 1996. *The Rise of the Network Society*. Vol. 1 of *The Information Age: Economy, Society and Culture*. Cambridge: Blackwell.

Chaudhuri, Shohini. 2005. *Contemporary World Cinema: Europe, Middle East, East Asia and South Asia*. Edinburgh: Edinburgh University Press.
Cunningham, Stuart, and John Sinclair. 2000. *Floating Lives: Media and Asian Diasporas*. St. Lucia: University of Queensland Press.
Curtin, Michael, and Hemant Shah. 2010. *Reorienting Global Communication: Chinese and Indian Media Beyond Borders*. Champaign: University of Illinois Press.
Desai, Jigna. 2004. *Beyond Bollywood: The Cultural Politics of Diasporic South Asian Film*. London: Routledge.
Durovicova, Nataa, and Kathleen Newman. 2009. *World Cinemas: Transnational Perspectives*. Oxford: Routledge.
Ezra, Elizabeth, and Terry Rowden, eds. 2006. *Transnational Cinema: The Film Reader*. New York: Routledge.
Fung, Anthony. 2008. *Global Capital, Local Culture: Transnational Media Corporations in China*. New York: Peter Lang.
Giddens, Anthony. 2002. *Runaway World: How Globalisation is Reshaping Our Lives*. London: Routledge.
Gittings, Christopher E. 2002. *Canadian National Cinema*. London: Routledge.
Hake, Sabine. 2002. *German National Cinema*. London: Routledge.
Hassam, Andrew, and Makarand Paranjape, eds. 2010. *Bollywood in Australia: Transnationalism and Cultural Production*. Crawley, Perth: UWA Press.
Hayward, Susan. 1993. *French National Cinema*. London: Routledge.
Higson, Andrew. 2000 "The Limiting Imagination of National Cinema." In *Cinema and Nation*, edited by Mette Hjort and Scott Mackenzie, 63–74. London: Routledge.
Huffer, Ian. 2013. "A Popcorn-free Zone: Distinctions in the Spaces, Programming and Promotion of Independent Cinemas in Wellington, New Zealand." In *Watching Films: New Perspectives on Movie-going, Exhibition and Reception*, edited by Albert Moran and Karina Aveyard. Bristol: Intellect.
Iwabuchi, Koichi. 2003. *Recentering Globalization: Popular Culture and Japanese Transnationalism*. Durham, NC: Duke University Press.
Jarvie, Ian. 2000. "National Cinema: A Theoretical Assessment." In *Cinema and Nation*, edited by Mette Hjort and Scott Mackenzie, 75–87. London: Routledge.
Karim, Karim. 2006. *The Media of Diaspora: Mapping the Globe*. London: Routledge.
Kaur, Ravinder. 2002. "Viewing the West through Bollywood: A Celluloid Occident in the Making." *Contemporary South Asia* 11(2): 199–209.
Kerrigan, Fiona, and M. F. Ozbilgin. 2002. "Art for the Masses or Art for the Few? Ethical Issues of Film Marketing in the UK." *International Journal of Nonprofit and Voluntary Sector Marketing* 7(2): 195–203.
Kumar, Ranjit. 2011. "Crossovers and Makeovers: Contested Authenticity in New Indian Cinema." PhD diss., University of Wollongong, New South Wales, Australia.
Lewis, Justin. 1990. *Art, Culture and Enterprise: The Politics of Art and the Cultural Industries*. London: Routledge.
Moran, Albert, and Michael Keane. 2004. *Television Formats across Asia: TV Industries, Programme Formats and Globalization*. New York: Routledge.
Rajadhyaksha, Ashish. 2003. "The 'Bollywoodization' of the Indian Cinema: Cultural Nationalism in a Global Arena." *Inter-Asia Cultural Studies* 4(1): 25–39.
Robertson, Roland. 1994. "Globalization or Glocalization?" *Journal of International Communication* 1(1): 33–52.
Said, Edward. 1978. *Orientalism*. New York: Pantheon.
Schlesinger, Philip. 2000 "The Sociological Scope of National Cinema." In *Cinema and Nation*, edited by Mette Hjort and Scott Mackenzie, 63–74. London: Routledge.
Smith, Anthony. 1999. *Myths and Memories of the Nation*. Oxford: Oxford University Press.

Straubhaar, Joseph. 1991. "Beyond Media Imperialism: Asymmetrical Independence and Cultural Proximity." *Critical Studies in Mass Communication* 8(1): 33–59.
———. 2007. *World Television: From Global to Local*. Thousand Oaks, CA: Sage.
Tomlinson, John. 1991. *Cultural Imperialism: A Critical Introduction*. London: Continuum.
———. 1999. *Globalisation and Culture*. Polity Press: Cambridge.
Vasudevan, Ravi S. 2000. "The Politics of Cultural Address in a 'Transitional' Cinema: A Case Study of Indian Popular Cinema." In *Reinventing Film Studies*, edited by Christine Gledhill and Linda Williams, 130–64. London: Arnold.
Vertovec, Steven. 1999. "Conceiving and Researching Transnationalism." *Ethnic and Racial Studies* 22(2): 447–61.
White, Amanda, and Pratap Rughani. 2003. *ImagineAsia Evaluation Report*. BFI. http://www.bfi.org.uk/about/imagineasia-evaluation/imagineasia-evaluation.pdf. Accessed March 4, 2004.

10 Seduced "Outsiders" versus Skeptical "Insiders"?

Slumdog Millionaire through Its Re/Viewers

Shakuntala Banaji

Slumdog Millionaire (Boyle 2008) is now best known for winning numerous awards at the BAFTAs (British Academy of Film and Television Arts), Golden Globes, and the Oscars. After being publicly championed by an unprecedented number of film critics, it caused something of a media sensation when celebrities in Bollywood and some (but not all) viewers in India publicly labeled it exploitative and unfair to India and Indians. Told in flashback from the point of view of a young man, the film narrates the story of two brothers from a shantytown in Bombay, who choose different pathways in life. In the opening sequence of the film, one of the brothers has reached the final of the much-vaunted TV quiz show, the Indian version of *Who Wants to Be a Millionaire?* Arrested, apparently for cheating, Jamal Malik explains to his police interrogators how it is possible for someone like him, a slum child with little formal education, to know the answers to the most seemingly esoteric questions: he has learned the answers through bitter experience. And in the process of recounting these, he opens for the audience a window on the world of two Muslim children born in a Bombay shantytown in the 1980s. Via fast-paced sequences full of jump cuts—depicting communal riots, professional begging, and child-molesting gangsters—the boys and the camera travel across India and back again. They return in search of an old girlfriend as Bombay's/Mumbai's economy goes neoliberal and gated communities spring up, isolating the rich from the poor. In tandem, the younger brother, Jamal, stays honest, innocent, hardworking, and loyal—a tea boy in a call center; the older brother becomes a gangster's lackey, corrupt and aggressive, taking the quickest possible route to what seems like financial success.

A viewing of the film during a year of media hype, followed by a series of random but heated discussions about it, crystallized into an urge to discover whether and how different kinds of *knowledge* and *experience*—about cinema, Hindi cinema, India, Bombay, and urban poverty (Indian style)—played into critical responses to the film by its viewers. Saying that the same film and the same set of circumstances can call up wildly different, even contradictory, viewpoints from people or from the same person at different times should no longer be much of a surprise. Meaning does not reside solely in media texts; this has been established over the decades via painstaking theoretical critique and empirical scholarship (see, among others, Austin 2002; Buckingham 1993; Barker and Brooks 1998; Mankekar 1999; Staiger 2000). What is interesting about people's reactions to this particular film is not, in fact, the divergence of opinion per se. What is intriguing is, first, the vehemence and types of the feelings called forth by what might seem a fairly prosaic rags-to-riches story, albeit set in an (to most Western audiences) exotic setting: delight and jubilation, inspiration, tears, disgust, anger, and humiliation are only some of the emotions expressed by those who watched it. Second, and more confusingly, perhaps, it was read as an educational—almost an ethnographic—tale by some re/viewers, a contrast to Bollywood glitz and to the mawkish sentimentality of documentaries about India. Additionally, and more problematically, perhaps, opinions expressed about the film contained tropes of quasi-orientalist (Said 1978) or reorientalist (Lau 2009) cultural and political discourse. Indeed, the quaint assumption of an ethnographic subject when a film or book happens to feature nonwhite and non-Western protagonists is a classic feature of such discourse in relation to fiction genres. In a fascinating paper delivered on this subject, Ellen Dengel-Janic (2009) argues that "[w]hat the film negates and helps to mask in a pleasurable visual manner is a translocated fear of poverty and the abject . . . The film's appeal reflects not only the West's exoticism of India but also its repressed fear and paranoia of becoming abject and poor." But given the wide range of viewers who ultimately encountered the film, can such a critical reading be sustained? Understanding the combinations of *circumstance* and *experience*, *contextual* and *technical knowledge*, and *generic expectation* that lead to particular discourses or technical sequences in films being picked up and enjoyed or selectively critiqued has been the aim of much of my work on Hindi cinema to date (see Banaji 2006, 2008) and remains at the core of this chapter. However, even these combinations do not capture fully the investments people have in their judgments about films, or indeed the complexity of the emotional and cultural histories that inflect these judgments.

RESEARCH QUESTIONS

Following my first viewing of the film—which, to lay my own cards on the table, was shot through with a mixture of great enjoyment (the editing, the child actors, and the music), recognition (places I saw growing up, familiar iconography, and known political events), and disappointment (implausible romance, weak women characters, British accents, and pseudo-Bollywood ending)—an analysis of reviews, and casual conversations with a number of fellow viewers, new questions began to emerge:

1. Who is more likely to judge the visual and other cinematic pleasures offered by this film positively?

a. Re/viewers familiar with popular Hindi cinema or viewers familiar with India?
   b. Those with an interest in offscreen politics or those with little interest?
   c. Those living in India or those living abroad?
   d. Those who have experienced something akin to shantytown poverty?
   e. Lower- and middle-class viewers who do not live in slums but have some direct experience of them?
   f. Or transnational urban viewers (carefully excluded from the film's narrative)?
2. What role can anthropological notions of "insider knowledge" and "outsider gaze" play in film studies' analyses such as this one: can re/viewers' self-positionings vis-à-vis the film or its subject matter contribute to an understanding of its reception?
3. How do re/viewer's preexisting worldviews, ideological standpoints, and intersecting identities inflect responses to the film?

These questions—which are not necessarily specific to this film but could be asked about our responses to melodramas that build their narratives around gay American cowboys or Japanese geishas or American soldiers at war in Iraq—are evidently much broader than this study; all aim to explore the relationship between what might be deemed "insider" knowledge and value judgments made about films purporting to convey such insider knowledge. Relating as they do to people's individual experiences, life trajectories, and expertise, these questions did not appear to be answerable by analyzing reviews in film journals or by viewers writing on the Internet Movie Database (IMDb). The following section therefore outlines the chosen methodology of this study and the theoretical framework via which analysis of emerging themes was carried out.

DATA COLLECTION

While written reviews available online in scholarly and film journals, newspapers, and the IMDb, for instance, form the backdrop to ideas in this study, the primary method of data collection was via twenty-five half-hour qualitative interviews, which took place either via Skype or face-to-face, and fifteen in-depth qualitative questionnaires (administered over the Internet) in the spring and summer of 2009. Respondents were recruited via requests to random viewers at showings of *Slumdog Millionaire* and other films in Bombay and London, questions to friends circles on a number of social network sites, written requests to randomly selected reviewers on IMDb, and verbal requests to auto and taxi drivers and shop assistants in Bombay in the summer of 2009. I ended up recruiting seventeen respondents actually living in

Bombay, three living in the United States, ten living in the United Kingdom, and ten from around Europe and Asia. There were seventeen respondents who identified as female and twenty-three who identified as male. In terms of class self-descriptors, saliently, participants in India who were evidently working class by background, education, and/or current occupation were the least likely to describe themselves as such, using terms like "doing okay," "fifty-fifty," or "in the middle" to describe their financial circumstances, while a few called themselves "workers." In the United Kingdom, participants in middle-class or professional occupations tended to stress that their roots/parents were working class. This qualitative study of forty interviewees, though far from representative of any particular group, is therefore somewhat diverse in terms of social class, gender, age, nationality, country of residence, cinematic knowledge, education, and experience of Hindi cinema. The oldest interviewee was seventy and the youngest seventeen, but most fall into the age group of twenty-five to fifty. My work with young viewers in India and the United Kingdom over the past ten years was immensely helpful in suggesting ways of approaching specific cinematic topics through what amounted to self-narration (Shotter and Gergen 1989, 255).

ANALYSIS AND THEORETICAL INTERPRETATION

Interviews took place in Hindi and/or in English, and while some were written down by respondents, the rest remain untranscribed. All were coded for key themes and crosscutting discourses by me at the time of the interviews and again, subsequently, recoded once all the data had been collected and different types of "insiderhood" had emerged. Given the significance of interconnected factors such as ethnicity, gender, and national identification for respondents, the interviews and written responses were tied firmly to respondents' self-descriptions in this regard. In this, I followed Shotter and Gergen (1989) and contributors to their collection *Texts of Identity*. Like Celia Kitzinger (1989, 82) who writes about the discursive construction of lesbian identities, I wished to use this approach to focus not on the accuracy of accounts of identity and identification by research subjects but on the social and political (or in this instance critical and evaluative) functions served in relation to their readings of *Slumdog Millionaire* and their responses to the depictions of India and slum children therein.

Further, and in particular, notions drawn from critiques of ethnographic film, now circulating in visual anthropology (Martinez 1992; MacDougall 1995; Pink 2001), provided an interesting lens for examining some of the anxieties caused by the film around notions of representation, class politics, nation, and authenticity. While *Slumdog Millionaire* had no overt pretensions to being an ethnographic account of life in Indian slums and was, in fact, openly touted by its makers as a "feel-good film," many of its re/viewers implicitly used criteria from ethnography or realist criteria from social science to evaluate, understand, and comment on its qualities and their reactions to it. Sarah Pink's (2001) discussion of current scholarship on audiences of ethnographic film and video is illustrative of why this approach can prove fruitful:

> Visual anthropologists now pay serious attention to the politics of ethnographic film representation and spectatorship. . . . Wilton Martinez has shown how individuals' readings of ethnographic films are embedded in complex sets of existing power relations and cultural narratives that "conventional" ethnographic film narratives and pedagogic strategies do not challenge. (145)

Paying attention, then, to power relations, pleasures, individual self-narratives, and the groups of discursive readings emerging from viewings of the film, the following section presents a snapshot of the data collected.

GOING ON A JOURNEY, BEING SURPRISED, AND LEARNING SOMETHING

One of the largest groups amongst my respondents (roughly fifteen out of the forty) were those who lived primarily in the West and had enjoyed the film and saw it as an example of cinema that has the potential to surprise and teach something previously unknown, to make them think in new ways. Their commentaries on form and content were integrated and are presented here following from self-descriptions elicited via opening questions. Civic, social, and intercultural investments in being surprised by films, and in discovering new knowledge through the films they watch, can be seen to flow directly into aspects of the movie that these viewers enjoyed or focused on as being particularly salient for them. All of these are also implicitly political, in line with their self-descriptions as highly educated, and in the cases of the excerpts chosen here, also educators.

Excerpt R (written, English)

> I grew up in middle class, white, suburban, mid-western America. I am white. . . . My family was extremely conservative and religious and we attended (Baptist) church three times a week and I went to a private religious school. . . . There are many fascinating cultural differences [between my life in the West and what I experienced when visiting India]. . . . I very much enjoy traveling and all the experiences that global visits bring but am very uncomfortable with what I represent to the people in these countries (generally speaking). I often find myself torn between a curiosity and a sympathy for people living in poverty and an annoyance at how I am approached. I have assumed that my

skin color identifies me as someone from the rich west and with this comes a great deal of guilt. I wish I could just blend in and observe—but instead I become the center of attraction. In India, people would simply stop whatever they were doing, take a seat and stare. How to best handle these situations? I still don't know, but I want to learn. . . . I really enjoyed *Slumdog Millionaire*—it was well-constructed, suspenseful, and made a great story. Mainly I recognized the country that I'd visited briefly. I liked that a great deal, because I recognize that although film may be set in "real" locations, watching something on the screen is never the same as experiencing it in real life. For example, the smells of a place are not present. On my trip to India, I saw beggars in the street coming up to the cars, particularly in Delhi. *While watching the film* [my emphasis] I was skeptical—and also horrified by the idea that these child beggars were so centrally organized. I thought the depictions of the slums were quite real and of the cities—it reminded me very much of my experience in other Indian cities. But are there adults that are so evil to use orphans for their own gain? I thought that may stir cynical feelings from Western viewers. I also found the story of the main character inspiring—how much he had overcome to make it as far as he did, but the fact that the TV host was so determined to put him in his place—I wondered if this was some kind of commentary on Indian society?

In the previous excerpt, viewer R moves through a wide range of emotional investments in watching films, many of which are explicitly connected to her enjoyment of travel and of learning about "people from different cultures" and "how to handle" situations in which she is perceived as the rich, white foreigner. The language in which R describes her impressions of places, film sequences, and emotions is vivid: "torn" between "curiosity," "sympathy," and "annoyance." Being inspired, feeling guilt, skepticism, and horror also feature, alongside a sense of recognition that facilitates and enhances her enjoyment of the movie: "it reminded me very much of my experience of other Indian cities." Notably, and confirming work done elsewhere on viewers' responses to modality issues in media texts (Ang 1985; Banaji 2006), the notion of realism comes up repeatedly: "I thought the depictions of the slums were quite real and of the cities"; "I wondered if this was some kind of commentary on Indian society." This particular comment also carries within it a clue to the way in which the film has been categorized here as potentially able to illuminate real offscreen circumstances and situations. R's comments on films in general and *Slumdog Millionaire* in particular are connected by references to and a narration of her travels. Although this was how the questioning set up the discussion, more than two-thirds of the viewers I spoke with and wrote to did not respond in this manner, which thus constitutes a peculiarity both of this individual viewer and of a couple of other viewers who share certain characteristics with her, notably that they had experience of living in different cultures and had a strong sense of reflexivity about the intersections of national identification, class, and ethnicity prior to viewing the film. Perhaps most interestingly for the purposes of this paper, R expresses a wish to "just blend in and observe without becoming the center of attention" while touring other countries. For her, and perhaps for a number of other Western viewers (both white and diasporic), the film became a "window on the world" that allowed an emotional engagement with uncomfortable and perhaps hidden aspects of India without the accompanying practical complications.

Viewer Q, like viewer R, liked the film but is also conscious of the surrounding hype and how it affected his expectations.

Excerpt Q (written, English)

My mother is a house-mom, my father is unemployed since I was 2, so rather low class. Money difficulties throughout my youth. . . . Mine is a very religious family, father is imam, mother wears headscarf. Every problem had to be solved religiously . . . I reacted against that, kept thinking, and now agnostic, since my 23rd year. Politically rather leftist, although I have some more "right" views, although in my opinion they are not right but left. I vote left nevertheless. In films I look for the surprise, something that makes you think, laugh etc. . . . Something new. Something well said, well acted. . . . The only thing I know about these films [Bollywood] is they are very long, a lot of dancing and music, love plots, tradition versus modernisation, etc. The reason why I hesitated to see it was the way it was presented in the Belgian media, and especially in the weekly film section on Wednesday during the news on the Flemish public broadcast VRT [Vlaamse Radio–en Televisieomroep]. It was presented as if it was just a kind of success story, very media related. He plays a televised game, wins and hurray all for the best. I don't like the game show either, never watch it when it is on, although I generally like quizzes. It's a bit fake. The trailers they showed seemed so superficial, so Hollywood, or rather Disney. . . . I was surprised that it was better than I thought, the song at the end seemed too much "made," it was like an obligation, with little reference to the rest of the movie. I was surprised that there were more layers, more depth than showed before in the trailers. I felt rather as it showed a country in transition, separate worlds, rich and poor—new buildings versus slums. The fact that the mobster kids, from the slums, are only able to be in those new buildings when they are still being built, was a nice contrast.

Q's background is working class, and, more explicitly, his youth was lived in a context of continued financial insecurity. He too lives primarily in the West. However, unlike R, Q is of ethnic minority origin and has experienced life as a working-class immigrant, outside the mainstream majority community in his Belgian home city. He has worked with refugees and has some experience of Hindi films, which have not made him a fan. This experience of a marginal position is reflected by a quick and critical reception of the hype around *Slumdog Millionaire* in the mainstream media of his country of residence. Although he makes no connection between discourses in the Belgian media about the success of the film and the success of its protagonist in a media quiz show and his own experiences of childhood poverty, it is clear that the film's running motif about financial success is a weakness rather than a strength. His awareness of class contrast colors the moments that stand out for him. In a similar vein, his comment that the program *Who Wants to Be a Millionaire?* is "fake" and hence unlike other quiz shows links neatly to his distaste for the hype, the Disney-like superficiality of what was shown of the film in its previews. Nevertheless, he finds things to like in the film, particularly what he takes to be its less obvious commentary, played out through visual references of class politics and uneven modernization in India.

NOTHING SPECIAL

Unsurprisingly, for a number of viewers in this study, it emerged that the film was "nothing special." They neither liked it immensely, nor disliked it intensely. There were a few young women in this group, but the majority were youngish men (in the age group fifteen to thirty-five), who had extensive experience of Hindi cinema, had grown up in and/or lived in South Asia (and Bombay in particular), and had experienced or still experience life within a working-class community. These young men could be classed as "insiders" in the sense that they are intimately familiar with a number of the contextual aspects of the film—including, in some cases, the violence and the childhood in a slum setting.

Excerpt B (spoken, face-to-face, Hindi)

I've lived in Bombay all my life—never been out of the city. I'm twenty-seven and I share this auto [rickshaw] with my brother-in-law. I've been driving since I was seventeen. I live in a shanty-town in [names suburb] and my family lives there also. I saw that *Millionaire* film with my wife when it released because she and I share a passion for films. We must have seen more than one hundred films together. We saw it but we didn't go back to see it again. Usually we go to see good films again and again. We found the children very good—they were not actors, did you know that? They were just real kids. The director must have done a lot of work with them, credit to him. One thing that irritated my wife very much with the film was that it is named about people who live in the huts [*jhopdis*] but actually the children become orphans and most of the time they are without a home in the film, wandering from place to place. I grew up here [in a shanty-town] and the worst we do is we drink a bit; we don't join in a gang and we didn't suffer like some of the children on the street. Their life is ten times as bad. Maybe this director did not understand the difference between us, because we are all poor in his eyes and he wants to make the American people feel pity on us all. There were some bad things shown in the film but these are nothing unusual for us [poor people in India]. Have you seen *Company* or *Zeher*? So many Hindi pictures are made on interesting topics.

In B's description of his viewing and his own history, the fact that he watches and enjoys Hindi films stands out. He positions himself as an ardent film fan but claims no authority further than that of knowing which films he likes and which do not merit a second viewing. He names his wife as a viewing companion and speaks about her also in his description of responses to the film. However, at one point, he clearly distinguishes his wife's opinion—and her feeling that the film smudges out important distinctions between different strata and lives amongst those who are poor in urban India. He goes on to support his wife's opinion about *Slumdog*'s clichéd reduction of urban slum poverty to a gangster-victim binary by referring to his own experience. Here both knowledge of films and of life work to de-exoticize the narrative and techniques of *Slumdog*. Also, another common discourse emerges that views the director as "inauthentic" in a way that, perhaps, even the most elite Hindi film directors might not be regarded.

F, a viewer raised in relative poverty in a small village in South Asia, exhibits similar feelings and opinions.

Excerpt F (spoken, face-to-face, English)

I grew up in Bangladesh, in a village, not Dhaka . . . My father is dead. I have an uncle in Dhaka, so yes, I have been there and it is not quite like Bombay but it is—there are same kinds of places [slums]. I've never been to India. I just came to UK, something, now maybe three years ago. I've worked in this place [London fast food restaurant] since then. I went to see *Slumdog Millionaire* because it was like a Bollywood film and I am a big fan of Bollywood films. Did I like it? Why not? What was there not to like? It had a happy ending, didn't it, so we can forget the bad things shown in the beginning—they actually do not leave much of an impression on the mind because it happens very fast and we know that he is telling the story now so he is alive. He didn't die in childhood, so that is good. But actually, now you ask, I found [the film] quite normal [average]. The music was not much good . . . the songs were very few. Then it became boring with the same question answer, question answer again and again—that thing I found interesting at the beginning I found tiring by the end. In the middle I was thinking about getting up for my shift in the morning and I was wanting to sleep [laughs]. . . . Yes, I was alone watching it. I prefer to watch real Bollywood films—*Singh is King!*

F's pointedly sardonic summary of one of the film's significant pulling points—its telling of the horrors of Jamal's childhood in flashback—is striking. It is possible to see what F means when he says "so we can forget the bad things shown in the beginning." The events taking place in the "present," for instance, the gangster Jamal's brother is involved with or the policemen questioning Jamal, are so much less intensely unsettling than the riots or the cartel that turn orphans into disabled beggars. As in B's commentary, F's comments about the film are framed by the reality of a working-class life— driving a rickshaw or waking for an early shift in a kitchen. These comments are also set within a shared Hindi cinema fandom, by whose standards *Slumdog Millionaire* falls somewhat short. In a similar manner to several of the other working-class South Asian interviewees in this study, F began by making neutral or politely positive statements about the film, hoping to ascertain my taste and impressions and not to contradict me. However, by the end of our interview, which in his case was conducted in an intermittent manner as he served customers at his place of work, his feelings about the film had become much more apparent—from "What's not to like?" he had moved to "boring," "tiring," and "not real Bollywood."

UNABLE TO "LET GO"

Another subset of viewers within my study was united by their dissatisfaction with the film. I quote here only two excerpts, as these were some of the longest and most heated analyses provoked by my questions. These excerpts are characterized less by the implicit class politics that animates some of the preceding accounts and more by quite specific and detailed references to aspects of *Slumdog Millionaire*, which prevented these viewers from enjoying it or from relaxing and being entertained during their viewing.

Excerpt M (spoken, face-to-face, Hindi)

I'm 39, I work part-time, my husband is quite strict but I can work from home and I also get to watch a lot of movies. We are from a good—I mean middle-class family. It's surprising to me how much everyone likes this picture. I went with my husband and son (he is grown up) and his friend. We paid a lot for the tickets and I felt that we had wasted the money. Yes, it shows a very bad side of Mumbai. We all know Hindi pictures do not tell the whole story. Yes, some people live like that also. But that was not my main reason for not liking. It mixed up everything—children and poor people and gangs and rioting and religion and brothers and betrayal and begging. It never stopped to consider each thing. Life is a mixture. What I like about Hindi pictures is that they don't just remain in the same style—there are so many new and interesting topics coming out . . . but this Danny Boyle *Slumdog* picture became so famous. I was upset about the way this picture got so many awards but it had no heart, unlike our pictures. I couldn't relax when I was watching. I was very furious and irritated.

M, who locates herself as middle class (and is indeed middle class in terms of education and income), contests almost every aspect of *Slumdog Millionaire* from its representations and its structures of feeling to the way in which it appears to her to have grabbed praise and renown from Hindi films that are more deserving. She situates her criticisms of the film within the context of the debates she has encountered about its supposed misrepresentation of India and Indians, its portrayal of unmitigated filth and corruption, distancing herself from what she thinks might be interpreted as middle-class chauvinism and narrow-mindedness. M's critique raises issues related to a perceived correspondence between reality and the film and related to the film's style. Like some of the viewers in the previous group, she points out that if realism or social critique is something one looks for in films, there are Hindi films too that deliver, in a variety of styles and genres. Her critique is also leveled at the exploitative way in which she felt the director used stock ingredients (or masala) to spice up the film, and in this critique M is not alone. Several other interviewees commented on the pace of the film in dealing with the "serious" issues, that "might entertain some people but made me first sea-sick and then just sick" (as one viewer asserted). Evidently, a number of viewers felt the film's voice and perspective was that of a voyeuristic outsider, one who grabbed and narrated bits and pieces for effect but did not have any lasting emotional investment in the subject matter of the film.

The first group of viewers quoted in this paper—R, P, and Q—are outsiders to the film's context in numerous ways but relate to and enjoy it because to them it both entertains and informs in an ironic and socially critical way. T is also an outsider to India and to Hindi films. She engages fully with *Slumdog*'s setting, only to be "embarrassed" and "depressed."

Excerpt T (spoken, face-to-face, English)

I'm 48, single, female. I grew up in South Africa and came to UK when I met my ex-husband. I should explain probably that my knowledge of poverty like that shown in *Slumdog* dates back to my time in SA. I was growing up at a time of struggle and economic transition, I recognize some of that from the film, the buildings built on places that have been bulldozed so that you can wipe out the memory of the people who lived there before and the people who made them live like that. I'm not saying it is the same in Mumbai, there's no apartheid, but there is a kind of class partition . . . I worked at a rape crisis centre for some years. *Slumdog Millionaire*—you can tell full well that it is made by a man, and for men and it has very unexceptional characterizations of masculinity and femininity—that is something that I usually wish films to challenge if they are to grip my emotions. How can I explain this? I watched it, and I was enjoying it a bit—rather I felt entertained, and I was also feeling very upset at the same time and angry with the filmmaker because he puts across the boys' experience and the men's experience but it isn't real. It is pretending to be something. And I know this because of the girl. They just drop her in the middle just like that. She is the bravest character and then suddenly she is a nothing, a pathetic woman who needs to be saved by someone who looks much younger and weaker than her. . . . I could honestly say I had stopped enjoying the film, I was no longer gripped, I was just embarrassed and depressed. I recognized this kind of film immediately like the one where there is a happy ending because finally the African boy can marry the white girl—Romeo and Juliet—while apartheid continues around them.

While her comment that the film is "pretending" to an authenticity of experience that it fails to represent strikes a chord with earlier critiques, the most poignant of all here is T's sense of the ways in which sites of struggle and oppression are erased in similar ways in countries like India and South Africa as neoliberal economic policies are entrenched by the elites. Her second point too, that the film may seem to play fair in representing some poorer Indian boys and men, but that it does so at the expense of poor Indian girls and women, speaks to the experience of a number of other women viewers. T's commentary intimates that insiderhood can transcend nationality and ethnicity, as well as age, class, and place. Also, her sense of an ending that does not match the beginning and that undermines the avowed motives for the film's initial representations of slum life has been picked up by other critics (see Beck 2009).

DISCUSSION

When we encounter *Slumdog Millionaire* through its re/viewers, a number of discourses on film style and social authenticity emerge. Listening to interviews such as the one with T, I am acutely aware of the fact that many of us seem to be taking this film very *seriously*, as if it represents an intervention in politics rather than "mere entertainment." Looking back through the transcripts and notes to find instances of people who had watched the film as "mere entertainment," I discovered one or two, but these were exceptions. In my study, most viewers' accounts revolved around meanings connected both to their own experiences of reality and of film, and to their preexisting ideological frameworks. In most cases, these are deeply political—whether with reference to cultural politics and globalization, or to the politics of religion, gender, and social justice. So, what if anything do these re/viewers tell us about films such as *Slumdog Millionaire* and about film more generally? Are insiders critical and outsiders complimentary?

Looking across the group of viewers in this study, an intersection of cultural knowledge and social class clearly inflects the ways in which this particular film's depictions and stylistic features are enjoyed or rejected. In tandem, there are evident connections between the ways in which respondents encounter films collectively and the ways in which they allow themselves to feel and make meaning at an individual level. Partly because they are keenly aware that some re/viewers experience *Slumdog Millionaire* as an entertaining but authentic account of social reality in impoverished urban India—a spicy, modern ethnographic film—others recoil from it. On a similar note, whether or not the film sets itself up as "feel-good movie of the year (2008)," the fact that it made millions by representing the gravest poverty emphasizes its hypocrisy and inadequacy for some viewers. Most of these critics, and the unimpressed, detached, or neutral viewers, could be described as cultural "insiders" in relation to Hindi cinema and to this film's subject matter. And yes, this is a simplistic and perhaps misleading description in the world of popular cultural consumption.

Even working with such a simple notion of insiders and outsiders as an axis along which to code a range of perceptions and declarations about the content and form of *Slumdog Millionaire*, it is possible to see that vis-à-vis the film there are a range of different ways of being an insider or an outsider. Clearly, knowledge of street life and poverty counts as one type of "insider" experience; while knowledge of the conventions of cinema generally, and Hindi cinema more specifically, counts as a very different type of "insider" knowledge. Knowledge and experience of poverty or working-class life differ in the West and in India, in ethnic minority communities in the West and amongst communities in locations such as Bangladesh or South Africa. The commonalities between these experiences, however, appear to be a factor connecting a sizable portion—perhaps twenty viewers—of participants in my study who, for various reasons, recognize and feel connected to or recognize but distance themselves from the representation of the children's experiences in *Slumdog Millionaire*. The children who act in the film were seen as one of the film's most praiseworthy features even by less enthusiastic viewers. Overlapping this knowledge, but quite different from it, is experience of Hindi films and filmmaking. A smaller proportion of my respondents had such accumulated fan, producer, or viewer experience, and almost uniformly, they were less congratulatory about, and thus less enamored of, the film. Basically, they could take it or leave it. One could see this as a more sophisticated view of the film that positions it accurately between Hollywood and Bollywood. But this is not the whole story. Simply thinking of those with more or greater knowledge and experience on which to base judgments about "authenticity" does not do justice to this or any other film.

Quite understandably, a number of viewers spoke about how they were engaged by aspects or sequences of the film but were skeptical about the neatness of the ending. The lack of solidarity and the shallowness of the success depicted was pleasing for some while irritating to others. As one viewer put it: "Feel-good film? The ending was the only feel-good aspect of the film and I hated it." The number of different positions from which pleasure and entertainment are experienced and constructed in relation to the film is at once constrained and multiplied by its public (marketing) and critical context. Those who might simply have dismissed the film as good or bad entertainment engaged more fully with its narrative and representations because it was a commercial and critical success. The opinions most heard in the public debate about *Slumdog Millionaire* were generally not particularly nuanced—and regardless of what they said, they helped to market the film. However, viewer discussions of the film outside the limelight elicit critiques about life and cultural production that would not otherwise have been made.

CONCLUSION

Discourses around the ethnicity of *Slumdog Millionaire*'s director, which played a role in polarizing opinion and drove yet more viewers to see the film, are ultimately not the primary concern of most viewers in the study discussed here. Ethnicity itself or rather some particular, essential Western and non-Western way of viewing did not stand out as much during in-depth discussions as it threatened to in media sound bites or in the early reviews of the film. Representation, however, proved to be an issue that could not be sidestepped. Discussions of representation—which included both overt and more guarded questions about ways of seeing the world—provided a focal point for those viewers interested in gender, ethnicity, and justice, as well as globalization, poverty, and childhood. Although the group of viewers in this paper is too small to provide any statistically significant pointers with regard to gender and reception, it may be interesting that only women interviewees commented on the misrepresentation of women by the film and decried the pathetic excuse for a woman character. Few interviewees, however, failed to comment on the child actors as one of the film's avowed strengths. The film takes a group of disenfranchised people—impoverished children—who are by and large given meager space in either fiction or nonfiction media or in civic life and acknowledges their existence. Whatever the film's failings in representation and emotion, and whatever one's anxieties about the increasing links between visibility in the media and a consideration of the group's human rights, being portrayed in fiction is not necessarily a bad thing for the millions of children falling into this category.

To expand on this, growing up without ever seeing yourself or someone like you represented coherently in any fictional cultural form—particularly at a historical moment when cultural representations circulate via the most ubiquitous technologies and almost all leisure is given over to their consideration—has many possible consequences, psychological, social, and educational. bell hooks (2009) passionately describes some of these consequences in her piece on Black female spectators of Hollywood films in the 1950s and 1960s. I have written elsewhere (Banaji 2010) of the urgent need for the realistic, nuanced, and wide-ranging representations of children from different classes, communities, and locations in India. In this context, *Slumdog Millionaire*, like its (more downbeat) predecessor *Salaam Bombay* (Nair 1988), plays a role in introducing relatively psychologically coherent and appealing Indian child characters to an international audience in the context of a film that successfully negotiated, even transcended, a usually entrenched popular culture/elite culture divide. There is no doubt that *Slumdog Millionaire* could have been more emotionally realistic, respectful, and moving in its treatment of its subject. There is no doubt that many reviewers were and still are ill informed about Bollywood and about wider Indian cinema—and that they judge from positions of ignorance. But whether greater knowledge on the part of reviewers or affective engagement and respect on the part of the director would have curtailed or increased *Slumdog*'s appeal for the broad range of viewers encountering it is something that another film, and another director trialing such subject matter, will have to discover.

Returning to the question of whether *Slumdog Millionaire* lends itself more problematically than other recent popular films in the West to charges of orientalism, it is worth considering some people's tendency to view it as entertainment but also as ethnographic documentary within a broader historical and theoretical context. The reflections of several writers in Stokes and Maltby's (2004) collection, *Hollywood Abroad*, emphasize that the use of popular fiction films to "access" and gaze at "the Other" is distinctly not a one-way process, although the actual power of those who gaze and those represented on-screen varies widely in different situations and should always be borne in mind. Nezih Erdogan (2004), writing more of the whole institution of cinema rather than of individual cinematic moments in the context of conflicting national cultures and settings, argues that "wherever national culture has to articulate a difference and fantasy has to play on this difference, the distance between the object . . . and the subject must be continuously and carefully maintained and disavowed at the same time" (126). Arguably, this dialectic in opinion formation between (national, rational) self and the (exotic or despised) Other is common to ethnographic documentary and to fiction film, thus making it far less noteworthy than it might seem when some viewers apply an overtly ethnographic or sociological imagination in assessing *Slumdog Millionaire*. I suggest, then, that instead of simply accusing Danny Boyle's film of contributing to orientalist discourses—which it does at times, for a variety of reasons mentioned by viewers in this article and for some that are not—it is equally important to recognize the moments in his film and in others like it that draw us into dialogues, both real and imaginary but always political, about things and with people we never realized we hold at arm's length; and herein lies the crossover potential of the film.

REFERENCES

Ang, Ien. 1985. *Watching Dallas: Soap Opera and the Melodramatic Imagination*. London: Methuen.
Austin, Thomas. 2002. *Hollywood, Hype and Audiences: Selling and Watching Popular Film in the 1990s*. Manchester: Manchester University Press.
Banaji, Shakuntala. 2006. *Reading "Bollywood": The Young Audience and Hindi Film*. Basingstoke: Palgrave Macmillan.
———. 2008. "Fascist Imaginaries and Clandestine Critiques: Young Hindi Film Viewers Respond to Violence, Xenophobia and Love in Cross-Border Romances." In *Filming the Line of Control: The Indo-Pak Relation through the Cinematic Lens,* edited by Meenakshi Bharat and Nirmal Kumar, 1–25. New Delhi: Routledge.
———. 2010. "Adverts Make Me Want to Break the Television: Indian Children and their Audio-visual Media Environment in Three Contrasting Locations." In *South Asian Media Cultures: Audiences, Representations, Contexts,* edited by Shakuntala Banaji, 51–72. London: Anthem Press.
Barker, Martin, and Kate Brooks. 1998. *Knowing Audiences: Judge Dredd, its Friends, Fans and Foes*. Luton: University of Luton Press.
Beck, Bernard. 2009. "Angels with Dirty Faces: Who Invited *Slumdog Millionaire* and *The Visitor?*" *Multicultural Perspectives* 11(3): 146–49.
Boyle, Danny, dir. 2008. *Slumdog Millionaire*. London: Celador Films.
Buckingham, David. 1993. *Reading Audiences: Young People and the Media*. Manchester: Manchester University Press.
Dengel-Janic, Ellen. 2009. "Bringing the Slum to Your Doorstep: New Modernity in *Slumdog Millionaire*." Paper presented at the Annual Conference of the Association for the Study of the New Literatures in English, Münster, Germany, May 21–24.
Erdogan, Nezih. 2004. "The Making of Our America: Hollywood in a Turkish Context." In *Hollywood Abroad: Audiences and Cultural Exchange,* edited by Melvyn Stokes and Richard Maltby, 121–35. London: BFI.
hooks, bell. 2009. *Black Looks: Race and Representation*. Illustrated ed. London: Turnaround.
Kitzinger, Celia. 1989. "The Regulation of Lesbian Identities: Liberal Humanism as Social Control." In *Texts of Identity,* edited by John Shotter and Kenneth J Gergen. London: Sage.
Lau, Lisa. 2009 "Re-Orientalism: The Perpetration and Development of Orientalism by Orientals." *Modern Asian Studies* 43(2): 571–90.
MacDougall, David. 1995. "The Subjective Voice in Ethnographic Film." In *Fields of Vision: Essays in Film Studies, Visual Anthropology and Photography,* edited by Leslie Devereaux and Roger Hillman, 217–55. Berkeley: University of California Press.
Mankekar, Purnima. 1999. *Screening Culture, Viewing Politics: An Ethnography of Television, Womanhood and Nation in Postcolonial India*. Durham, NC: Duke University Press.

Martinez, Wilton. 1992. "Who Constructs Anthropological Knowledge? Towards a Theory of Ethnographic Film Spectatorship." In *Film as Ethnography*, edited by Peter Crawford and David Turton, 130–61. Manchester: Manchester University Press.
Nair, Mira, dir. 1988. *Salaam Bombay*. New York: Cinecom Pictures.
Pink, Sarah. 2001. *Doing Visual Ethnography: Images, Media and Representation in Research*. London: Sage.
Said, Edward. 1978. *Orientalism*. London: Routledge & Kegan Paul. Reprint, London: Penguin Classics, 2003.
Shotter, John, and Kenneth J. Gergen, eds. 1989. *Texts of Identity*. London: Sage.
Staiger, Janet. 2000. *Perverse Spectators: The Practices of Film Reception*. New York: New York University Press.
Stokes, Melvyn, and Richard Maltby, eds. 2004. *Hollywood Abroad: Audiences and Cultural Exchange*. London: BFI.

Note

A version of this chapter first appeared in the journal 'Participations' in 2010 (volume 7, issue 1).

11 *Control Room*
Film and Websites

Emanuelle Wessels

THEORETICAL GROUNDINGS

This project's approach to film spectatorship takes an initial cue from Emmanuel Levinas's thoughts on visual ethics. For Levinas, the event that breaks the closed loop of totality—the subject's bounded ego—is the face. Levinas's notion of the face contains an element of excess, a component that eludes total capture, recognition, or understanding by the perceiving ego. The face, according to Levinas (1969), "resists possession . . . resists my powers" (187). For Levinas, a first ethics is rooted in one's encounter with the face. The face is a construct, a discursive visuality, which, figuratively, by revealing itself, speaks ethical obligation to the subject to respect the Other as self.

Levinas (1969) distinguishes the encounter with the face from typical visual experiences, asking, "How does the epiphany as a face determine a relationship different from that which characterizes all our sensible experience?" (187). For Levinas, part of the difference lies in the face's impact on perception as something distinct from the conventional visual process of taking outside phenomena as objects. The encounter with the face is distinct from the process of subsumption, for such an instance brings the consciousness of the perceiver into contact with a sense of absolute alterity, which escapes the mind's attempt to take it as an object. In encountering alterity from outside, the subject cannot wholly represent it, ascribe it fixed and certain meaning, and make it completely intelligible or sensible. There is a sense of the unknowable, and this sense is necessary for an ethical encounter to occur. I cannot fully comprehend or understand what I see, and this element that escapes "my powers" is what I must respect. Discourse, then, serves as a bridge that hails the Other as a self, for "speech cuts across vision" (Levinas 1969, 194) to alter the relationship from the typical encounter between a mind and its object.

Utilizing a Levinasian ethic to analyze film viewing and engaged spectatorship is especially productive when dealing with films that deal with moral issues. Ann Kaplan (2005) understands the ethical spectator vis-à-vis film viewing as a witness. The cinematic witness views the Other from an open place, resisting the desire to interpret or categorize them under some framework, subsuming them into the subject's ego (see Oliver 2001). The look of the witness is empathetic. This mode of looking and encountering difference has been used to argue for the ethical and political importance of viewing atrocity from a standpoint of morality and shared humanity; commonality is seen as rooted in the precariousness of life and the potential for human suffering (see Durham Peters 2005). Adopting witnessing as a way of theorizing film viewing is productive insofar as it offers an alternative to understanding spectatorship as a passive and ideologically fraught process, while also taking ethical responsibility for others into account. Traditional psychoanalytic film theory has, from its inception, understood the medium of film as defining the ways in which viewing subjects were sutured into ideological operations by ways of symbolic identification (see Metz 1974). Ethical witnessing, as an approach to film spectatorship, focuses on how the viewer is enjoined to experience events and emotions in the film. This mode of viewing, then, resists ego-centric identification and shifts the register of response from ego identification to a more affective, presymbolic manner of making sense of events. Witnessing, as a mode of spectatorship, trades primarily in presymbolic affects, not representations.

Ethical witnessing functions as the precursor to "response-able" witnessing, a notion that demands political responsibility to act. As John Durham Peters (2005) discusses, witnessing is enabled by access to information and exposure. Seeing in this way need not be understood as beholding and contributing to spectacle (see Debord 1999) but as accessing the information necessary to take further action. Durham Peters, for example, argues that viewing disturbing material can prompt a subject to clarify his or her ethical values. He adds, "Exposure to suffering is an excellent test case for the notion, so central to the liberal project, that consorting with the dark can be ethically inspiring" (Durham Peters 2005, 205). For the viewing of suffering to inspire ethical response, it must "bear a moral witness, not produce an aesthetic spectacle" (Durham Peters 2005, 222). It must present information factually and offer possibilities for closing the distance between observer and observed. Ethical witnessing must force an encounter with the face of the Other—for Levinas a discursive and visual event—and it must resist reifying them into a spectacle. It is from within this framework that this project begins. Although witnessing has been explored as a model to study new takes on active viewing, the ways in which audience participation intersects with the primary text has been underexamined from the perspective of the possibilities of ethical viewing and spectatorship. It is from this standpoint that this project begins its examination of *Control Room* and the interactive platforms with which it converges.

CONTROL ROOM AND "RESPONSE-ABLE" WITNESSING

Control Room is a documentary film directed by Egyptian-American filmmaker Jehane Noujaim (2004) and coproduced by the U.S. production company Magnolia Films and Noujaim's independent production company,

Noujaim Films. Since the film, Noujaim has won an award from the nonprofit organization TED (Technology, Entertainment, Design), and launched the project Pangea Day, a 2008 film festival event designed to fulfill the director's great wish to "unite the world through film" (*Pangea Day* 2012). Noujaim (2006), in her TED Prize Wish speech, stated her hope for "global acceptance of diversity, mediated through the power of film." *Control Room*, which was the starting point and inspiration for Noujaim's subsequent endeavors, is shot from U.S. Central Command headquarters in Qatar, where journalistic coverage of the wars takes place. CNN, MSNBC, and the BBC all have offices at Central Command, and Al Jazeera is located twenty miles away. *Control Room* follows the goings on at Central Command, interviews reporters for Al Jazeera and U.S. military personnel, covers press announcements, and documents reactions and responses in the newsroom to the bombings in Iraq. *Control Room* is guided by questions including perceptions of Al Jazeera around the world, possibilities and limitations of journalistic objectivity regarding the war in Iraq, and Arab-world reactions to the U.S.-led wars in the Middle East, September 11, and the coverage of these events by Western outlets.

Control Room is notable for many textual features, particularly insofar as they attempt to produce and activate a globally aware, responsible witnessing viewer. The first is the complete absence of narration from Noujaim or anyone else, which creates the look of a passive camera. As John Durham Peters (2005) states, "Playing dumb can reveal the stupidity of those who presume to know best" (273). Noujaim's silent presence and observant, yet disengaged camera are aesthetic strategies that situate the film, and by extension the viewing position offered by it, as an ethical witness primed to respond. Absence of narration denies narrative closure by ostensibly refusing to interpret events and thus supplies viewers with access to a scene, a situation, and an event.

Control Room uses these techniques to situate its viewer as an observant witness and a rational subject evaluating arguments and reasoning *within* the film, not one processing arguments from the film itself. In one scene, for example, Noujaim films a debate between Lieutenant Josh Rushing, a U.S. soldier, and Hassan Ibrahim, an Al Jazeera journalist. The exchange is filmed in a series of longer shots, several seconds each, preferring pans and zooms over quick cuts and lacking music, narration, or postproduction effects. The camera ostensibly does not interpret or manipulate the facts; it simply observes them, thereby performing its technical recording device function in a manner similar to how Durham Peters understands the mechanical nature of the witness. "Passivity," Durham Peters (2005) explains, "is another source of believable witnessing. Mechanical witnesses can be preferable to smart ones" (251). This semiotic element, through conveying a disengaged look, disarticulates the recording device from the interpretive choices and actions of a filmmaker. In doing so, viewers are hailed to understand the events recorded as preexisting the selection and deflection in which journalism and documentation engage. In arranging the shot in this manner, Noujaim produces the look of the detached witness, seeing events from a "neutral" standpoint from which they can make ethical determinations. In the absence of someone telling them what to do with these "facts," viewers must ascertain on their own how to respond to them, how to take the revelation into account. A detached camera folds neatly into this system, producing a look of disengaged engagement.

Textually, *Control Room* positions its viewer as a subject capable of crossing over, of encountering the face of the Other. Through their detachment, and the degree of "control" that the film deliberately abdicates, a witnessing viewer is produced. Primed to evaluate both sides objectively, this viewer is positioned to be able to "cross over" from one side to the other, respecting the other opinion, while simultaneously performing robust, factual evaluation. Viewers are not goaded into initially identifying with one side or the other because identification would undo the witnessing event. In this sense, *Control Room* does crossover work on the narrative level through its technical and aesthetic choices. Through the silent filmmaker and calm camera, *Control Room* quietly shepherds its viewers into a position from which they can "cross over" to the other side and see a perspective other than their own.

This film hails viewers as ethical witnesses by way of the detached subject and its commitment to notions such as democracy, objectivity, rationality, and fairness. Early in the film, journalist Samer Khader states that the project of Al Jazeera is to contribute to the function of democracy by cultivating "respect for the other opinion." *Control Room* invites its witnesses to link events on their own and to draw conclusions from the incongruity present in the gaps between the images. The sense of responsibility cultivated by the film aligns with the notion of cosmopolitan citizenship discussed by Martha Nussbaum. Cosmopolitan citizenship derives from automatic birthright membership in "the community of human argument and aspiration that is truly great and truly common . . . It is this community that is, fundamentally, the source of our moral obligations" (Nussbaum 1996, 7). The work that this film does mobilizes the cosmopolitan citizen through its enactment of pastoral power, with the film as a witness in its own right playing the role of the pastor shepherding its flock of viewers into the channels of proper ethical citizenship. The notion of pastoral power as a rationale for citizen governance has been utilized by contemporary scholars to analyze the didactic role of instructional YMCA films (Greene 2005). Channels into which ethical energies can be shepherded materialize in the networked nodes of the web spaces into which *Control Room*'s narrative aims to cross over, where viewers are invited to do ethical work both on themselves and in the service of the global human community.

CROSSING OVER: *CONTROL ROOM'S* MULTIPLATFORM PRESENCE

Control Room's website is first mentioned in the credits at the end of the film. The website contains a myriad of additional content, including an interview with the director; articles about Al Jazeera and *Control Room*; links to Al Jazeera English, CNN, and Central Command; and a form to fill out for volunteer opportunities. Website users must remain aware that they are watching and operating media technologies—changing channels and looking at screens by pushing buttons on their computer or phone. Using the little graphics of televisions foregrounds the apparatus of viewing, producing an awareness of the passivity involved in being immobilized in front of a screen. Leaving the *Control Room* space allows the witness to build linkages with content bundled by this platform in a manner that creates similarity and nodal network connectivity. Manuel Castells's (2004) notion of network is useful to discuss this multiplatform transmedia event, to paraphrase Henry Jenkins (2006). Castells points out that a network is composed of a series of interconnected nodes, lacking a center, with nodes being of varying degrees of importance to the network. *Control Room* enjoins viewers to engage and participate in their own self-work of becoming ethical, cosmopolitan citizens. In this sense, it is best understood as more of an interconnected network than a discrete text. Hailed by the text as ethical cosmopolitan citizens and witnesses, viewers enter participatory media invited, not told, to "see for themselves" what Al Jazeera is all about. *Control Room*'s interactive space disavows the viewer of an unethical viewing position, further building an ethical witness responsive to "both sides" of the issue; one who can respond to the matter of war and humanity without defaulting to an oppositional mentality or preset ideological script. Crossing over and empathizing with the Other—what Levinas understood as encountering the face—is productive of an affective shock. In addition to Levinas's work, this reading is indebted to the notion of affect as theorized by Gilles Deleuze (1990), which posits that affect is a presymbolic, primary experience that does not signify, yet is felt profoundly and jarringly in the body. Applying sound reasoning to affective shock is to result in ethical awareness; this entails the transformation of the witnessing event into a subject position. The affective shock of the face arrests the viewer at the moment of witness. From there, the viewer must choose where and how to route this affect. Choosing the interactive channels offered by the film—its crossover spaces—enables the completion of the constitution of interactive subjects into cosmopolitan citizens.

Interactive, crossover spaces are the sites in which *Control Room*'s pastoral power is actualized through its formation of witnessing affect into cosmopolitan subjectivity. The "volunteer" tab of the site, where viewers are asked to provide contact information to sign up for local volunteer opportunities, is paired with clips on the little television (in an Arab home) where an American and Al Jazeera journalist discuss possibilities for journalistic objectivity when both sides hold political opinions on the wars. With this tab, viewers are hailed to contribute their labor to advancing the scope and reach of the primary film text. *Control Room* mobilizes audience participation as volunteer work, a type of viewer/user involvement directly predicated on the film's "do something" ethos that flows from the position of ethical, responsible witnessing. The website comprises the channels and pathways into which affects produced by the film are to be routed. *Control Room*'s pastoral power shepherds active viewers into manners of interactivity conducive to the cultivation of global citizenship and ethically responsible behavior enabled by the film's crossing into other platforms and opportunities for engagement. By being called to see through the screen as a window to the other side, witnesses are put to work by being asked to register their support in a carefully legitimated manner.

In the "Interview" section of the website, Noujaim sums up the goal of presenting inclusivity and balance as deriving from her own hybridized subjectivity as an Egyptian-American "growing up and going back and forth in two worlds; gaining different perspectives on events." Noujaim, through her self-identification as a subject used to crossing back and forth between "two worlds," writes her subjectivity and personal experience with crossing over into the convergent terrain that *Control Room* traverses, supplying added credibility from her persona. She explains that the goal of *Control Room* is to foster dialogue between the West and the Middle East regarding September 11 and the subsequent wars, a mission inextricable from journalistic aims and the presentations of events from multiple perspectives. This is important, Noujaim explains, for "how are people supposed to communicate if basic perspectives on the world are different?" ("Control Room Movie" 2012). Whereas Noujaim's voice was absent from the film, it is audible in the space of the website. Faith in dialogue is an organizing principle that defines the ethic of *Control Room*'s witness. Engaging in antiwar dialogue, from this standpoint, defines the political action built into the interactive space.

Hyperlinks to *Control Room*'s press coverage provide participants with access to reviews, interviews at DemocracyNow.org and Salon.com, which further build on the statements and standpoints made about the film in the tabs. The first interactive feature, a digital graphic of an older-model television and remote control supplies a trailer for the movie with embedded reviews. One, from the UK newspaper the *Independent*, praises the film as "a transformative work of political art that will change the way you view the world forever." Through this platform, reviews are selected and presented that allow the viewer, through their participant activities, to quickly and immediately access preaggregated information that invites them to confront the film with a prefigured viewing experience: that which is transformative, radically altering, unprecedented. The website, in this sense, prefigures the film and offers a properly disciplined interpretation of it. The "response-able" witness is not merely positioned by the film, she or he emerges out of the interaction of film plus website. No longer involved with a singular, centralized text, spectators are activated across a network of nodes, each containing a different component of the cultural story and speaking to one another in various ways.

What I ultimately wish to argue is that there is an ethically palpable dimension to the interactive work invited by the platforms into which

Control Room crosses over. In addition to structuring a witnessing viewing experience and supplying the techniques of citizen self-governance, the crossover properties of *Control Room* expand its purview and reach of reception, as well as offering hope that ethical witnessing has indeed been activated as a mode of reception. The latter possibility is evidenced by perusing user comments offered online, a feature enabled and supported by YouTube (a platform that plays a substantial role in distributing and exhibiting Noujaim's work). By opening up the project to a multiplicity of channels, Noujaim greatly increases the possibilities for the film's reach and reception, as well as gently shepherding the reception through her own ethical lens and mission of cultivating cosmopolitan citizenship. This is achieved, in part, through the broadcasting of her TED Talk, endeavors with Pangea Day, and allowing the entire film to remain accessible via YouTube. As I demonstrate in the next section, these ancillary projects link up to *Control Room* in important ways. They inhabit, if you will, the same discursive universe, and exemplify another sense in which possibilities for reception are both opened and carefully structured through the film's crossing over into convergent, interactive multimedia platforms.

CONVERGENCE, CROSSOVER, AND *CONTROL ROOM*: EXPLORING RECEPTION

Noujaim's 2006 TED Prize speech is available in video form on TED's website (http://www.ted.com). TED then uploaded the video onto YouTube. In the talk, Noujaim opens with a statement of her dream to "unite the world through film." She goes on to explain that this mission entails facilitating the ability of people to "travel" and "meet each other" in a virtual context, through the act of seeing film (Noujaim 2006). Recognizing that financial and monetary realities impose limitations on the feasibility of material, physical travel, Noujaim invests faith in the virtual as the domain in which transformative meetings, witnessing encounters with the Other, can be arranged. This intermingling of deep human emotion and technological sophistication presents exciting potential for the ethical dimensions of technology, particularly the ways in which widespread viewing of film can be productive of a global politics of peace predicated on ethical witnessing. This notion is in line with David Gunkel's (2007) injunction to "think otherwise" (10) as a strategy of escaping the notion that material and virtual are diametrically opposed, fundamentally distinct categories. He explains, "Virtual realism is described as a new, third term that would overcome the mere difference of network idealism and naive realism and, at the same time, preserve their differences in a careful balancing of one against the other" (Gunkel 2007, 10).

Noujaim, in her TED Talk, advocates precisely this sort of virtual realism, offering the hope that transformative, ethical encounters with the Other can be meaningfully achieved through cinematic spectatorship. Not only does her project strive to cross boundaries and borders of self and Other, but it also flows between material and virtual, as the two swirl together, enabling encounters and possibilities for reception and awareness. Freeing the virtual domain from its "Othered" status, in this sense, supplies a language through which film viewership can be discussed as a deeply meaningful and transformative act, and certainly not subservient to material travel and meeting. Noujaim backs up this philosophy throughout her talk. It is clear throughout that she believes deeply in the power of pictures, as she shows her audience a slide show of her favorite photographs of Donna, an exchange student that her family hosted years ago. Looking at the photos of Donna reminds Noujaim again and again of the need to *see* Others—not as objects or spectacles, but as expressions of difference to be respected, as the embodiment of potential for growth. In these moments she is reiterating Levinas's ethical injunction to encounter the face of the Other. After sharing photos from an early shoot in Cairo, Noujaim turns her attention to *Control Room*, which, as her first film, was the catalyst for her awakening to the power of cinema. Noujaim states in the talk that she has delivered the video to her audience to view prior to the talk and appears happy that a number of them have indeed viewed it prior to the assembly. "Some of you watched it!" she exclaims, sounding a bit relieved. Noujaim then shows several extended clips from the film, supplying additional narration that puts it into context with her larger mission of uniting the world through film by using the medium as an opportunity to foster encounters and virtual dialogue with those having different views (Noujaim 2006).

Noujaim's use of *Control Room* in her TED Talk extends the virtual scope of the film by sending it into more nodes of the network, thereby increasing its reception. The space of film reception has been redefined through this act. Not merely confined to the movie theater or even the couch, the audience of *Control Room* now includes the TED Talk audience, as well as everyone who watches the TED video from TED's website or on YouTube. From a reception standpoint, this is significant because as theater attendance has declined, home viewing has increased, and digital files comprise a bigger piece of the reception puzzle. A film's virtual life can, thanks to the speed, transferability, and portability inherent in digital technologies, be substantially lengthened (see Klinger 2006; Rodowick 2007). Noujaim's willingness to creatively utilize digital platforms to increase *Control Room*'s reception speaks to, on some level, the significance of film's crossing over into online spaces. The TED talk has more than 132,000 views on TED's website, and hosts a number of comments indicating that the mode of reception structured and encouraged by Noujaim has been adopted by the audiences. One comment, from Honghai Lee, praises the talk, stating:

> Connect people through the power of movie, i agree. And if her wish come true, "MOVIE DAY" like Christmas, will make a difference in creating some new movements. Specially us, china. We maybe need this

kind of "DAY," to connect people to know truth what the govement [*sic*] really done, to stand up to make some change. (Noujaim 2006)

Lee's comment was posted on August 3, 2012—more than eight years after the film was released. This extended virtual life, enabled by its crossing over into online formats, is indicative of one way in which digital platforms can effectively open and extend possibilities for reception, viewing, and audience activity and interaction. *Control Room* certainly enjoyed respectable success in its initial run. It grossed more than US$2 million, a robust fiscal gain in proportion to its $60,000 budget. It was initially released at the Sundance Film Festival and traversed the art-house cinema circuit in the United States and the cinemas of numerous countries in the Middle East (Solomon 2004). It cannot be ignored, however, that this was a small film with a limited release. The domain of the virtual, however, acts as a powerful supplement that extends this scope, while offering possibilities for viewer interaction and participation that are conducive to the mission and goals of the film. In this sense, the film's crossing over into the Internet ought to prompt scholars to rethink our definition of what constitutes film exhibition, as well as continue to look to the output of interactive viewers who "talk back"—input which can supply valuable insight into whether the viewing position produced by the film is a tenable one.

YOUTUBE AND TECHNOLOGIES OF WITNESSING

Control Room's appearances in interactive media spaces are not limited to the TED site. It has established a toehold in a highly popular Internet space—YouTube. Not only is the TED Talk available for viewing on YouTube, but the full-length *Control Room* film is there as well. As a relatively new, and highly complicated, cultural technology, YouTube has been difficult for scholars to get a handle on in terms of cultural significance, contribution to democracy, implications for capitalism, and other issues. Aaron Hess, for example, has argued that, although YouTube shows some promise as a technology with potential to reinvigorate the public sphere in virtual form, conventions endemic to its use as a platform, including dissemination of silly viral videos, flaming and name-calling, and overall lack of seriousness, significantly constrain this potential. Hess (2009) cites anonymity and lack of governmental oversight and regulation as the main culprits for these problems. Others are more cautiously optimistic. Burgess and Green, for example, suggest that, as an "accidental archive," YouTube's relatively open, accessible, and easy-to-use format enables a panoply of participation practices that may have been previously off limits to a variety of uses, such as people with disabilities (Burgess and Green 2009, 141). YouTube, perhaps, fills a gap for these groups that the culture industry—and its "mainstream" channels of media distribution—has left open. The argument that interactive, "new" media platforms have the potential to enrich democratic participation did not, of course, begin with YouTube. Jenkins (2006) and McLeod (2005) have suggested that bottom-up, grassroots cultural participation should be encouraged as modes of creative and engaged cultural citizenship. Others are more skeptical, suggesting that interactive practice has been effectively annexed by capitalism as a new form of pleasurable, digitally oriented free labor (see Terranova 2004; Andrejevic 2007). The nuances of this debate, while significant, are outside the scope of this chapter. Rather, in analyzing the role of YouTube in Noujaim's project, I wish to focus on the sense in which the platform does, in the manner suggested by Burgess and Green, effectively fulfill its function as an alternative channel of distribution, thus broadening the scope of *Control Room*'s reception. Further, as demonstrated by user comments, and the way in which Noujaim carefully marshals YouTube as a platform of distribution, the stated ethical mission of *Control Room* is preserved as it crosses over into another space of the Internet. In this sense, this project concludes not so much with an end or final word, but with a possible starting point for future work on cinema and viewing, interactivity, and convergent technologies.

YouTube moves the "top comments" to the top of the page based on ratings from other users. The top comments for Noujaim's TED Talk include the following two posts. The first, from user thunderbrow, reads: "Absolutely brilliant. So wonderful when technology is used for benefit of all life. Peace be with you all." Another, by nofx2211984, says that "it is a shame that more people don't subscribe to this channel. We need this sort of involvement when it comes to the sharing of thought" ("Jehane Noujaim" 2008). Although this user is right to point out that the TED Talks are certainly not as numerically popular as more "standard" YouTube fare—viral videos and the like—it is nonetheless important that *Control Room* continues to enjoy a long virtual life in this space. Although the views and comments are not in the millions, a good number of them, especially the top-rated ones, indicate that Noujaim's ideal, ethical viewer has indeed been successfully produced by the *Control Room* narrative. Moreover, significantly, these viewers are engaging virtually, posting comments and engaging with other users; these are modes of interactive participation that further structure and facilitate the desired reception and engagement with *Control Room*, thereby engaging in robust, ethical debate and dialogue with those who hold different views. This uptake of reception can be found upon examination of *Control Room*'s exhibition on YouTube, where it is permanently accessible in its entirety. Available in nine parts, *Control Room*'s segments have between 7,000 and 27,000 views on YouTube. The top-rated comments, like the ones that follow the TED Talk, indicate an overall positive reception of the film. Moreover, there is a pattern amongst the comments of lively debate between the YouTube users concerning the issues presented in the film, which is conducive to the project of the film and supports the notion that the type of viewer positioned by it has been activated. For example, following the third segment of the film, two highly rated commenters discuss the culpability of the United States in the Iraq war. Their exchange is as follows:

> The American people and the American government are two different things. People need to stop saying Americans are power hungry, Americans are bad people. You do not know us, you know what you hear about our Government on TV. Most of us are just as outraged with this war as you are, we just want our loved ones home. Think about that before you start talking about how awful we are as people.

Response:

> But this applies to ALL nations not just america, governmens [sic] are meant to be public servans [sic]! what are they in reality? the truth is rumsfeld u r one of the bggest [sic] war criminals on earth, just like u treat your prisoners mr bush? Gitmo? but tying iraqi prisoners n walking them like dogs NP we are the nation of the free, lies to shame even the devil by the "honourable politicians" wheather [sic] ameicans [sic] iraqis or whatever politics stings bloody lying crooks running the world no wonderppl [sic] hate politics. ("Control room-aljazeera-part 3" 2008)

What is promising about this interaction is that, despite palpable frustrations with the issues presented and differing views, these two interactive viewers are able to engage in a dialogue about the content consumed without resorting to name-calling, flaming, or other activities that Hess argues fundamentally inhibit the potential for YouTube to function as a virtual public sphere. Like Rushing and Ibrahim, these two commenters have been activated by the witnessing stance of *Control Room* and moved to utilize its interactive, crossover qualities to robustly engage with difficult issues.

CONCLUSION

The analysis presented in this chapter explores how viewer energies can be produced and mobilized through a film's interaction with the spaces of participation. In the case of *Control Room*, such a convergence works in accordance with the filmmaker's ethical imperative. I have shown that Noujaim's projects, through the working of pastoral power and commitment to cosmopolitan citizenship, activate an ethical witness and supply, through digital technologies that intersect with the film, opportunities to actualize this ethical stance.

Although we must, of course, remain careful to guard against naive optimism, it is my hope that investigating this small slice of crossover cinema has provided some insight into the ways in which thinking of active viewership though the lens of ethical responsibility, and interrogating the extent to which participatory technologies can support this perspective, is useful when continuing to examine the political and ethical potential and the stakes of viewing film. Perhaps Noujaim's goal of uniting the world through film is not that far-fetched—interactive spaces could further support, and be mobilized in the service of, actualizing this goal. *Control Room*'s crossover is certainly not the last word on this process. Instead, it gestures to a starting point for thinking of new directions for scholars studying film viewership, interactivity, and subjectivity.

REFERENCES

Andrejevic, Mark. 2007. *I Spy: Surveillance and Power in the Interactive Era*. Lawrence: University of Kansas Press.
Burgess, Jean, and Joshua Green. 2009. *YouTube: Online Video and Participatory Culture*. New York: Polity.
Castells, Manuel. 2004. *The Network Society: A Cross-Cultural Perspective*. Northhampton, MA: Edward Elgar Publishing.
"Control room-aljazeera-part 3." 2008. YouTube video, 9:29. Excerpt from Jehane Noujaim, dir., *Control Room*, 2004, posted by sameeh86, February 28, http://www.youtube.com/watch?v = T6aaRieWr2Q&feature = relmfu.
"Control Room Movie." 2012. *Noujaim Films*. http://www.noujaimfilms.com/. Accessed August 30, 2012.
Debord, Guy. 1999. *The Society of the Spectacle*. New York: Zone Books.
Deleuze, Gilles. 1990. *The Logic of Sense*. Translated by Mark Lester. New York: Columbia University Press.
Durham Peters, John. 2005. *Courting the Abyss: Free Speech and the Liberal Tradition*. Chicago: University of Chicago Press.
Greene, Ronald Walter. 2005. "Y Movies: Film and the Modernization of Pastoral Power." *Communication and Critical/Cultural Studies* 2(1): 20–36.
Gunkel, David. 2007. *Thinking Otherwise: Philosophy, Communication, Technology*. Lafayette: Purdue University Press.
Hess, Aaron. 2009. "Resistance Up in Smoke: Analyzing the Limitations of Deliberation on YouTube." *Critical Studies in Media Communication* 26(5): 411–34.
"Jehane Noujaim: TED Prize Wish: Unite the World on Pangea Day." 2008. YouTube video, 26:24, from a TED Talk delivered in Monterey, California, February 2006, posted by "TEDtalksDirector," April 15, http://www.youtube.com/watch?v= QCFSrb6B5nw.
Jenkins, Henry. 2006. *Convergence Culture: Where Old and New Media Collide*. New York: New York University Press.
Kaplan, E. Ann. 2005. *Trauma Culture: The Politics of Terror and Loss in Media and Literature*. New Brunswick, NJ: Rutgers University Press.
Klinger, Barbara. 2006. *Beyond the Multiplex: Cinema, New Technologies, and the Home*. Berkley: University of California Press.
Levinas, Emmanuel. 1969. *Totality and Infinity: An Essay on Exteriority*. Translated by Alphonso Lingis. Pittsburg: Duquesne University Press.
McLeod, Kembrew. 2005. *Freedom of Expression®: Overzealous Copyright Bozos and Other Enemies of Creativity*. New York: Doubleday.
Metz, Christian. 1974. *Film Language*. Chicago: University of Chicago Press.

Noujaim, Jehane, dir. 2004. *Control Room*. Los Angeles: Lions Gate Home Video.
———. 2006. "Jehane Noujaim Wishes for a Global Day of Film." Filmed in February. TED video, 25:42, posted July, http://www.ted.com/talks/lang/en/jehane_noujaim_inspires_a_global_day_of_film.html.
Nussbaum, Martha. 1996. "Patriotism and Cosmopolitanism." In *For Love of Country: Debating the Limits of Patriotism,* edited by Joshua Cohen, 2–17. Boston: Beacon Press.
Oliver, Kelly. 2001. *Witnessing: Beyond Recognition*. Minneapolis: University of Minnesota Press.
Pangea Day. 2012. http://www.pangeaday.org/. Accessed August 3, 2012.
Rodowick, David Norman. 2007. *The Virtual Life of Film*. Cambridge, MA: Harvard University Press.
Solomon, Deborah. 2004. "Inside Al Jazeera: Questions for Jehane Noujaim." *New York Times,* April 25. http://www.nytimes.com/2004/04/25/magazine/25QUESTIONS.html.
Terranova, Tiziana. 2004. *Network Culture: Politics for the Information Age*. Ann Arbor, MI: Pluto.

12 *Desi* Turns Malay
Indian Cinema Redefined as Crossover in the Malaysian Market

Sony Jalarajan Raj and Rohini Sreekumar

As twenty-first-century India aspires for First World status and emerges as a global economic power, its media and cultural industries are also expanding rapidly to meet escalating domestic demands for entertainment products. In particular, Indian cinema has been one of the most visible creative industries expanding its operations to cater to an emergent Indian leisure economy. With a sizable Indian global diaspora (nonresident Indian [NRI] or people of Indian origin communities) keen to engage with the popular cultural products of India, a ready-made market exists for these products in foreign countries. Alongside this diasporic or NRI demand, there exists a complementary rising interest amongst non-Indian audiences for Indian popular cultural products like cinema—dubbed the "Slumdog effect" in reference to Danny Boyle's (2008) India-set, but not Indian-made Academy Award winner, *Slumdog Millionaire*. This transcultural reach and appeal make the reception of Bollywood in Malaysia an apt illustration of the crossover phenomenon. Before proceeding, two terms that need to be defined are *Bollywood* and the *crossover wave*. Bollywood can be categorized as a global Indian industry, "spinning the screen fantasies" of millions of fans around the world (Rajadhyaksha 2003, 25). With its unique mix of song, dance, melodrama, sentiments, and fights, it made an enormous global impact and developed into a strong brand (Lorenzen and Taeube 2007).The emerging middle class in the 1990s also placed a demand on Bollywood films as their essential entertainment media (Kaur 2002). The term *crossover* encompasses a wide range of features ranging from content and theme crossovers to production crossovers. For many years, after 1991, crossover was more or less applied to the diaspora-themed films that attract mainly the diasporic population (such as the film *Dilwale Dulhaniya Le Jayenge* [Chopra 1995]). Later on, filmmakers like Mira Nair and Gurinder Chadha, Deepa Mehta and Anoop Kurian, and other UK- and U.S.-based Indians ventured into some crossover movies made in English that served to appeal to a largely Western audience. Films like *Salaam Bombay* (Nair 1988) and *Water* (Mehta 2005) are fine examples for this trend of crossover cinema.

Desi in Hindi (the national language of India) denotes something belonging to the country. It can be used as a synonym for *indigenous*.

Though the commercial success of these films was minimal, the coverage in film festivals was enormous. However, *Lagaan* (Gowarikar 2001), a Bollywood film based on India's colonial history, was successful with a global audience outside of film festival circuits. Some years later, the film *Slumdog Millionaire* (Boyle 2008) digressed further from the diasporic definition of crossover by being a UK-financed film with an Indian codirector and stars. Hence, now the crossover film is not just defined by its audience, but its definition also includes production, distribution, and technical or artistic collaboration.

Since Southeast Asian countries form one of the largest bases for the Indian diaspora, the international consumption of Indian cinema is often associated with geolinguistic, geocultural, and georegional patterns of consumption in those regions. This chapter examines both Tamil and Bollywood films since they constitute the majority of crossover ventures out of the different regional language films of India. Malaysia serves as a distinctive example for two dynamic perspectives of crossover—Bollywood and its borderless audience, and local Tamil cinema productions (which is a recent and distinctive approach to crossover cinema in production).

Here local Tamil film production is vested with the plaque of crossover as it manifests one of the first instances in which a diasporic population ventures into making ethnic language films in their residing land. Malaysia has the highest Tamil diasporic population apart from Sri Lanka, and so, it is quite explicit that "Kollywood" (that is, Tamil language) films will enjoy popularity there. However, this article is concerned mainly with the Tamil films made in Malaysia by the diasporic population, which has also influenced non-Indians to step into this venture. Moreover, these films speak to the local population on their local issues or about their past. Though only an evolving phenomenon, it has widened the ambit of crossover films.

While the Bollywood crossover audience has been explored many times in different contextual frameworks, in Malaysia, this particular crossing over is a historical phenomenon rather than a postglobalized Bollywood trend. Since its inception, Malay cinema has displayed a certain affinity with Indian culture and the early influx of Indian directors in Malaysian cinema ensured that the content reflected Indian cinema and mythology (Van der Heide 2002). Indeed, Bollywood has been popular with Malay audiences since the 1950s because of its emphasis on movement, spectacle, melodious songs, and beautiful stars. Thus, Indian cinema in Malaysia has become more than Indian and gets redefined as a crossover cinema.

INDIAN CINEMA IN MALAYSIA: A HISTORICAL CROSSOVER

The presence of an Indian diaspora in Malaysia, many of whom originate from migrant workers recruited under colonial rule to work on tea, palm oil, and rubber plantations in the early 1890s after the abolition of slavery, can be seen as the original impetus in the success of many Bollywood (and more broadly Indian) films there (Lal 2006). Even before that, Malaysia, being an archipelago and the center of major sea routes, witnessed a constant cultural interaction as Indian traders began to settle there. This was bidirectional rather than a sort of domination, where Indian traders settled for business purposes in Malaysia, and Malay traders came back from India laden with Indian customs and cultures (Van der Heide 2002). The result was the transformation of the coastal land into "Indian-style city states, in which the ruler was defined as 'god on earth,' as the reincarnation of the Hindu gods of Shiva and Vishnu" (Van der Heide 2002, 66). The narratives of *Mahabharata* and *Ramayana*, the great epic texts of Hinduism, have thus been incorporated into the traditional art forms like *Wayang* (puppet show) and *Bangsawan*. In fact, the credit of introducing Indian movies to Southeast Asian audiences is attributed to Abdulallyi Esoofally, "the tent showman" and one of the pioneers of film exhibition/distribution in the early 1910s, who traveled through the Far East, including Burma, Ceylon, Singapore, and Indonesia, with a tent bioscope, introducing film to these regions (Burra and Rao 2006). After colonization, this cultural inspiration and invasion was even more substantial, and this led to the first film in Malaysia in 1933, *LailaMajnun* (Rajhans 1933).

A historical consideration of the Malaysian film industry is necessary since the genesis of crossover is entwined with the very history of the Malaysian film industry. The Malaysian film production sector is traditionally divided into two historical periods—the studio era (from 1947 to 1977) and the independent phase (from 1974 onward). The crossover phenomenon in Malaysia has thrived since 1933 when *Laila Majnun*, the first Malay film, was made by Indian businessman K. R. S. Chisty under the direction of B. S. Rajhans with Malay *Bangsawan* actors. Being an adaptation of the Indian movie *Laila Majnu* (Madan 1931), the Malaysian *Laila Majnun* has been described as having all the characteristics of a typical Indian film of that time, including song and dance sequences. Indeed, since its inception, Malay cinema has displayed a certain affinity with Indian culture, with Khoo (2006) noting that Indian directors in Malaysian cinema ensured that the content reflected Indian cinema and mythology. Because of this cultural affiliation and industrial familiarity, Indian films remained very popular with Malaysian audiences from then on, extending to the non-Indian population as well. Moreover, even though the studio era was dominated by two Chinese organizations, Shaw Brothers and Cathay-Keris, the films were almost always made by Indian directors like B. S. Rajhans and Lakshmana Krishnan. Besides the Indian-Malay cultural connection, Indian directors were preferred because of India's well-developed film industry, familiarity with English, and the filmmakers being less expensive to employ than Hollywood ones (Kanda 1995). Even though earlier films dealt with Indian myths and folklores, directors of major studios in Malaysia and Singapore did eventually make films based entirely on local issues and racial themes. For instance,

Rajhans's (1947) *Singapuradi Waktu Malam* deals with the problems of Malay youths leaving for the city from their kampong. Lakshmana Krishnan, an Indian-born director who is considered as the father of Malay films, started his filmic career in the Tamil industry in Chennai (then Madras) as assistant director. In 1949, he joined Malay Film Productions as its residential director. He made a local version of the 1936 Tamil film *Devdas* (Barua 1936) (based on a popular Bengali novel of the same name frequently filmed in India), called *Selamat Tinggal Kekasihku* (Krishnan 1955), but changed the class theme to an interracial love story of a Malay boy and a Chinese girl. Hence, at the earlier stage of the development of the Malaysian film industry, the films looked similar to Indian movies, yet also displayed a local flavor. Moreover, these films competed with Bollywood films from India and Chinese films from Hong Kong, with both commanding fairly good audiences. This helped the audience to be at ease with considering both the language films as their own, thereby making space for Bollywood to enjoy a similar reception ground as in its homeland.

BOLLYWOOD AND ITS MALAYSIAN AFFILIATION

The Bollywood connection with Malaysian cinema, which kicked off with *Laila Majnun*, laid a solid foundation for the success of Bollywood film in redefining itself as a crossover film in Malaysia. Even the legendary Malaysian actor and director P. Ramlee is compared to (and said to be inspired by) Bollywood classic heroes like Raj Kapoor, MGR (M. G. Ramachandran), and singer Muhammad Rafi, mainly for the romantic and melodramatic characters he enacted while taking on the role of a singer as well (Van der Heide 2002). Furthermore, the earlier Malaysian films had a tendency to adapt Bollywood-style narration and even stories. For instance, films like *Ibu Mertua-ku* (Ramlee 1962) and *Penarik Beca* (Ramlee 1955) are compared to Indian films *Deedar* (Bose 1951) and *Awara* (Kapoor 1951), respectively (Samad 1994). Alongside these historical connections, the global value attained through strategic branding already attached to the Bollywood films brings a certain global visibility to Malaysia such that the country acquires some of the brand aura, thus making its films more than foreign films. Indian film premieres, award nights, and cassette releases are spread over a number of locations, with Malaysia now a regular venue for such events. The Third International Indian Film Awards were held at Malaysia Genting Highland and Resorts, which was subsequently followed by dance nights, cassette releases, and similar events in the following years. To pick a few contemporary examples, Malaysia hosted the 2007 Zee Cine Awards, the 2002 International Indian Film Academy Awards, and dance-musical shows like *The Merchants of Bollywood* and the Zee Bollywood Night in 2012.

Apart from this, the presence of the Indian diaspora, which forms a significant section of the population and social setup of Malaysia, also serves as a crucial factor for the success of Bollywood movies. Bollywood adopts narrative structures reflective of the Hollywood model and incorporates stories that reflect the nation's transition to social and economic modernity (Vasudevan 2000). For the diaspora and the Indian population, depictions of "the shame, guilt and consequent low self-esteem associated with the poverty, corruption and caste oppression in their home country, could be replaced with strategic and economic success stories" (Kaur 2002, 200). This is the typical characteristic that makes Bollywood films different from Tamil movies, which are very much based on local issues. It can be argued that people of Indian origin in the diaspora, widely dispersed, share a similar experience while watching Indian movies, which thus contributes to the construction of a global "public culture" and an "imagined community" (Anderson 1991, 7). Scholars argue that Indian popular movies are one of the most significant and visible components of Indian popular culture both at home and in the diaspora, and that mainstream Indian movies epitomize the cultural flow of images across the globe. This, they add, is a characterizing feature of globalization, but in a direction counter to the normative West-to-East media flows. This diasporic appeal, together with the global appeal of Bollywood, makes the same a popular source of entertainment in Malaysian society.

The success and failure of any movie industry outside its homeland largely depends on the local entertainment industry with which it is competing. When compared with the Indian film industry, Malaysia's film industry is rather small (with not more than twenty-six films in 2009) and tied with stringent laws and regulations that demand 70 percent of content and dialogue to be in the national language *Bahasa Melayu*. They also require that the films adhere to noninflammatory, nonpolitical, and religiously sensitive story themes in order to get approval from the government fund. Postcolonial Malaysia initiated its own policies, like *Rukunegara* (Pillars of the nation), the New Economic Policy, and the National Cultural Policy, which postulated the formation of a national culture based on the culture of the indigenous people, that is, the Malay or *Bhumiputras*. By that time, the Malaysian state had undergone Islamic revivalism and renewal, which influenced the cultural policy. Van der Heide (2002) says, "Universities encouraged research in Malay folk arts, festivals were organized to promote traditional Malay performing arts and certain Malay popular arts were selected to exemplify traditional Malay culture" (96). There is insufficient representation of Chinese and Indian characters and cultures in contemporary Malay films, making it an ethnicity-specific film industry. For a multiracial country like Malaysia, having a substantial population of Chinese and Indians, this policy was more or less unwelcoming, yet films in both these languages continue to flourish in Malaysia. With the overwhelming influx of Hollywood, Bollywood, and Chinese movies, and the preference for Hollywood over indigenous films among Malaysian audiences, Malaysian films are in a constant struggle for audiences and international acclaim. Moreover, according to renowned Malaysian film director Amir Muhammad, the Malaysian film industry is said to be shackled by Indian culture, and the "audiences are being lulled by the specter of Indian directors' imagination" (interview with the author, 2012). At this juncture, the Malaysian local industry is struggling to produce and exhibit films in a market dominated by imported cinematic products (McKay 2011).

So there are only a few independent directors who form the third-wave directors, that is, filmmakers who come forward to experiment with new story lines. Even though a few like Yasmin Ahmad and Amir Muhammad have ventured into new story lines and multiracial themes, and have entered international film festivals, the box-office collection and viewership for these films has been negligible. This has become an ideal setting for the Bollywood movies to flourish since they are supported by huge production companies. While a strong local production culture and a sizable domestic population are beneficial to any film industry, they also provide a strong platform for export and distribution activities. This can be applied to the reception of Indian cinema in Malaysia. BIG Cinemas (Reliance) Lotus Five Star is an international cinema chain that is growing fast in Malaysia with around twenty outlets, and Bollywood superstar Shah Rukh Khan has already promised to start a studio in Malaysia. Both of these can be considered big steps toward increasing ties between Bollywood and the Malaysian film industry. To achieve more cultural accommodation, Indian films have attempted to incorporate more open and occidental views of life. For instance, Mumbai-based Reliance Big Picture's feature *Kites* (Basu 2010) became notable in the Malaysian market because it overrides cultural barriers and integrates Western culture, language, and even attire into its narrative. Such "Hollywoodizing Bollywood" films are popular in Malaysia as Hollywood itself is the largest-grossing industry at the Malaysian box office.

Bollywood is the other name for entertainment and fun, particularly for those who need a casual visual experience unlike Hollywood, which usually appeals to a serious audience because of its "high-tech spectacles" (Vieira and Stam 1985, 37). This indeed is the reason for the explosion of Bollywood film DVDs, both pirated and copyrighted, in Malaysia. As Malaysian filmmaker Muhammad Fadhil al-Akiti says, not only is the Indian channel Zee a popular media outlet, but most of the national newspapers and magazines churn out news about Bollywood films, stars, and fashion frequently (interview with the author, 2012). It is the song and dance sequences that facilitate the entertainment quest effectively as they use nonverbal communication to empathize, relate, and connect with a diverse nation, enabling "the creation of a common culture in a linguistically fragmented nation" (Gopal and Moorti 2008, 14). In this sense, the song and dance sequences in Bollywood films have become arguably one of the most powerful tools of nationalism, operating as "capillaries" through which ideas of national belonging are circulated, consumed, and reproduced (Agostino 2010). As such, Malaysia is the seat of numerous Bollywood dance schools and body workout classes, one of which is by the leading Bollywood choreographer Saroj Khan. Indeed, as already mentioned, Hindi cinema has been popular with Malay audiences since the 1950s (Van der Heide 2002). It has created an "imagined space"—a space that exists outside the parameters of realism, with musicals generating a unique space constructed from generic conventions and the inventions in choreography, sound, and cinematography (Kao and Do Rozario 2008). Often, Bollywood films are broadcast on Malaysian television channels without subtitles despite the fact that many in the Malaysian Indian community do not speak the languages of India anymore. Instead, they take pleasure in the song and dance, fetishizing them as cultural links to their own people (Manuel 1997). This entertainment value is also linked with the fashion industry that these films are promoting. According to Koya (2002):

> So obsessed the directors are with these developments that the film world soon merged with the fashion and beauty pageant industries, forming an unholy alliance to make Bollywood what it is today: an unstoppable lust-generating super-factory. Frivolity, sensuality, indecency, appalling illiteracy and endless platitude, these are the marks of Bollywood.

As a result, concept beauty parlors, wedding planners, and dance schools based on Bollywood are very popular in Malaysia, with one particular brochure reading thus:

> Ever wonder how the Bollywood actresses can achieve such radiant, flawless skin? Is it something in their skin regime or skin care, perhaps? Wonder no more as Bombay Beauty, the very first authentic Mumbai beauty parlor, is helping to solve the beauty puzzle. (Bombay Beauty Parlor 2011)

Deepak Kumaran, a Malaysian film director, opines that the Malaysian film industry faces Malay-language movie crossover content producers from India in films like *Cinta* and *Sepi* by Kabir Bhatia (2006, 2008) and *Lagenda Budak Setan* and *Diva* by Sharad Sharan (2007, 2010), which can merge funding from India and talent and content from Malaysia (interview with the author, 2012). Both of these films follow the typical Bollywood formula of youth, melodrama, and love. With the vertical integration of production, distribution, and exhibition being the key driver of U.S. cinematic success in world markets (Hoskins, McFadyen, and Finn 1997), the same phenomenon is evident in the nature of cinematic trade between India and Malaysia. Crossover takes on a new dimension when it is looked at from a business perspective, as done by Martin Jones in analyzing the mutual economic benefits between India and Scotland in making the latter a shooting location (Martin-Jones 2006). When viewed from this angle, Bollywood in Malaysia unveils an intricate relationship as it is more of a mutually benefiting business entrepreneurship built on the identity and popularity of Bollywood film stars and movies. For instance, in 2008, Shah Rukh Khan was awarded the Darjah Mulia Seri Melaka by the government of Malacca, which conferred him the title of *Datuk*, akin to the British knighthood, for indirectly promoting Malacca through six of his films. The decision to award Khan with the Datukship was received with much criticism from across the country, with local artists and the public noting that the award could have been given to a local actor or artist. However, John (2008) reported that Malaysia and the Malaccan state authorities have defended their decision, saying it earned them more publicity and tourists than sponsored advertising on any international TV channel could. Hence, this felicitation "will certainly help promote both Malaysia and Malacca" and will "be the bridge for more movies to be shot at the historical city" (Malacca chief minister; as quoted in John 2008).

If, for a star like Shah Rukh, it is a way to make a permanent base of fandom and honor in a foreign land, for Malaysia it is a boost in tourism from across the world as Khan is an international brand in his own right. Hence, the Malaysian administration seems to support Bollywood movies as a means of promoting tourism since such movies surpass geographic boundaries, even at the cost of their indigenous movies. Moreover, the Malaysian government anticipates that it will become a source of income and infrastructure for boosting local film production. Apart from the studio venture by Shah Rukh Khan and the aspirations brought about for Indian directors in making Malay movies, talents from the Malay industry are given opportunities to showcase their talent in Bollywood films like Ady Putra in *Don 2*, in which he had a minor role as an advocate.

TAMIL CINEMA

Unlike Bollywood, Tamil cinema was always inwardly focused, giving little concern to diasporic sentiments. Analyzing the history of Tamil cinema, it is quite clear that the diasporic Tamil population is almost absent and insignificant in the movies, and if they are portrayed, it may take a backseat in the development of the plot. Hence a crossover or at least a revival in theme, as Bollywood did after 1990s, is not visible in Tamil movies even though the Tamil diaspora has been widely spread across the world since before the British colonization. As Velayutham (2008) notes, since Indian Tamil films are largely based on local issues and are for local release, the overseas release is limited to a few films and a few places. Moreover, these overseas releases are restricted to Tamil audiences alone as subtitling is not common for theater releases. The trend is no different in Malaysia where the Tamil population forms the majority of the Indian diaspora. Even though Bollywood identifies Malaysia as a potential market, Tamil cinema has not yet been redefined as a major entertainment medium for the Malaysian audience. For this reason, only selected films, such as those of stars like Rajnikanth, Kamal Hassan, Ajith, and Vijay, find a place in the theaters.

This issue needs particular consideration in Malaysia as in the history of the Malaysian film industry it was the Tamil talent that reigned supreme. Whether considering the first Malaysian film director or the earlier popular directors, Tamil talent was prominent in the Malaysian film industry. Despite a strong foundation for crossover Tamil film production, the phenomenon seems to be arising only gradually.

Because of the lack of subtitles, along with the absence of a globalized theme or perspective, Tamil cinema fails to attract the borderless audience that Bollywood garners. This can be attributed to the desire for some local Tamilians to produce and view Tamil-language films in a Malay majority land. Here crossover takes an entirely new meaning where the members of a diaspora (which is a minority) venture into making films in their home language meant for local release. It is worth noting that most of the films thus made are not closed to other ethnic communities in their production and reception. Tamil-language filmmaking emerged in 1970s when Felix Anthony, a British-educated film student, produced two films, *Thun Bangal Urangu Vathillai* (Sorrow never sleeps) and *Anbe En Anbe* (My love), in a studio he set up by himself (Chen 2011). It can be said that Tamil-language production emerged simultaneously when the independent era emerged, succeeding the studio era when more Malay directors ventured into film production by setting up home studios.

This period witnessed some remakes of Indian movies in Malay by Indian directors, like *Melati Putih* (Raj 1984), a remake of Tamil movie *Pathinaru Vayathinile* (Rajaa 1977), and *Suami, Isteri da* (Pansha 1996) adapted from *Mouna Geethangal* (Bhagyaraj 1981). However, these films met with failure due to lack of funding and screening options, and little has been mentioned about them in film records.

In 1991, the first locally produced Indian movie in Malaysia, *Naanoru Malaysian* (I'm a Malaysian), hit the screens in thirty-five millimeter and made history in Tamil film production by being successful as an out-of-India Tamil venture. According to Malaysian film director Hassan Muthalib, the third-generation Indian film directors in Malaysia catered to a Malaysian audience by featuring their stories and concerns, rather than a closed artistic venture aiming at the Tamil community. The reason lies in the fact that their life span coincided with the Malaysian independence and its aftermath, and this naturally evoked a sense of patriotism and affection toward the country (Muthalib 2012). These films, hence, were never aimed at the Tamil community alone, but at Malaysians as a whole. For Malaysian Tamil directors, Tamil cinema does not represent their homeland or nostalgic imagination but is a platform for portraying their hybrid identity as Malaysians. The distinctive characteristics of Chennai-based Tamil films are adapted by Malaysian Tamil films in portraying localized themes and concerns. However, it took almost twenty-one years for the local Tamil industry to witness another thirty-five millimeter, which came out in 2010 and was titled *Appalam* (Shauki 2011) (a remake of the Malay movie *Pappadam*). With *Appalam*, for the first time, a local Tamil video compact disk (VCD) distribution was established. Even before that, many young directors actively made Tamil movies, but these remained in digital format only as television feature films and for home screenings.

The fourth-generation Tamil filmmakers, most of them well trained and educated in the field, like Deepak Kumaran, began to engage with more critical issues of the Tamil community in a diasporic land, mainly Malaysia. This can be considered as a response to mainstream Kollywood films that gave negligible space to diasporic Tamil issues. Films like *Chemman Chaalai* and *Chalanggai*, both by Deepak Kumaran (2005, 2007), and *Ethirkalam*, a telemovie, portray the trials faced by the Indian community in Malaysia. *Chemman Chaalai* (2005), which is the first Malaysian feature film made entirely in Tamil, *Ops Kossa Dappa* (Joseph 2005), and *Chalanggai* (2006) are notable not only for their reception but also for the acclaim they have received in local film festivals. For instance, while *Chalanggai* received the best digital film award at the Twentieth Malaysian Film Festival, *Chemman Chaalai* won the special jury award in the Nantes Festival in France in 2005. Interestingly, *Ops Kossa Dappa*, an action drama, set the Malaysian record for having the largest number of actors in a movie even though it was a direct-to-video movie. The movie was well received because of the involvement of two Indian actors—Priyanka Kothari and Dhandapani—as major actors in it. Hence, it can be assumed that local Tamil films began poaching mainstream Indian movie stars and technicians with the intention of being crossover films. For instance, Malaysian production house Lotus Group fully financed an Indian movie, *Muniyandi Vilangyial Moonramandu* (Thirumurugan 2008), which added further layers to the definition of the crossover phenomenon. Kollywood has identified the potential Malaysian market and the developing Malaysian local Tamil industry. The South Indian Film Artistes Association (Nadigar Sangam) has said that it will help to market the Malaysian-made movies in India, as well as provide actors and technicians from Kollywood so that it can improve the quality and the marketing of the films as the Indian audience easily accepts films with familiar faces. Making this foundation even stronger, 2011 witnessed the first Malaysian Indian film festival in Chennai, where ten local Tamil films from Malaysia made between 2001 and 2011 by Malaysians were screened (Ramli 2011).

Even though there is a slew of locally made documentaries and feature films, the limited screening options render these productions unseen and unrecognized. According to Hassan Muthalib, a Malaysian film director and academic, the main expectation from this local Tamil film production is that it will get involved on all terms with the Kollywood of Chennai, so that it has wider possibilities of international release (interview with the author, 2012). However, one name that is associated with the distribution of Tamil films, precisely classics, is Columbia Video and Films, which is the largest copyright owner of Tamil films worldwide. It has procured the license of DVDs of classic films that are not even available in India. Apart from providing Tamil films for channels like Astro Thangathirai (the exclusive Tamil movie channel), it is also dedicated to making Tamil documentaries and telemovies for Malaysian channels. The CEO of Columbia Film and Video, Christopher Ravin Thomas, says that the majority of Bollywood movies enter the Malaysian media market through informal channels like pirated DVDs from China and Nepal and illegal Internet downloads, whereas the lion's share of the Tamil movies in Malaysia are distributed by major distributors like Columbia Films and Lotus Five Star as theater releases and original DVDs, which makes those films less popular even among the Tamil diaspora (interview with the author, 2012). They play a significant role in promoting Tamil films in Malaysia, even though they say that the present-generation Tamil diasporic community in Malaysia is least interested in the classic literature and films in their language (interview with the author, 2012).

The other hurdle faced by these local Tamil industries is the unavailability of funds from either the government or the government-aided National Film Development Corporation of Malaysia. Since most of these films are independent productions or part of the Little Cinema of Malaysia, they don't always have the financial might to fight with the mainstream Malaysian films. So, most often, they are shot either with digital or personal camcorders and are meant only for television or DVD sale; hence, they are lacking in quality and financial stability. The Malaysian Indian Art Activist Association president Gana Pragasam voiced that the Tamil films or documentaries are not getting ample broadcasting space in local channels and that these channels must allocate private production companies to produce documentaries and dramas to expand the industry (Chen 2011). The major source of revenue for such local Tamil movies is through DVD sales, and promotion of these movies is done by installing stalls at the Thaipoosam Festival ("Malaysian Indian Film Festival Opens" 2012). A governing body of the local Tamil movie industry is lacking in Malaysia, thereby leading to a disorganized and fragmented industry.

Though arriving late in the field, Singapore has also begun to identify the potential of local Tamil movies. In 2010, a local English-Tamil movie became the first Singapore film to be nominated for the prestigious Palme D'Or Award for the Best Film at the Cannes Film Festival. Even though the film did not win the award, it attracted great attention from a number of film critics (Tan 2008).

CONCLUSION

Comolli and Narboni's (2000) assertion that each film is reflective of the particular ideology that produces it suggests a connection between how meaning is expressed in a particular film and the nation, region, governance, or industry with which it is directly or indirectly affiliated. Because of the cross-cultural flow and increased interconnectedness in today's world, it is no longer easy to conform to an ideal type of a local (Hannerz 1992). The success of crossover films thrives on this ideology unleashed by the dislocation of culture and globalization. Since diasporas are the exemplary communities of the transnational moment, culture cannot any longer be considered to be fixed in a particular area but is spatialized in new ways and simultaneously embedded in more than one society. This is where the success of crossover films lies. Even though a budding commercialized phenomenon, crossover in Malaysia brings hope and progress in the Malaysian film industry as a result of heavy investment plans by Indian multinational investors in the global entertainment spectrum. Crossover ventures with the Indian film industry endow the Malaysian film industry with opportunities for film release and exhibition in foreign countries, as well as a generous inflow of funds and access to facilities. Bollywood already serves as a tourism marketer for Malacca, Langkawi, and Kota Kinabalu, which now serve as internationally acclaimed shooting locations. Such an impression brings along funding and technological enhancements, like Shah Rukh's decision to start a studio in Malacca so that it can serve both Bollywood and the local productions. Hence, Malaysia hopes to serve as a brilliant instance of Indian film crossover in all its aspects with mutually endorsing relationships to develop the respective industries to further levels of production, distribution, and exhibition.

REFERENCES

Agostino, Alexis. 2010. "From Bombay to Bollywood and Beyond." Review of *Global Bollywood: Travels of Hindi Song and Dance,* edited by SangitaGopal and SujataMoorti. *Senses of Cinema* 54 (April 4). http://www.sensesofcinema.com/. Accessed December 21, 2011.
Anderson, Benedict. 1991. *Imagined Communities.* New York: Verso.
Barua, P.C., dir. 1936. *Devdas.* Mumbai, India: New Theatres Ltd.
Basu, Anurag, dir. 2010. *Kites.* Mumbai, India: Reliance Big Pictures.
Bhagyaraj, K., dir. 1981. *Mouna Geethangal.* Chennai, India: K. Bhagyaraj.
Bhatia, Kabir, dir. 2001. *Cinta.* Petaling Jaya, Malaysia: Grand Brilliance.
Bhatia, Kabir, dir. 2008. *Sepi.* Petaling Jaya, Malaysia: Grand Brilliance
Bombay Beauty Parlor. 2011. [Brochure] Jalan Ipoh, Malaysia.
Bose, Nitin, dir. 1951. *Deedar.* Mumbai, India: Filmkar Productions.
Boyle, Danny, dir. 2008. *Slumdog Millionaire.* London: Fox Searchlight Pictures, Warner Bros Pictures.
Burra, Rani Day, and Maithili Rao. 2006. "Cinema." In *Encyclopedia of India*, vol. 1, edited by Stanley Wolpert, 252–59. New York: Charles Scribner's Sons.
Chen, Grace. 2011. "Malaysian Masala." *The Star Online,* October 24. http://ecentral.my/news/story.asp?file = /2011/10/24/movies/9733260&sec=movies.
Chopra, Aditya, dir. 1995. *DilwaleDulhaniya Le Jayenge.* Mumbai, India: Yash Raj Films.
Comolli, Jean-Luc, and Jean Narboni. 2000. "Cinema/Ideology/Criticism." In *The Film Studies Reader,* edited by Joanne Hollows, Peter Hutchings, and Mark Jancovich, 197–200. London: Oxford University Press.

Gopal, Sangita, and Sujata Moorti. 2008. *Global Bollywood: Travels of Hindi Song and Dance*. Minneapolis: University of Minnesota Press.
Gowarikar, Ashutosh, dir. 2001. *Lagaan*. Mumbai, India: Aamir Khan Productions.
Hannerz, Ulf. 1992. *Cultural Complexity: Studies in the Social Organization of Meaning*. New York: Columbia University Press.
Hoskins, Colin, Stuart McFadyen, and Adam Finn. 1997. *Global Television and Film: An Introduction to the Economics of the Business*. Oxford: Clarendon Press.
John, Jason Gerald. 2008. "Malacca Wants More Films Shot There." *New Strait Times*, December 5, 17.
Joseph, K. Annan, dir. 2005. *Ops Kossa Dappa*. Petaling Jaya, Malaysia: SSK Resources Sdn Bhd.
Kanda, Tamaki Matsuoka. 1995. "Indian Film Directors in Malaya." In *Frames of Mind: Reflections on Indian Cinema*, edited by Aruna Vasudev, 43–50. New Delhi: UBSPD.
Kao, Kai-Ti, and Rebecca-Anne Do Rozario. 2008. "Imagined Spaces: The Implications of Song and Dance for Bollywood's Diasporic Communities." *Continuum: Journal of Media and Cultural Studies* 22(3): 313–26.
Kapoor, Raj, dir. 1951. *Awaara*. Mumbai, India: All India Film Corporation, R. K. Films.
Kaur, Ravinder. 2002. "Viewing the West through Bollywood: A Celluloid Occident in the Making." *Contemporary South Asia* 1(2): 199–209.
Khoo, Gaik Cheng. 2006. *Reclaiming Adat: Contemporary Malaysian Film and Literature*. Vancouver: UBC Press.
Koya, Abd Rahman. 2002. "Bollywood in Malaysia: Not Everyone Loves It." *Little Speck*. April 16. http://www.littlespeck.com/informed/2002/CInformed-020416.htm.
Krishnan, Lakshmana, dir. 1955. *Selamat Tinggal Kekasihku*. Singapore: Cathay Keris.
Kumaran Menon, Deepak, dir. 2005. *Chemman Chaalai*. Petaling Jaya, Malaysia: Tan Chui Mui.
Kumaran Menon, Deepak, dir. 2007. *Chalanggai*. Petaling Jaya, Malaysia: Golden Screen Cinemas.
Lal, Vinay. 2006. "Multiculturalism at Risk: The Indian Minority in Malaysia." *Economic and Political Weekly* 41(35): 3764–65.
Lorenzen, Mark, and Florian Arun Taeube. 2007. "Breakout from Bollywood? Internationalization of Indian Film Industry." *DRUID Working Paper No. 07–06*. http://www3.druid.dk/wp/20070006.pdf. Accessed March 9, 2012.
Madan, J. J., dir. 1931. *LailaManju*. Kolkata: Madan Theatres.
"Malaysian Indian Film Festival Opens." 2012. *The Hindu*, January 10. http://www.thehindu.com/news/cities/chennai/article2789826.ece.
Manuel, Peter. 1997. "Music, Identity, and Images of India in the Indo-Carribean Diaspora." *Asian Music* 29(1): 17–35.
Martin-Jones, David. 2006. "Kabhi India Kabhie Scotland: Bollywood Productions in Post-Devolutionary Scotland." *South Asian Popular Culture* 4(1): 49–60.
McKay, Benjamin. 2011. *Fringe Benefits: Essays and Reflections on Malaysian Arts and Cinema*. Compiled and edited by YeohSeng Guan and Jullian C. H. Lee. Petaling Jaya, Malaysia: Strategic Information and Research Development Centre.
Mehta, Deepa, dir. 2005. *Water*. California: Fox Searchlight Pictures.
Muthalib, Hassan. 2012. "Voices of the Fourth Generation of the Malaysian Indian Filmmakers." In *Glimpses of Freedom: Independent Cinema in Southeast Asia*, edited by M. A. Ingawanij and B. McKay, 15–30. Ithaca, NY: Southeast Asia Program, Cornell University.

Nair, Mira, dir. 1988. *Salaam Bombay*. London: Channel Four.
Pansha, dir. 1996. *Suami, Isteridan*. Kuala Lumpur, Malaysia: Pansha.
Raj, M., dir. 1984. *Melati Putih*. Petaling Jaya, Malaysia: Asli Film Production.
Rajaa, Bharathi, dir. 1977. *Pathinaru Vayathinile*. Chennai, India: S. A. Rajkannu.
Rajadhyaksha, Ashish. 2003. "The 'Bollywoodization' of the Indian Cinema: Cultural Nationalism in a Global Arena." *Inter-Asia Cultural Studies* 4(1): 25–39.
Rajhans, B. S., dir. 1933. *LailaMajnun*. Singapore: Chisty.
———. 1947. *Singapura di Waktu Malam*. Singapore: Malay Film Productions.
Ramlee, P., dir. 1955. *Penarik Beca*. Singapore: Malay Film Productions Ltd.
———. 1962. *Ibu Mertua-ku*. Singapore: Malay Film Productions.
Ramli, Nurhidayah. 2011. "First Malaysian Indian Film Festival in Chennai on Jan 9." *The Star Online,* December 31. http://thestar.com.my.
Samad, Said. 1994. *Between Art and Reality: Selected Essays*. Kuala Lumpur: Dewan Bahasa Dan Pustaka.
Sharan, Sharad, dir. 2007. *Diva*. Kuala Lumpur, Malaysia: Sony Pictures Releasing International.
———. 2010. *Lagenda Budak Setan*. Selangor, Malaysia: Astro Entertainment Sdn Bhd.
Shauki, Afdlin, dir. 2011. *Appalam*. Kuala Lumpur/Petaling Jaya, Malaysia: Lotus Five Star.
Tan, Kenneth Paul. 2008. *Cinema and Television in Singapore: Resistance in One Dimension*. Leiden, The Netherlands: Brill.
Thirumurugan, dir. 2008. *Muniyandi Vilangyial Moonramandu*. Chennai, India: Lotus Five Star and Thiru Pictures.
Van der Heide, William. 2002. *Malaysian Cinema, Asian Film: Border Crossings and National Cultures*. Amsterdam: Amsterdam University Press.
Vasudevan, Ravi. 2000. *Making Meaning in Indian Cinema*. New York: Oxford University Press.
Velayutham, Selvaraj. 2008. "The Diaspora and the Global Circulation of Tamil Cinema." In *Tamil Cinema: The Cultural Politics of India's Other Film Industry,* edited by Selvaraj Velayutham, 172–88. Oxon, NY: Routledge.
Vieira, João Luiz, and Robert Stam. 1985. "Parody and Marginality: The Case of Brazilian Cinema." *Framework* 28(1): 20–49.

Contributors

THE EDITOR

Sukhmani Khorana lectures in media and communication at the University of Wollongong. Previosuly, she was a Postdoctoral Research Fellow at the Centre for Critical and Cultural Studies, University of Queensland. With a PhD from the University of Adelaide on Indian-Canadian filmmaker Deepa Mehta's elements trilogy, Khorana considers her intellectual role as that of a mediator between cultural discourses. She has also programmed for international festivals and worked as a media practitioner and is currently co-convenor of the Asian Australian Film Forum and Network. Sukhmani's work on contemporary Australian and Indian cinemas has appeared in *Senses of Cinema*, *Studies in Australasian Cinema*, *Metro*, *Screen Education*, *Outskirts*, and *Continuum*.

CONTRIBUTORS

Adrian Athique is currently Chair of the School of Arts, University of Waikato. Prior to this, Adrian was director of Media, Culture and Society in the Department of Sociology, University of Essex and a postdoctoral fellow at the Centre for Critical and Cultural Studies, University of Queensland. Adrian holds a BA (Hons) in Media Arts from the University of Plymouth and a PhD From the Centre for Asia Pacific Transformation Studies, University of Wollongong. Adrian has written extensively on Indian cinema and on transnational media consumption in *Continuum, Media Culture and Society, South Asia* and other leading journals. Adrian has written a number of recent books on the sociology of media, including *The Multiplex in India: A Cultural Economy of Urban Leisure* (with Douglas Hill, Routledge, 2010), *Indian Media: Global Approaches* (Polity, 2012) and *Digital Media and Society* (Polity, 2013).

Shakuntala Banaji holds a BA in philosophy and literature from the University of Warwick, a Postgraduate Certificate in Education from Goldsmiths College, an MA in English studies in education, and a PhD in media and communication from the Institute of Education, University of London, where she worked as a lecturer and researcher from 2004 to 2010. Before entering academia in 1999, she was a teacher of English and media studies in London schools through the 1990s. She is currently a lecturer in the Department of Media and Communications at London School of Economics.

Aisha Jamal holds a PhD in German studies from the University of Toronto. Her dissertation focused on German films by directors with an immigrant background. Currently, she is an Assistant Professor in the Department of Modern Languages at Trent University in Peterborough, Ontario. Her research interests include narratives of migration, German and world cinema, contemporary art, and popular culture. Her intellectual curiosities have also led to a documentary and experimental film practice.

Olivia Khoo is a senior lecturer in film and television studies at Monash University, Australia. She is the author of *The Chinese Exotic: Modern Diasporic Femininity* (Hong Kong University Press, 2007) and coeditor with Sean Metzger of *Futures of Chinese Cinema: Technologies and Temporalities in Chinese Screen Cultures* (Intellect, 2009).

Granaz Moussavi is an Iranian-Australian poet, filmmaker, and screenwriter. An alumnus of Flinders University and the Australian Film, Television and Radio School, she is currently a doctoral candidate at the University of Western Sydney. Her debut feature film, *My Tehran for Sale*, won the Independent Spirit Award at the Inside Film Awards 2009.

Peter C. Pugsley is Senior Lecturer in Media at the University of Adelaide where he teaches Asian screen media and advanced media theory. He holds a PhD from the University of Melbourne's Department of English (Cultural Studies) and Asia Institute. He is the author of *Tradition, Culture and Aesthetics in Contemporary Asian Cinema* (Ashgate, UK, 2013) and has published on Asian media in a range of journals, including and *Asian Studies Review, Continuum: Journal of Media and Cultural Studies, Scope: Online Journal of Film and TV Studies,* and *International Communication Gazette.*

Sony Jalarajan Raj is an Assistant Professor in the Department of Mass Communication at St. Thomas University. He has worked as a journalist for NDTV, *Doordarshan*, Asianet News, All India Radio, and Hindu Business Line. His research interests include communicative rationality, information flow, digital divides, and news media influences on the public sphere. In 2008, he was a Thomson Foundation (UK) Fellow in Television Studies with the Commonwealth Broadcasting Association. He has lectured at Mahatma Gandhi University, Kannur University, University of Kerala, Curtin University of Technology, and Monash University. He has published research in the *Journal of Communication Studies, Journal of Science Communication,* and *Mass Communicator*.

Kevin Smets is a postdoctoral fellow at the Department of Communication Studies, University of Antwerp. His dissertation deals with Turkish and Moroccan diasporic film cultures. His main research interests are cultural media studies, transnationalism and the Middle East.

Rohini Sreekumar is pursuing her PhD in the School of Arts and Social Sciences at Monash University. She obtained her master's degree in mass communication and journalism from Mahatma Gandhi University, India, with a gold medal. Sreekumar is the recipient of a National Merit Scholarship and Junior Research Fellowship from the University Grants Commission of India. She has worked as a lecturer at the Little Flower College in Kerala. Her research interests include journalism practice, mediated public sphere, and diasporic studies.

Emanuelle Wessels is an Assistant Professor of Communication Studies at Augsburg College in Minneapolis, Minnesota. She obtained her PhD in communication and critical media studies from the University of Minnesota in 2010. Her research interests include the ethics of viewing and spectatorship, media convergence and interactivity, and new media and social movements.

Gertjan Willems holds a master's degree in communication sciences (Ghent University, 2009) and a master's degree in film studies and visual culture (University of Antwerp, 2010). Since October 2010, he has worked as a PhD researcher at the Centre for Cinema and Media Studies in the Department of Communication Studies at Ghent University. In his doctoral research, he is focusing on the relations between the nation, film, and film policy, mainly in Flanders.

Noah Zweig is a PhD candidate at the University of California, Santa Barbara. Currently, he is working on a dissertation provisionally titled "Inverting Hegemony: Understanding Bolivarian State Satellite Footprints in Latin America." His work has been published in *Situations: Project of the Radical Imagination* and the *Journal of Popular Film and Television*.

Index

accented English 68–70, 72, 74, 76–7, 79–80
Accident (Yi ngoi) 51, 53–5, 62, 64
aesthetics 51–2, 61, 64; *aesthetic moment* 51; Hong Kong 51–3, 55, 61, 63–4; transnational 51
affect 144
Akin, Fatih 83–92
Al Jazeera 142–4, 150
Altiplano 96, 99–103
Appardurai, Arjun 114–15, 117
asylum seekers 17, 26
authenticity 126, 134, 136

Bangsawan 155
Belgian cinema 94–5
Belgium 94–5, 97, 99–102
biopic/biographical film 37, 40–3
Bolivarian Alliance for the Americas (ALBA) 36, 38, 46
Bolivarianism 39–40
Bollywood 4–5, 32–3, 110, 112–13, 123–4, 131–2, 135, 137, 153–64
border narratives 90–1

Canada 27, 30, 34–5
Chávez, Hugo 36, 39–40
Chen, Joan 70–3, 78
childhood 130–2, 136
citizenship 143, 145–6, 149–50
class politics 130, 132
Confession of Pain (Seung sing) 51, 55–6, 60, 62, 64
Control Room 140–51
coproduction 15–16, 21, 25
cosmopolitanism 59
creative process 20
crossover actress 66–7, 69–74
crossover audience 107–20

crossover cinema 153–64
cultural policy 99, 102

dialogue 145, 147, 149–50
diaspora 6–7, 11, 68–9; Indian 153–4, 156–7, 160
diasporic filmmaking 95–8, 101

elements trilogy 27–35
English language 66, 68–9, 71, 76, 78
ethics 140
ethnicity 126, 129, 134, 136
ethnography 126
European identity 83, 89, 92
European Union 83

femininity 66–7, 70, 73–5, 79–81
filmmaking 32, 35
film policy 94, 96, 98–9, 101–2
Flanders 94–6, 98, 100, 102–3
Flemish cinema 94–7, 99, 101–2
funding 95, 98–9, 101

García Canclini, Néstor 40
Germany 83–4, 86–7, 89–91
globalization 3–5
Gramsci, Antonio 40–1

Heaven on Earth 27, 29–33
Hindi cinema 123–6, 130, 132, 135
hybrid 3–8

Indian cinema 109–10, 112, 116
In July 83–92
Iranian identity 14, 17, 21

Japan 51, 54–6, 59–60, 62

Kiarostami, Abbas 15, 20, 24
Kurosawa, Akira 61–2

Levinas, Emmanuel 140–1, 144, 147
Li, Gong 66, 70–1, 74–8, 80–1
Los Libertadores 36–46
Lowenthal, Leo 42–3

Madame Butterfly 67, 72, 79–80
Malay 153–7, 159–62
Mehta, Deepa 27–35
Memoirs of a Geisha 66, 71, 74, 78, 80
mimicry 72–3
Miramax 4, 6, 51, 53, 63
multiculturalism 110–12, 115
My Tehran for Sale 14–26

national cinema 107–8, 110
nationalism 59; cultural 53, 55, 57, 64; technocratic 52, 55–6
nonresident audience 118
Noujaim, Jehane 141–2, 145–9, 151

Other 140–1, 143–4, 146–7, 148–9
Overheard (*Sit yan fungwan*) 51, 56–7, 62

Persian poetry 14, 21
poetic cinema 14–26
poetics 8

road movie *83, 90*

Slumdog Millionaire 6, 11, 113, 123–39, 153–4

Tamil cinema 154, 160–3
Televisión Española (TVE) 37–9
translingual stardom 66–7, 69–72, 79–81
transnational cinema 3–8, 11
Turkey 83–7, 89, 91–2
Turkish-German films 83–92
Turquaze 95–8, 101–2

viewers 123–38; diasporic 129; transnational 125; Western 128–9

Water 27–8, 31–4
Wayang 155
witnessing 141–4, 146, 148, 150

Yeoh, Michelle 66, 70, 81

Ziyi, Zhang 66, 70–1, 78, 80–1

For Product Safety Concerns and Information please contact our EU
representative GPSR@taylorandfrancis.com
Taylor & Francis Verlag GmbH, Kaufingerstraße 24, 80331 München, Germany